Natural Law Today

Natural Law Today

The Present State of the Perennial Philosophy

Edited by Christopher Wolfe
and Steven Brust

LEXINGTON BOOKS
Lanham • Boulder • New York • London

Published by Lexington Books
An imprint of The Rowman & Littlefield Publishing Group, Inc.
4501 Forbes Boulevard, Suite 200, Lanham, Maryland 20706
www.rowman.com

Unit A, Whitacre Mews, 26-34 Stannary Street, London SE11 4AB

British Library Cataloguing in Publication Information Available

Library of Congress Cataloging-in-Publication Data

ISBN: 978-1-4985-7642-0 (cloth : alk. paper)
ISBN: 978-1-4985-7643-7 (electronic)

∞™ The paper used in this publication meets the minimum requirements of American National Standard for Information Sciences Permanence of Paper for Printed Library Materials, ANSI/NISO Z39.48-1992.

Printed in the United States of America

Contents

Introduction

Steven Brust and Christopher Wolfe

The natural law tradition has its origins in the natural right tradition in classical Greek thought—especially of Plato and Aristotle—and was developed in the natural law of the Roman Stoics, and later by canonists, jurists, theologians, and philosophers of the Middle Ages, most famously by St. Thomas Aquinas. Even as the modern thinkers turned away from this premodern notion of natural law, they still relied on it. In fact, many Enlightenment thinkers attempted to expound complete theories of natural law even if their understanding of it began to differ in substance from the traditional notion. Accompanying this transformation was an emphasis on a modern notion of natural rights—both by modern political thinkers and by political movements such as the French and American Revolutions. Yet, natural law was still embedded in the European and American cultures, however much deformed or diminished. The history of both modern Europe and the United States has witnessed a steady decrease in the acceptance of the natural law.

One of the most prominent American jurists, Chief Justice Oliver Wendell Holmes Jr., disdainfully dismissed the notion of natural law in a 1918 *Harvard Law Review* article, maintaining that "jurists who believe in natural law seem to me to be in that naïve state of mind that accepts what has been familiar and accepted by all men everywhere." He argued that "it is true that beliefs and wishes have a transcendental basis in the sense that their foundation is arbitrary. You cannot help entertaining and feeling them, and there is an end of it."[1] Holmes's relativism—the notion that there is no objective morality and each individual decides for himself what is morally good or bad based on his or her preferences—steadily expanded its influence in American life. Ironically, moral relativism has become dogmatic, attacking natural law arguments while promoting its own moral absolutes based on an assumption of the equality of all lifestyles.

In the face of these tendencies, there has been something of a "renaissance" in natural law, in both ethical and political thought. Those oriented toward the natural law tradition see this as inevitable, as there is always an "eternal return of the natural law"[2]—most especially when it is faced with fierce opposition.

Adherents to natural law are usually engaged on two fronts. The first is a dialogue with contemporary schools of thought that reject natural law, holding rival moral and political theories. The challenge for proponents of natural law in that case is to argue for the truth and rightness of the natural law, while simultaneously discerning what elements of the opposing theories can be accepted—or at least conditionally accepted—in hopes of coming to some common agreement. Given the trenchant analysis of outstanding contemporary natural law thinkers, one hopes that opponents of natural law would likewise show a willingness to engage representatives of the natural law tradition.

The second front of engagement is the often intricate and subtle (but important) debates among natural law adherents themselves, who are constantly striving to clarify and deepen their understanding of natural law in its breadth and depth, and to apply it to contemporary moral and political challenges. It should be noted that these two fronts of dialogue are not mutually exclusive, but, in fact, overlap to a significant degree, each enriching the other.

Today, there exist deep divisions in America over a variety of issues: the status of same-sex relationships, embryonic stem cell research and abortion, euthanasia, gender identity, cloning, the use of drones, care for the environment, capital punishment, economic crises, and government involvement in health care. These issues are bound up with ideas of "equality," "dignity," "liberty," "rights," and "the good" that are often understood to have widely divergent and even contradictory meanings.

This volume presents a number of essays relevant to these contemporary challenges in morality and politics, not primarily by addressing specific political and moral issues, but by exploring the fundamental principles by which one should approach them. The essays, then, cover a variety of important topics, including interpretations of the classical natural law theory found in its most famous proponent (Thomas Aquinas), the relevance of God and theology to natural law, the metaphysical foundations of the natural law, especially the meaning and importance of nature and reason, the role of inclinations in natural law, the relationship between natural law and natural rights, and a more specific treatment of natural law in relation to the contemporary political order and civil law.

Some of these topics are addressed in reference to the critics of the natural law tradition, but others concern the debates among fellow adherents. The contributors to this volume intend to defend, in one way or another, the importance of natural law for both the individual and society, as a response to the dogmatic relativism of our day. They also propose natural law as the means by which common agreement on moral issues can be achieved and which can provide the best foundation for a morally fulfilling life and for a just social order.

The book is divided into two parts, the first of which focuses on natural law in theory. The second part covers natural law in relation to history and to contemporary thought and political circumstances.

Steven Long leads off by providing a basic summary of Thomistic natural law, responses to objections to the natural teleology which undergirds it, and an argument that it is still relevant today for public and political life despite its theistic source and contemporary secularism's resistance to anything theological. Professor Long provides a very helpful distinction between natural law as passive and active participation in the eternal law of God. Passive participation is where we recognize that we have certain ends according to our human nature which cannot be chosen. We are active participants in natural law insofar as we actively use our reason to know and understand the precepts which help conform our reason to the divinely created order of ends. In the second part of the essay, Long refutes the purported "naturalistic fallacy" by arguing that it contains its own fallacy because it is an undue rejection of teleology in human nature. He claims that one can derive an *ought* from an *is*, or, in other terms, a value from a fact, because of the very "fact that nature is ordered to certain ends in relation to which the proper functioning of the nature is defined."

In the third section of his chapter, Long asks whether natural law doctrine is useful today for politics if it is "essentially theistic in character" and there exists a common sociological viewpoint of a "self-limitation of secular regimes to avoid any reference to God in their public moral reasoning." He argues that a complete natural law doctrine should serve as the context of political and legal judgments, but it is not necessary to present a full-blown theory of natural law with reference to God while making political arguments, because judgments according to the natural law are not primarily a matter of presenting this whole truth doctrine but rather are very much a matter "of prudence and particular virtues." And, he continues, since the secular state can never interfere with this judgment of conscience, then the full theistic character of natural law can never be eradicated by the secular state. He does note one area—bioethics—where the rapid increase in new technologies and biological, medical, legal, and moral complexities require a more complete argumentation with a comprehensive understanding of human dignity, body–soul composite, and the full teleological order of natural and supernatural ends.

The next article by Michael Pakaluk explores Aquinas's precise meaning of the natural inclinations that are central to his discussion of natural law. His intent is to demonstrate how they are rooted in Aquinas's natural philosophy, which he inherited from Aristotle, and, as such, have their source in man's metaphysical structure: "Nature acts for an end or goal, and because to be a goal is to be a good, the nature of each thing aims at some good. The tendency to achieve its end which is imparted to a thing in virtue of its having a nature is what Aquinas refers to as a natural *inclinatio*." Pakaluk argues that knowledge of man's nature gives rise to knowledge of the natural law as law. Thus, one must discover the natural inclinations proper to man by looking at the natural forms as revealed both in the genus and species of the definition of man—"rational animal"—as well as the category of substance. These forms correspond to the hierarchy of inclinations posited in question 94, article 2.

Essential to Pakaluk's argument is both a correction of a commonly used translation of Aquinas's question 94, article 2, and a clarification of the difference between the speculative and the practical reason. The difference between speculative and practical knowledge resides not in the content of the knowledge, but in the purpose for which the knowledge is used: "if something is held or asserted merely because it is true, and not for any direct purpose other than its truth, then that act is an act of speculative reason; otherwise it is assignable to practical reason." Pakaluk demonstrates that knowledge of the inclinations is like other kinds of knowledge acquired in everyday life, through the use of speculative reason. Contrary to certain natural law theorists who want to claim you can't derive a moral *ought* from an *is*, "for Aquinas, a finding about what things are naturally good for us implies precepts for us. The precepts hold for us because they command that which contributes to what we are inclined to, as members of the kind, and because we are members of the kind, we can be presupposed to have the requisite goals." Thus, in agreement with Long, Pakaluk concludes that "there is no gap between *is* and *ought*."

The next essay by Fulvio Di Blasi follows Long in focusing on important conceptual distinctions related to natural law, natural right, and natural rights. First, he provides a definition of the very term *natural*: "When *natural* qualifies *law*, *right*, or *rights*, it is meant to refer the conventional aspects of human law(s) and legal systems to a necessary and noncontingent source able to shed light on their goals, structures, and limitations."

Di Blasi makes specific distinctions with respect to the terms *ius naturale* and *lex naturalis* in order to clear up conceptual differences across languages and among thinkers. Lex naturalis—natural law—concerns the objective order of justice but must include a reference to the Legislator, God, who created and arranged the objective order. Ius naturale—natural right—is the intelligible and objective order of justice in the universe according to which something is due or belongs to someone. In addition, he notes that natural right as an objective order of justice can further "refer to the concepts of *facultas* and right/just action." The notion of natural right as a claim or faculty has been one of considerable debate, especially as it relates to modern natural rights and premodern natural law. He claims that with the modern social contract theorists such as Hobbes, Locke, Pufendorf, and Rousseau, the meaning of natural right as a claim or faculty defines "natural rights [as freedoms and powers] that people possess in the state of nature prior to, and independently of, the existence of any authority and law" and they therefore end up being "powers to do what whatever one wants to." It is this modern notion of a claim right detached from any objective order of justice based on human nature (as it was in the premodern world) that has come to dominate the contemporary world.

In the final part of the essay, Di Blasi also takes sides in the debate over the "new natural law theory" as expounded by John Finnis in his book *Natural Law and Natural Rights*. Most notable is that Finnis and others who hold this new theory accept the argument of the naturalistic fallacy (which, we have seen, Long rejects). According to Di Blasi, the new theory of natural law wants to propose an ethical foundation for human rights which is not subject to the naturalistic fallacy, is opposed to utilitarianism, neocontractualism and, in general, to minimalist liberal positions. It does this by attempting to ground an objective ethics in practical reason which intuitively identifies basic reasons for action—basic human goods—and not by first having a metaphysical understanding of human nature. According to Di Blasi, the new theory ends up "rejecting two essential elements of his [Aquinas's] concept and of the entire classical tradition of natural law: the existence of an ultimate end for man, and an objective hierarchy of values."

In the following chapter, moral philosopher J. Budziszewski offers a challenging argument on the epistemological status of the natural law, defending Thomas Aquinas's view that everyone knows the natural law. He begins by first establishing that Aquinas does, in fact, hold the view that everyone knows the natural law. In order to do this, he provides a "corrected" interpretation of an oft-quoted passage from Aquinas that the Germans did not think that theft was wrong.

He then proceeds to make the case for why Aquinas's view is right, in principle, by responding to five possible objections to whether all really know the natural law. Ultimately, he concludes that "the obstacles that prevent him [anyone] from acknowledging true moral universals lie less in the realm of the intellect than in the realm of the will. He may even desire to concoct intellectual obstacles, because they give him a pretext for refusing to admit to himself that he knows what he does, in some sense, know."

Budziszewski examines the controversial act of abortion, providing evidence that post-abortion signs of guilt in those who have undergone or performed abortions, lead to the conclusion that the action was known to be wrong, and not that those who have had abortions or perform abortions, were ignorant of the knowledge that abortion is wrong.

Finally, Budziszewski asks that if it is the will rather than the intellect which prevents persons from doing the right thing, then what can be done to reach such persons? The solution is to combine both an education in truth with that of moral virtue, building up the moral character of the person. Without the good character, then the person will be less apt to accept the truths of the moral law, but instead will try to offer justifications for violating it.

Steven Brust takes up the issue of human knowledge of natural law, and, in particular, the question of the role of divine law in knowledge of the natural law. The natural law is a dictate of reason and it is therefore knowable by human reason, even apart from divine revelation. But this fact has to be qualified in light of Aquinas' discussion in I-II, Q. 91, A. 4 of the *Summa Theologiae* of the reasons why divine positive law is necessary. Among the reasons is human uncertainty, especially with respect to particular and contingent moral judgments. This reinforces Thomas' discussion at the beginning of the Summa of why divine revelation is necessary: not only does it provide us with knowledge of things beyond reason, but it also gives greater clarity and certainty to those things that can be known by reason in principle but that are often not known by many in practice.

A careful analysis of Aquinas' discussion of the Old Law (especially the Decalogue) and the New Law make it clear that there is greater or lesser certainty with respect to different kinds of particular and contingent matters. Divine law is especially helpful for achieving moral certitude more so when those particular and contingent matters are those which directly implicate universal moral principles, especially the negative moral norms, and much less so when they concern the myriad of actions of daily life determined by the virtue of prudence.

Brust argues that there is reason to be pessimistic today about how much of the moral law is known by a majority of the populace, regarding some very grave matters (e.g., basic natural law understandings of human sexuality, marriage, and the family). This suggests that natural knowledge of the moral law can be obscured, as Aquinas argued, by sin and passions and corrupt customs, and that reason may need to be purified by grace. Natural law thinkers who follow Aquinas have to be sensitive to the fact that, however much unaided reason is capable, in principle, of making sound moral judgments, they cannot ignore the importance of the divine law in the knowledge of morality as well.

Leading off the second part of the book, which focuses on historical and contemporary thought and politics, is a contribution by Protestant theologian J. Daryl Charles, who focuses on the relationship between the Gospel, God's order of creation, natural law, and Christians' relationships with nonbelievers. He primarily defends natural law against many Protestant theologians' unwarranted rejection of it due to their "marked ethical discontinuity [with the original Protestant Reformers] in their understanding of Scripture." Thus, Charles's essay moves to another battleground on which natural law must contend with respect to theology: not that its theological foundations make it impermissible in political arguments, but that it is not theological enough to contend with the political challenges.

Charles provides ample evidence to demonstrate that Luther, Calvin, Zwingli, and Bullinger all believed that the natural law is a part of God's created order, included in the Old Testament's Ten Commandments, applicable to all men, and is in conformity with the Gospel. In contrast, recent Protestant theologians Karl Barth, Jacques Ellul, H. Richard Neibuhr, John David Yoder, and Stanley Hauerwas, who reject natural law, are not in continuity with their predecessors and distort the Christian tradition in one way or another—whether it be regarding Christian social ethics, or the relationship between nature and grace, or the Gospel and God's metaphysical order. Charles concludes with a defense of the universality of natural law and a warning that the posture taken by those who reject natural law "prevents us—and those falling under our influence—from entering into responsible and heartfelt dialogue with unbelievers."

Hadley Arkes argues for the very "ground" of natural law in the context of judicial interpretation. This ground, he emphasizes, is not so much a grand theory, but a set of necessary truths, consisting in principles of reason which ordinary people can grasp in commonsense judgments about everyday circumstances. These first principles of reason allow one to have "an awareness . . . that there are certain things so wrong that their wrongness will not be diminished even if they are done only occasionally, in small doses." Arkes then applies this "commonsense" reasoning to a critique of the work of judges and lawyers—whether liberal, or conservative (like his friend, the late Justice Antonin Scalia)—exhorting them to overcome their rejection and or skepticism of natural law, and to recognize the principles of reason which are implicitly operating in certain constitutional cases.

To explain why these are principles of reason, Arkes appeals not so much to Thomistic natural law as to Kant (whom Ralph McInerny characterizes in his essay later in this volume as a "bottomless source of error"), who equated "moral laws" with the "laws of reason," or more precisely, the "laws of freedom." Aware of this purported conflict with traditional natural law, Arkes claims that in substance, Kant found the ground of moral judgment "in the same nature that provided the ground for Aristotle."

The final contribution by Christopher Wolfe offers a provocative rapprochement of natural law with classical liberalism. His thesis is sure to stimulate debate not only with liberals, but also among other believers in natural law. Wolfe's thesis is that natural law theorists can be good liberals—

in the sense of accepting liberalism's original (limited) notions of freedom and equality, and its promotion of tolerance and peace, and respect for human dignity and rights. Yet at the same time, natural law theorists can't be simply liberals because "if the liberal tradition has grasped much of the truth about political life, it has also found it difficult to embrace some elements of that truth—elements found especially in Thomas Aquinas's concept of natural law." And current or contemporary forms of liberalism tend greatly to exacerbate the weaknesses of liberal political theory. These weaknesses are first, its narrowing of the common good and its inability to recognize sufficiently that a liberal (or any other) political regime influences (for better and/or worse) the people's understandings of themselves and what is a good life, and second, and more particularly, their attitudes toward truth, the family, and faith.

Despite these shortcomings, Wolfe warns against a return to a pre-liberal past, but instead offers his "natural law liberalism." A correct understanding of natural law (separated from its accidental features associated with certain social and political practices of pre-liberal regimes) supports liberalism's separation of powers, political equality, limited government, a broad range of liberty, etc. Yet, natural law can help liberalism be self-critical in order to stave off its unhealthy tendencies—which are merely tendencies and not essential elements to liberalism.

Many of these essays were originally presented at a conference entitled "Natural Law Today," under the auspices of the Thomas International Center (at that time, the Ralph McInerny Center for Thomistic Studies). Therefore it is quite fitting that we include the keynote address to the conference participants as an afterword. Ralph McInerny provides us with a brief (and partly autobiographical) historical narrative touching on some of the themes covered by the contributors. He describes the rise and fall—and rise once again—of Thomistic natural law in Catholic universities during the twentieth century within the context of the demise of ethics and natural law thinking in university philosophy departments specifically, and the retreat from the liberal arts education in the American university generally.

The turn from natural law thinking is evidenced in the influence of analytic philosophers such as G. E. Moore and A. J. Ayer, who ultimately grounded their rejection in the "so-called 'naturalistic fallacy.' " This so-called fallacy consisted "in assuming that the natural properties of what you called good were the basis for calling it good." In other words, one could know what one ought to do, by knowing what human nature is. The fallacy was rejected by most moral philosophers, and as a result, McInerny notes, "if calling a thing good or bad cannot be explained by features of the thing being evaluated, value terms express our subjective attitude of approval or disapproval." The natural law tradition looks to the features of human nature in order to provide an objective ground to the good, in opposition to merely subjective grounds.

McInerny concludes by provocatively suggesting that Christian philosophers are at an advantage in ethical reflection because they have faith to guide them in their "existential circumstances," which govern every philosopher.

The American Public Philosophy Institute offers this volume as an opportunity for scholars and generally educated citizens to confront once more the question of the foundations of moral principles and action, in the light of the ever-returning natural law.

NOTES

1. Oliver Wendell Holmes Jr., "Natural Law," *Harvard Law Review* 32 (1918–19): 40–44.

2. Yves Simon, *The Tradition of Natural Law: A Philosopher's Reflections*, ed. Vukan Kuic (New York: Fordham University Press, 1992), 3–4. Heinrich Rommen, *The Natural Law: A Study in Legal and Social History and Philosophy*, trans. Thomas R. Hanley, OSB, PhD (Indianapolis: Liberty Fund, 1998). Originally published in Germany, Rommen's book was titled *The Eternal Return of the Natural Law*. Also, John Courtney Murray titles one of his chapters in *We Hold These Truths: Catholic Reflections on the American Proposition* (New York: Sheed and Ward, 1960), "The Eternal Return of Natural Law."

WORKS CITED

Finnis, J. M. *Natural Law and Natural Rights*. Oxford: Clarendon Press, 1980.

Holmes, Oliver Wendell Jr. "Natural Law." *Harvard Law Review* 32 (1918–19): 40–44.

Simon, Yves. *The Tradition of Natural Law: A Philosopher's Reflections*. Edited by Vukan Kuic. New York: Fordham University Press, 1992.

Rommen, Heinrich. *The Natural Law: A Study in Legal and Social History and Philosophy*. Translated by Thomas R. Hanley, OSB, PhD. Indianapolis: Liberty Fund, 1998.

Murray, John Courtney. *We Hold These Truths: Catholic Reflections on the American Proposition*. New York: Sheed and Ward, 1960.

I

Natural Law Theory

Chapter One

God, Teleology, and the Natural Law

Steven A. Long

The purpose of this essay is to take up one central element of the teaching of St. Thomas Aquinas, whose theology and philosophy remain a source of sure instruction and authoritative teaching.

The central element here to be considered is St. Thomas's understanding of the natural law. In particular, I will consider the pivotal issue of the relation between God and the natural moral law. What is this relation? This issue is of great importance for religion, morality, and public life, and it is definitive for the character of the natural law. Yet often this issue is clouded by the portrayal of natural law as exclusively a set of rules for moral problem-solving. On such a view, natural law would be simply a collection of protocols for addressing particular moral issues in precision from metaphysical truth or theology: a moral problem-solving device.

To the contrary here I will argue that for St. Thomas Aquinas, natural law is the *precondition* and *foundation* for right exercise of practical reason. It is the normative theological and metaphysical order that undergirds, makes possible, and flows into our moral logic. On this older Thomistic view, our practical reasoning is epistemically and ontologically derived from the natural law. It is derivative of the larger cosmic story rather than supplanting it. While through our practical moral reason we actively participate in the divine government of our own actions, the precondition for this active participation is the mind's prior *adaequatio* or conformity to the right end. For it is knowledge of the end which is the root of right appetite, and all practical moral judgment must be conformed to right appetite. As St. Thomas writes in the *Summa theologiae*,

> Now in regard to the means, the rectitude of the reason depends on its conformity with the desire of a due end: *nevertheless the very desire of the due end presupposes on the part of reason a right apprehension of the end.*[1]

This paper offers a rudimentary account of three important conclusions about God and natural law that flow from this Thomistic conception of natural law. These are the following: (proposition 1) that natural law is genuine law, which carries the ancillary implication that the doctrine of natural law is theistic; (proposition 2) that the knowledge and love of God are the capstone of natural law even considered in precision from grace; and finally, (proposition 3) that the epistemology of natural law loses nothing by acknowledging the aid we receive from grace in knowing the natural law. I will begin with the preambular consideration of the traditional definition of natural law and its explication through natural teleology in terms of the passively participated teleological order. Here I also offer a (necessarily) very brief argument against a total separation or dichotomy of fact and value). The exposition then will turn straightaway to the three aforementioned conclusions.

WHAT IS THE NATURAL LAW?

St. Paul, in his Letter to the Romans (2:14–16, New American Bible Revised Edition) adverts to the natural law when he writes,

> For when the Gentiles who do not have the law by nature observe the prescriptions of the law, they are a law for themselves even though they do not have the law. They show that the demands of the law are written in their hearts, while their conscience also bears witness and their conflicting thoughts accuse or even defend them on the day when, according to my gospel, God will judge people's hidden works through Christ Jesus.

This law which is written in hearts, and to which conscience bears witness both through remorse and integrity, is not a law known exclusively through book learning. It is *lex non scripta*, unwritten law. Or, perhaps more truly, it is law written in human nature by the finger of God. It is said to be natural for various reasons: because it is the law that measures the perfection of human nature; because it is known "naturally," that is, it is at root accessible to the reason of all persons; because human persons are subject to this law by nature and not from any antecedent consent; because it is distinct both from the positive law of the state and from the canon law of the Church, as well as from the *lex nova* of divine charity revealed in Christ. So viewed, natural law is a theme of theological and metaphysical profundity. It is a providential mode of the divine government of creation, most particularly of the rational creation.

Regarding law generally, St. Thomas writes that law is "an ordinance of reason for the common good, promulgated by him who has the care of the community."[2] It is God who has the care of the community of being and who promulgates the natural law from creation. St. Thomas Aquinas defines the natural law as follows: "The natural law is nothing else than the rational creature's participation of the eternal law."[3] In the previous article, St. Thomas defines eternal law as "the very Idea of the government of things in God the Ruler of the universe."[4] We may consider natural law in a variety of ways, but when it comes to defining natural law in the strict sense, St. Thomas defines it as "nothing else" than a rational participation of the eternal law.

All creatures are by nature subject to divine governance. They derive the inclinations to their proper acts and ends from the "impress" of that eternal law which is the creative ordering wisdom of God. But the subrational creation is subject to this divine governance in a diminished and purely passive way, in accord with its merely physical nature. St. Thomas will say that subrational creatures are subject to natural law only by "passive participation and similitude." This means that nonrational beings are governed by God solely by being passively subject to the divine ordering of nature. While all creatures—including human persons—derive their inclinations to their proper acts and ends through passive participation of the eternal law, rational creatures are not only passive recipients of the divine governance, but also actively participate in this governance through the light of reason. The eternal law is impressed on human nature, and the mind's natural reception of this impressed teleological order as giving reasons to act, and reasons not to act, is a rational participation in the eternal law. This light of reason is by its very nature a finite participation in the divine wisdom, mediated by the impress of the ordering wisdom of God on creation. Thus, St. Thomas teaches that "the natural law is promulgated by the very fact that God instilled it into man's mind so as to be known by him naturally."[5]

Thomas writes that " human reason is not, of itself, the rule of things: but the principles impressed on it by nature, are general rules and measures of all things relating to human conduct, whereof the natural reason is the rule and measure, although it is not the measure of things that are from nature."[6] The human mind is what St. Thomas calls "a measured measure." This means that the mind is measured by reality as the very condition for its own true judgments which then in different ways "measure" things and actions. For us to discern the objective measure of right action, there must be a measure of such action to which the human mind may conform. In conforming to this measure, the human mind is then able to extend its judgment to govern practical conduct. This measure, that transcends the human mind while remaining accessible to it, is the natural law.

While the passively participated order is not *in itself* natural law, it *is* nonetheless a true participation of the eternal law, and constitutes the impress of the ordering wisdom of God in all things (for as Thomas teaches in the *Summa theologiae* , all things derive the inclinations to their proper acts and ends through the eternal law).[7] This passively participated order is a teleological order, order to an end. All efficiency implies finality or end: one cannot even define agency as opposed to non-agency without referring to end (as for instance "snow-shoveling" is, and is understood to be, action ordered to the end of shoveling snow). It may be that at times an action is itself the end, as when one simply wishes "to take a walk." But action as action can only be, and be known, in relation to end. Without the final cause or end, action would be either unceasing (in the sense of *never arriving at or terminating in any objective fulfillment*) or uninitiable (because there would be nothing *for the sake of which* to act). But neither of these options describes real action.

The human mind does not connaturally know the divine essence, an idea known as "ontologism." Nor is the eternal law possessed through an a priori knowledge (which would leave the mind incapable of genuinely *knowing* the truth even if it happened to *conceive* that which is the truth, because if the mind is limited to a priori categories it could not directly consider the actual nature and being of things which is the foundation for true judgments). Rather, when the mind receives the passively participated order of ends—the impress of the governing wisdom of God from creation—as giving *reasons* to act and *reasons* not to act, it receives this order "*preceptively*," literally *as* precept, articulating a normative direction or law. Thus, the whole content of the natural law is derived from the rational reception of the passively participated teleological order, an order that is not itself the natural law, but is a participation of the eternal law—indeed, is the impress of the divine wisdom in the order of things. Without the passively participated teleological order, the natural law would be bereft of normative content, just as without language a book has no literary content. Yet the book is only "doing literary work" when *read*, and the passively participated order articulates norms only to a mind that receives this order as authoritatively indicating *rationes* (ends) which are reasons to do and hence (in certain respects) reasons to *avoid* certain types of action.

For St. Thomas, knowledge of the truth is the root both of our contemplative and of our practical moral lives. Thomas maintains, as did Aristotle, that "the speculative intellect by extension becomes practical."[8] In other words, our practical moral judgments proceed from insights that are only accidentally ordered to action. St. Thomas articulates with precision both the nature and the distinction between the speculative and the practical in the following two quotations from the same article:

> Now, to a thing apprehended by the intellect, it is accidental whether it be directed to operation or not, and according to this the speculative and practical intellects differ. For it is the speculative intellect which directs what it apprehends, not to operation, but to the consideration of truth; while the practical intellect is that which directs what it apprehends to operation.[9]

In the reply to the second objection, he continues, writing, "The object of the practical intellect is good directed to operation, and under the aspect of truth. For the practical intellect knows truth, just as the speculative, but it directs the known truth to operation."[10] In other words, both our practical moral deliberation, and our speculative consideration of reality for its own sake, hinge upon our knowing the truth. Whether in its contemplative or practical aspect, the human mind is measured by truth founded in the eternal law.

St. Thomas's emphasis upon the importance of knowing the truth for our practical moral lives at times is thought to blur the distinction between facts and values. For St. Thomas does not accept an ironclad divide between nature and the good, between fact and value. Of course there is a distinction between the natural species of an action and its moral species—for example, between the physical character of an act and its moral character. The man who pushes an old lady into an oncoming bus and the man who pushes her *out* of the way, physically speaking, are both men who push old ladies around; but clearly there is a moral difference. Nonetheless, St. Thomas rightly holds that the natural species of an act plays an important causal role in defining the moral species, because it constitutes the matter of the act which we intend.[11] And we ought not do or even intend certain things, precisely because they are the kinds of things they are. For example, to say that one is not killing a child but only saving a kingdom from dynastic civil war when one murders an infant heir to the throne is self-deceit. Similarly, when the calipers crush the skull of an infant in utero in a craniotomy, we cannot avoid the datum that this is a directly homicidal act directed at an innocent.

But isn't it impossible to derive a value from a mere fact? It is true that we cannot logically derive ethical conclusions from premises containing no ethical content. But it is false to suppose that the teleological ordering of human nature is possessed of no ethical content. To the contrary, the order of ends provides the major premise in moral reasoning. Nature is only devoid of ethical content if we abstract it from this ethical content, but we need not perform this abstraction. Dichotomizing nature from the good is plausible only if we deny that the good is a function of natural teleological order. But if we reject the enlightenment reductionism which reduces nature exclusively to mere matter in motion, we find no probative grounds for denaturing the good and denying natural ethical teleology, the natural order to the end.

We have seen that for St. Thomas the light of natural reason "is nothing else than an imprint on us of the Divine light,"[12] a rational participation in the eternal law. Just as law in the strict sense derives from the mind of the governor, so properly speaking it prescriptively addresses the minds of those subject to it with authoritative determinations of the good to be sought and the evil to be avoided. These definitional traits of the natural law point toward a pivotal conclusion that is often obscured in meditations upon natural law. For the natural law is not only metaphorically law, but rather is law in the strictest and fullest sense.

NATURAL LAW IS TRUE LAW

Here we advert to my first proposition—that is, that natural law is true law. For many theists, the divine foundation of natural law has come to be viewed as an "extra," an aspect of natural law that may be of special interest to theists but that is not essentially definitive for the natural law. Hence, one major theorist of the natural law, professor John Finnis, maintains "the fact that natural law can be understood, assented to, applied, and reflectively analysed without adverting to the question of the existence of God."[13] In one respect this is true: by nature we know much of the content of the natural law before we realize it to be genuine law. We do not naturally begin with an intuition of God, from which we then deduce a list of commands and prohibitions. In the order of our discovery of natural law, and in precision from grace, our awareness of God comes later rather than earlier. Nonetheless, the words of Yves Simon, from his fine work *The Tradition of Natural Law*, are pertinent here. As he puts it, "from this logical priority in the order of discovery it does not follow that the understanding of natural law can be logically preserved in case of failure to recognize in God the ultimate foundation of all laws."[14]

Understandably, the designation of natural law as law will become rather shaky without reference to a promulgating divine authority. Thus John Finnis writes in *Natural Law and Natural Rights* that

> natural law—the set of principles of practical reasonableness in ordering human life and human community—is only analogically law in relation to my present focal use of the term: that is why the term has been avoided in this chapter on Law, save in relation to past thinkers who used the term. These past thinkers, however, could, without loss of meaning, have spoken instead of "natural right," "intrinsic morality," "natural reason, or right reason, in action," etc.[15]

Finnis cites the view of Mortimer Adler that natural law is "law" only by what is called an analogy of extrinsic attribution.[16] On such a view, natural law would be called "law" only because it provides some of the moral building blocks for positive civil law in political community. Just as we call medicine "healthy" because it is one of the causes of health, so on Adler's account we would call natural law "law" only because it contributes certain elements of true law—a true law that is identified with positive civil law. On this Adlerian view, natural law is a material contributor to law rather than being law in the strict sense.

However, from the perspective of St. Thomas natural law is more truly law than is civil law—for civil government pales in comparison with the divine government of creation, as does human wisdom in comparison with the divine wisdom, and the root principles of positive law are *derived* from the natural law. Without doubt natural law is a cause of positive law, but this does not mean that natural law falls short of the strict definition of law. It is an ordinance of the eternal law, promulgated from the moment of creation and governing the commonwealth of being and human agency: it, indeed, is that law which is naturally most worthy of the title.

By contrast with the Adlerian view, St. Thomas maintains that "the participation of the eternal law in the rational creature is properly called a law, since a law is something pertaining to reason."[17] Natural law is properly called law. If natural law were only "law" by a weak analogy of extrinsic attribution, we would be confronted with a natural law that was "law" in only the most attenuated sense. It would be law without a legislator, and without promulgation. Subtracted from its root in the eternal law, its normativity would be unclear. But to the contrary, it is in the most literal sense that we are subject to natural law. We are subjects of the commonwealth of being, and the law of our being is promulgated at creation by the author and supreme governor of our being.

Natural law is often thought of as equivalent with a doctrine of ethical objectivity as opposed to moral subjectivism and relativism. But if natural law were nothing but moral objectivity it would take us no further than do the conclusions of ethical rationalism. One need not look far to find agnostics and atheists who affirm elements of natural moral rectitude, and who insist upon the objective validity of certain moral insights. But such truncated moral objectivism need not be construed as *law*. It is actually more common for moral objectivism to abstract from the metaphysical and theological character of natural moral law than to affirm it. It is not Kantians alone for whom the regularity of moral phenomena fails to imply our subjection to any particular authority or government.

By contrast St. Thomas directs us to speak of the *natural moral law*. This reference to law is not a mere figure of speech. The human intellect does not by itself transform the water of human *inclinatio* into the wine of *lex*. Rather man falls within the jurisdiction of the divine government by virtue of his very being.

Neither the being nor the natural ordering of creation are self-originated. They are in the most literal sense possible ontologically *heteronomous from another*. Both our being and our order to the final end of human existence are received radically from the outside. Creatures *only are* because they receive the gift of existence (*esse*) from God. Similarly, their natures are conferred upon them at creation—there is no pre-creation poll soliciting prior consent. No social contract reduces the Creator to a mere participant in democratic polity. The presumption of secular states that claim authority to license others to commit wrongful homicide through abortion or euthanasia manifests the hubris of such an idea. For the state cannot license an act that no one has a moral right to perform. Practical reason does not define moral truth ex nihilo. Its spending capital is received from the divine ordering of creation, and this plan of ordering is not a suggestion—it is law. The very reason for the immutability of the natural law in its primary premises is the truth that it is nothing other than a rational participation in the eternal law. Far from being a mere doctrine of ethical objectivity, Thomistic natural law doctrine is rich with theological and metaphysical necessity.

As an objective law that measures the perfection of human nature, the natural law is distinct from the nature that it governs. Our knowledge of the law is not merely self-knowledge. For this reason St. Thomas in the prologue to his *Treatise on Law* in the *Summa theologiae* identifies the "extrinsic principles moving to good" as God, law, and grace.[18] Natural law does not mean that human nature—in the sense of the human essence and its properties—is a law to itself. If this were true, one would need only be human already to have achieved the perfection to which we are ordered through the natural law. Moreover, if human nature were a law to itself, it would designate a zone of human autonomy in relation to the divine jurisdiction. But to the contrary, the natural law is nothing other than a rational participation in the eternal law.

The distinction between human nature and the natural law does not mean that natural law fails to operate *within* human nature, nor does it mean that we fail to know the law through our own reason. Rather it means that the being and authority of the natural law are extrinsic to the human reason whereby we know its content. Any norm—let us say a norm of grammar—is distinct from what it governs. We would not say that a grammatically correct sentence *is grammar*, albeit we would say that it is *grammatical*. Similarly, we do not say that human nature when rectified from moral wrong is the law, save in a manner of speaking—rather, we say that it *is lawful*. The natural law is nothing other than the eternal law as naturally directive of the rational creature.

Law as rational precept properly derives from and reflects intelligence. It proceeds from the mind of the legislator, to the minds of the ones to whom it is promulgated. The recipient of the law receives legal precepts as interior reasons for conduct, as *reasons* for doing or not doing. This is to say that law is not merely physical force or threat.

Yet to say that the natural law is rooted in human intelligence is not to say that it is primarily or exclusively rooted in human intelligence. While the natural law is the *measure* of the perfection of the human mind, the human mind is not by itself the standard of its own perfection: it is not the summum bonum. Only the divine mind that creates human nature, that impresses upon it its natural inclinations, and that gives it the light of reason, thereby promulgates authentically natural law.

It is important to observe that for St. Thomas, law as such—including the natural law—is ordered to the common good. The common good is a good that is one in number, which by its nature is more diffusive and communicable to many, as opposed to individual goods which if one has, another does not. Private goods are ordained to common goods, and there is an order of common goods that terminates in God as the extrinsic common good of the universe. We see the theocentric character of the common good in the following lines of St. Thomas in *Summa contra Gentiles*:

> Further, a particular good is ordered to the common good as to an end; indeed, the being of a part depends on the being of the whole. So, also, the good of a nation is more godlike than the good of one man. Now the supreme good, namely God, is the common good, since the good of all things depends on him: and the good whereby each thing is good, is the particular good of that thing, and of those that depend thereon. Therefore all things are directed to one good, namely, to God, as their end.[19]

Further, the essential role of the common good in the moral life is manifest in *Summa theologiae*, *Prima secundae*, question 19, article 10:

> But a man's will is not right in willing a particular good, unless he refer it to the common good as an end: since even the natural appetite of each part is ordained to the common good of the whole. Now it is the end that supplies the formal reason, as it were, of willing whatever is directed to the end. Consequently, in order that a man will some particular good with a right will, he must will that particular good materially, and the Divine and universal good, formally. Therefore the human will is bound to be conformed to the Divine will, as to that which is willed formally, for it is bound to will the Divine and universal good.[20]

The universality in question is the universality of God as the ultimate common good. Thus, we have seen that natural law is true law; that God is promulgator and source of the natural law; that natural law is a rational participation of eternal law; that natural law serves the common good, and that God is the supreme common good; and that God as supreme common good is the final end and must be willed formally in every good act. Clearly, natural law is theocentric, and a non-theocentric natural law doctrine cannot rightly be said to be that of Aquinas.

WHAT IS THE CONTENT OF THE NATURAL LAW? THE PRIMACY OF OUR DESIRE TO KNOW AND LOVE GOD

What is the content of the natural law? Here one observes St. Thomas's stress upon the hierarchy of ends, and his teaching regarding the primacy of our desire to know and love God. Here we converge upon my second proposition, that the knowledge and love of God are the capstone of natural law even considered in precision from grace.

According to St. Thomas, by nature we share certain inclinations with all creatures (e.g., to persist in being); yet other inclinations we share with the animal creation (such as those toward food, or sex); while yet others derive from our specifically rational nature (such as desire for friendship, or the desire to know the truth about God). As Yves Simon puts it in *The Tradition of Natural Law*, "Thus everything that is right by nature is right either because the universal nature of being is such, or because the universal nature of animal is such, or because the rational nature is such."[21]

These inclinations are neither incomparable nor of equal dignity, but ranked according to their proximity to the final end. As St. Thomas puts it, "according to the *order of* natural inclinations, is the *order* of the precepts of the natural law."[22] Just as the human creature is more than a mere sum of his parts, so the good life for the human creature is more than a summing up of incomparable and teleologically disparate goods.

Human inclinations are more or less proximate to the final end of human living. Every human good derives its "appetibility," its desirability, from its relation to the ultimate good for the rational creature. As St. Thomas puts it, "Man must, of necessity, desire all, whatsoever he desires, for the last end" (Dicendum quod necesse est quod omnia quae homo appetit, appetat propter ultimum finem).[23] This final end, while at the level of nature formally distinct from the last end revealed through grace, is nonetheless God.

It is the way of attending to God—natural, or supernatural—that varies between imperfect natural happiness and perfect supernatural beatitude. The natural law and the *lex nova* of divine charity and wisdom converge, under diverse formalities, upon the same God. Indeed, only because we are directed to God by nature is our further—and formally distinct—direction to God in grace possible. As St. Thomas puts it in a decisively important passage of the *Summa theologiae*, "From natural love angel and man alike love God before themselves and with greater love. Otherwise, if either of them loved self more than God, it would follow that natural love would be perverse, and that it would not be perfected but destroyed by charity."[24] If one's acts do not reflect this rightly ordered *natural* love (distinct from *supernatural* charity), then they violate the natural law. St. Paul's Letter to the Romans insists (1:19–21):

> For what can be known about God is evident to them, because God made it evident to them. Ever since the creation of the world, his invisible attributes of eternal power and divinity have been able to be understood and perceived in what he has made. As a result, they have no excuse; for although they knew God they did not accord him glory as God or give him thanks. Instead, they became vain in their reasoning, and their senseless minds were darkened.

It is not the issue of the existence of God alone that is at stake in this passage. Nor is the issue here that of religion as a virtue that is part of natural justice (as St. Thomas teaches us).[25] Rather what is involved is the very character of the natural law. For this law has as its natural capstone the love and gratitude we owe to God by nature.

It cannot be plausibly supposed that the aboriginal ordering of rational nature to know and love God more than itself has no practical bearing on the natural moral life. *To* the *contrary, this ordering of the rational nature to God* is *the very natural purpose of the moral life*. Moral activity is not its own end: it is—even at the natural level—directed to something above itself. In the *Summa contra Gentiles*, book 3, chapter 34, St. Thomas reduces to absurdity the idea of moral activity as the ultimate good. He compares this notion with the idea that making war is for its own sake rather than for justice or peace—a nightmarish thought.

Moreover our happiness consists in an operation of the speculative rather than the practical intelligence.[26] We wish rationally to possess our happiness, to be happy and not merely to be *seeking* or *striving* for happiness. Hence for St. Thomas our final end in the actual economy of providence is twofold: imperfect natural happiness in the knowledge and love of God from afar mediated by creation, and perfect supernatural beatitude consisting in direct vision of God.

What all this means is that it is part of the content of the natural law itself—even apart from grace—that one love God more than oneself and above all things. And it is the derangement of this rational inclination to love God above ourselves that radically disorders the moral life. *There is simply no room for doubt about the teaching of St. Thomas on this point: it is with natural love, even prior to divine charity, that we aboriginally flow forth from creation loving our Creator above ourselves. When this rational inclination is diminished the whole ethical life shivers with the tremors of alienation.*

There is a tendency to be discerned in much contemporary moral theology and philosophy to treat the natural law as merely a compendium of practical rational exhortations possessing no divinely normative status. This is what becomes of natural law when it is disembedded from its definitively theological character. The spectacle of moral theologians exalting subjective conscience above the moral law flows from a failure to understand natural law as literal and nonmetaphorical *law*.[27] For many today, natural law seems to reduce to a collection of "rules of thumb" for a practical reason which by itself decrees the law. In this vision, man is left alone in the garden of his inclinations to devise rules befitting them. But this vision is metaphysically and morally false: man *discovers* a law that is not of his own making. The light of reason, which participates the eternal law, discloses the path of human obedience to God. The natural law is not a mere *instrument* whereby moral experience is organized by human intelligence: it is the ordering wisdom of God itself as participated by the rational creature. The natural law is in principle immutable because it is *nothing* other than the eternal law.

OUR KNOWLEDGE OF NATURAL LAW: IMPEDED BY SIN, VIVIFIED BY GRACE

Here we approach my third and final proposition, that we lose nothing by acknowledging the aid we receive from grace in knowing the natural law. St. Thomas makes clear that nature is, in *part*, destroyed by original sin.[28] He identifies three senses of human nature: first, the principles and properties of human nature; second, the natural inclination to virtue; and third, that gift of original justice conferred upon the first parents of the human race. He states that the third (the gift of original justice) is destroyed by sin; the second (the natural inclination to virtue) is diminished by sin; and the first (the principles and properties of human nature) is neither destroyed nor diminished by sin (after all, if they *were* diminished or lost, then human beings could not be damned—because the damned would not be human!). *Because* the root of our natural inclination to virtue is the rational nature, this inclination cannot be wholly extinguished: even the damned possess it, for it is the source of their unending remorse of conscience. The tendency of the rational creature to God cannot wholly be eradicated.

Yet our natural inclination to love God more than ourselves is diminished by sin. And, being the capstone of the law, this diminution in the natural love of God is bound to affect all lesser rectitudes, much as the weakening of gravitational force attracting a body toward a planet diminishes motion on the part of the totality of the object and not merely on its most advanced part.

Catholics rightly emphasize the distance between themselves and their Protestant brethren on the question of original sin's corruption of human nature. But if they follow St. Thomas, they will distinguish *what is known* when we know the natural law from *that set of conditions under which we best know this law*. For St. Thomas the latter conditions unabashedly are those of grace. While root knowledge of the natural law cannot be extirpated—because the rational form and its inclination to virtue can be diminished but not totally suppressed—nonetheless many of its real implications in virtue can be obscured and diminished. Rational inclination is wounded and weakened by sin.

Natural law loses nothing of its relative independence and autonomy by the realization that in this given order of providence it is inscribed in an economy of grace. It is the work of sin to diminish our natural inclination toward God, and the work of grace to restore it and elevate it in supernatural charity. One of the principal means of this restoration is the graced insemination of our minds with natural truths that we are wont to neglect. Many a conversion begins with humble acknowledgment and contemplation of the natural law, opening the way for greater mysteries. To know the original rectitude of nature is to taste the divine goodness and encounter the refreshing breezes of natural inclinations no longer fetid with self-love and timidity.

A perfect knowledge of natural law apart from grace in this economy of providence appears to be chimeric, owing to the darkening of the mind and will by sinful passions. Thus St. Thomas holds:

> Whence man in the state of integral nature referred the love of himself and of all things to the love of God as to the end, and thus he loved God more than himself and above all things. But in the state of corrupt nature man falls short of this according to the appetite of his rational will, which, unless it be healed through the grace of God follows its own private good because of the corruption of nature. And so we must say that in the state of integral nature man did not need the gift of grace added to his natural endowments in order to love God above all things naturally, although he needed God's help moving him to it; but in the state of corrupted nature, man needs, even for this, the help of grace healing his nature.[29]

CONCLUSION

What is required is less a moral calculus than the affirmation of natural law and divine law, the conformity of the mind to the ordered whole of the synthesis of nature and grace which exceeds the sum of its parts: a metaphysically rooted change of gestalt. The persistent obstruction to this is the discounting of natural truth as irrelevant, with the subsequent implication that the moral significance of the normative divine ordering of human nature is rejected.

A prudential advisement may be drawn from this consideration of the natural law: theological indifferentism in the teaching of the natural law wounds its very heart, and by consequence the life of the limbs is impaired. Whatever prudential "tacking" against the secular winds we do, our task is to teach and live the *whole* of the natural law. Abstraction from this reality, like a doctor's abstraction from the idea of health, amounts to losing the capstone and defining purpose of all the rest. Neither surgery nor moral reasoning and effort are ends in themselves: they are ordered to a health that is above them. A wounded, morbid, and moribund world begs not for moral guidance alone but to rediscover the possibility of health: a health that in every age begins with obedience to the divine government and ends in knowledge and love of God.

NOTES

1. Aquinas, *Summa theologiae* 2.1.19.3 (translation mine, derived from that of the Fathers of the English Dominican Province, rev. ed. [1920; public domain]; emphasis mine); "In his autem quae sunt ad finem, rectitudo rationis consistit in conformitate ad appetitum finis debiti. *Sed tamen et ipse appetitus finis debiti praesupponit rectam apprehensionem de fine, quae est per rationem.*" All Latin quotations are taken from the *Corpus Thomisticum: S. Thomae de Aquino opera omnia*, made available online by the University of Navarre (http://www.corpusthomisticum.org/iopera.html). This is not because the author fails to value the Leonine texts; but because (a) no sufficient difference in the cited material exists to weigh against relying on the editions cited, and (b) the editions cited are *actually accessible* to students who have neither the funds to afford Leonine folios nor proximity to libraries that possess them. The Leonine Commission was founded to make these texts available for theological and philosophic use, and while PDFs of Leonine texts are slowly being released, at the present moment—and in the judgment of the present author—the Navarre site may rightfully boast of having the most easily accessible collection of Thomas's texts.

2. Aquinas, *Sth* 2.1.90.4; "rationis ordinatio ad bonum commune, ab eo qui curam communitatis habet, promulgata."

3. Aquinas, *Sth* 2.1.91.2; "lex naturalis nihil aliud est quam participatio legis aeternae in rationali creatura."

4. Aquinas, *Sth* 2.1.91.1; "ideo ipsa ratio gubernationis rerum in Deo sicut in principe universitatis."

5. Aquinas, *Sth* 2.1.90.4; "quod promulgatio legis naturae est ex hoc ipso quod Deus eam mentibus hominum inseruit naturaliter cognoscendam."

6. Aquinas, *Sth* 2.1.91.3; "ratio humana secundum se non est regula rerum, sed principia ei naturaliter indita, sunt quaedam regulae generales et mensurae omnium eorum quae sunt per hominem agenda, quorum ratio naturalis est regula et mensura, licet non sit mensura eorum quae sunt a natura."

7. Aquinas, *Sth* 2.1.91.2.

8. Aquinas, *Sth* 1.79.11; "intellectus speculativus per extensionem fit practicus."

9. Aquinas, *Sth*; "Accidit autem alicui apprehenso per intellectum, quod ordinetur ad opus, vel non ordinetur. Secundum hoc autem differunt intellectus speculativus et practicus. Nam intellectus speculativus est, qui quod apprehendit, non ordinat ad opus, sed ad solam veritatis considerationem, practicus vero intellectus dicitur, qui hoc quod apprehendit, ordinat ad opus."

10. Aquinas, *Sth*; "Ita obiectum intellectus practici est bonum ordinabile ad opus, sub ratione veri. Intellectus enim practicus veritatem cognoscit, sicut et speculativus; sed veritatem cognitam ordinat ad opus."

11. See Aquinas, *Sth* 2.1.18.7:

> One and the same thing, considered in its substance, cannot be in two species, one of which is not subordinate to the other. But in respect of those things which are superadded to the substance, one thing can be contained under different species. Thus one and the same fruit, as to its color, is contained under one species, i.e., a white thing: and, as to its perfume, under the species of sweet-smelling things. In

like manner an action which, as to its substance, is in one natural species, considered in respect to the moral conditions that are added to it, can belong to two species, as stated above. [Ad primum ergo dicendum quod secundum substantiam suam non potest aliquid esse in duabus speciebus, quarum una sub altera non ordinetur. Sed secundum ea quae rei adveniunt, potest aliquid sub diversis speciebus contineri. Sicut hoc pomum, secundum colorem, continetur sub hac specie, scilicet albi, et secundum odorem, sub specie bene redolentis. Et similiter actus qui secundum substantiam suam est in una specie naturae, secundum conditiones morales supervenientes, ad duas species referri potest, ut supra dictum est.]

This is important because of Thomas's teaching that form is received, and matter is a receiving, potential principle. Here one sees that the natural species can receive diverse specific form owing to the moral conditions added to it, which however makes clear that the natural species is necessarily itself a material cause of the object of the external act. While prime matter can receive any form, in natural things Thomas teaches that the actual reception of form requires that the matter be disposed to receive the form. The matter of the diamond may admit of refracting light, but it does not admit of being cut with a plastic fork. The matter of an act of stabbing in the heart may admit of the moral relations of/orders to self-defense, killing in just war, or murder, but it does not admit of the moral relations of/orders to "friendly greeting" or "feeding the poor." The act itself, its integral nature, and its per se effects thus necessarily must be included within the object of the external act, under the *ratio* of appetibility under which the agent either prefers this act as a way toward the intended end, or at least is willing to accept this act in the case where there is no other way toward the end.

12. Aquinas, *Sth* 2.1.91.2; "nihil aliud sit quam impressio divini luminis in nobis."

13. John Finnis, *Natural Law and Natural Rights* (Oxford: Clarendon Press, 1980), 49.

14. Yves Simon, *The Tradition of Natural Law* (New York: Fordham University, 1992), 62.

15. Finnis, *Natural Law and Natural Rights*, 280–81.

16. Finnis, *NLNR*, 294nx.6.

17. Aquinas, *Sth* 2.1.91.2; "participatio legis aeternae in creatura rationali proprie lex vocatur, nam lex est aliquid rationis."

18. Aquinas, *Sth* 2.1.90, prol.

19. Aquinas, *Summa contra Gentiles* 3.17.6 (translation mine, derived in part from that of Vernon Bourke et al., eds. and trans. [Notre Dame, IN: University of Notre Dame Press, 1975]); Praeterea. Bonum particulare ordinatur in bonum commune sicut in finem: esse enim partis est propter esse totius; unde et bonum gentis est divinius quam bonum unius hominis. Bonum autem summum, quod est Deus, est bonum commune, cum ex eo universorum bonum dependeat: bonum autem quo quaelibet res bona est, est bonum particulare ipsius et aliorum quae ab ipso dependent. Omnes igitur res ordinantur sicut in finem in unum bonum, quod est Deus.

20. Aquinas, *Sth* 2.1.19.10; Non est autem recta voluntas alicuius hominis volentis aliquod bonum particulare, nisi referat illud in bonum commune sicut in finem, cum etiam naturalis appetitus cuiuslibet partis ordinetur in bonum commune totius. Ex fine autem sumitur quasi formalis ratio volendi illud quod ad finem ordinatur. Unde ad hoc quod aliquis recta voluntate velit aliquod particulare bonum, oportet quod illud particulare bonum sit volitum materialiter, bonum autem commune divinum sit volitum formaliter. Voluntas igitur humana tenetur conformari divinae voluntati in volito formaliter, tenetur enim velle bonum divinum et commune.

21. Simon, *The Tradition of Natural Law* (supra), 124.

22. Aquinas, *Sth* 2.1.94.2 (my emphasis); "Secundum igitur ordinem inclinationum naturalium, est ordo praeceptorum legis naturae."

23. Aquinas, *Sth* 2.1.1.6.

24. Aquinas, *Sth* 1.60.5; "quod naturali dilectione etiam angelus, et homo plus, et principalius diligat Deum, quam seipsum. Alioquin, si naturaliter plus seipsum diligeret, quam Deum, sequeretur, quod naturalis dilectio esset perversa, et quod non perficeretur per charitatem, sed destrueretur."

25. Aquinas, *Sth* 2.2.81.2.

26. Aquinas, *Sth* 2.1.3.5.

27. Of course, this is not to reduce the eternal law, the natural law, or for that matter the *lex nova* of grace (which is, itself, a *higher* participation of the eternal law than is even the natural law), to the status of a pure deontology. To the contrary, the passively participated teleological order is indeed that participation of the eternal law which contributes the content known through active rational participation of the eternal law: obligation specifies that which is necessarily required for the achievement of the end and the conformity of judgment, appetite, and action to the divinely impressed order of ends.

28. Aquinas, *Sth* 2.1.85.1.

29. Aquinas, *Sth* 2.1.109.3; Unde homo in statu naturae integrae dilectionem sui ipsius referebat ad amorem Dei sicut ad finem, et similiter dilectionem omnium aliarum rerum. Et ita Deum diligebat plus quam seipsum, et super omnia. Sed in statu naturae corruptae homo ab hoc deficit secundum appetitum voluntatis rationalis, quae propter corruptionem naturae sequitur bonum privatum, nisi sanetur per gratiam Dei. Et ideo dicendum est quod homo in statu naturae integrae non indigebat dono gratiae superadditae naturalibus bonis ad diligendum Deum naturaliter super omnia; licet indigeret auxilio Dei ad hoc eum moventis. Sed in statu naturae corruptae indiget homo etiam ad hoc auxilio gratiae naturam sanantis.

WORKS CITED

Aquinas. *Summa contra Gentiles*. Translated and edited by Vernon Bourke et al. Notre Dame, IN: University of Notre Dame Press, 1975.

———. *Summa theologiae*. In *Corpus Thomisticum: S. Thomae de Aquino opera omnia*. http://www.corpusthomisticum.org/iopera.html.

———. *Summa theologiae*. Translated by the Fathers of the English Dominican Province. Rev. ed. 1920.

Finnis, John. *Natural Law and Natural Rights*. Oxford: Clarendon Press, 1980.

Simon, Yves. *The Tradition of Natural Law*. New York: Fordham University, 1992.

Chapter Two

Natural Inclinations in Aquinas's Account of Natural Law

Michael Pakaluk

Inclinations are central to Thomas Aquinas's account of natural law. This chapter aims to clarify what the term "inclination" means and its role in natural law. What are human inclinations? Is there is an ordering of human inclinations? Is a human inclination a desire? Do we know about human inclinations in the same way we know about other things? Do we know about human inclinations through speculative or practical reason? How do we arrive at lawlike precepts from our natural knowledge of human inclinations?

WHAT DOES THE TERM *INCLINATION* (*INCLINATIO*) MEAN IN THE PHILOSOPHY OF AQUINAS?

Aquinas uses the term *inclinatio* in his account of natural law, when he says that precepts of the natural law are based on human inclinations (plural, Latin, *inclinationes*),[1] but it is important to understand that this term is not used solely or even primarily in the context of natural law, but rather it is something like a technical term in Aquinas's philosophy of nature generally.

To see that this is so, one should consider that Aquinas holds that a nature is an internal source of change and of rest in a thing. A nature belongs to a thing in virtue of the form that that thing has; and the change and rest which a thing's nature is responsible for are directed toward an end. Nature acts for an end or goal, and because to be a goal is to be a good, the nature of each thing aims at some good. The tendency to achieve its end which is imparted to a thing in virtue of its having a nature is what Aquinas refers to as a natural *inclinatio*. Thus, this notion of a natural *inclinatio* is basic to Aquinas's teleological understanding of nature.

Some significant passages from the *Summa* in which this conception is expressed are the following:

- "Upon the form follows an *inclinatio* to the end, or to an action, or to something of that sort; for everything, in so far as it is in actuality, acts and tends toward that which is in accordance with its form."[2]
- "It is common to every nature to have some *inclinatio*; and this is its natural appetite or love. This *inclinatio* is found to exist differently in different natures but in each according to its mode."[3]
- "It is necessary to assign an appetitive power to the soul. To make this evident, we must observe that some *inclinatio* follows every form: for example, fire, by its form, is inclined to rise, and to generate its like."[4]
- "Every *inclinatio* follows upon some form."[5]

It can be seen that for Aquinas the most important ideas are that an *inclinatio* follows upon form and that it tends to some end. It follows that the best way to identify the natural *inclinatio* (or, plural, *inclinationes*) of a thing would be to identify its natural form (or forms).

It should be noted that *inclinatio* is an analogical term for Aquinas, like many other important terms in Aristotelian philosophy. What this implies is that, for different kinds of things, and in different circumstances, correspondingly different phenomena will count as an *inclinatio*. A stone's falling toward the earth is an *inclinatio* for Aquinas, but also a dog's hungering for food, an angel's love of self, and a human being's love of knowledge. One kind of inclination is not exactly like another kind, and not entirely different, but rather the one varies relative to another in an understandable way given the difference in kind or circumstance. Like other analogical terms, then, *inclinatio* cannot be defined through identifying some common trait that is found in the same way in all cases of inclination. But one can clarify it through likenesses and closely related terms: thus, according to Aquinas, an inclination is like a relation to an end;[6] it is a tendency;[7] an impetus;[8] an ordering ("love is like an inclination or order in a natural thing");[9] an aptitude;[10] and even a kind of law, insofar as that which has an inclination is like something subject to a law directing it to that end.[11]

Aquinas's notion of *inclinatio* must be viewed in connection with his conviction that the realm of nature is a distinctive kind of reality precisely because it manifests change. Thus, anything in nature must, through the kind of thing that it is, be ordered toward participating somehow in movement and change. Its *inclinatio* is that through which it so participates. That to be a natural being is to be ordered toward movement and change is so central a conviction for Aquinas that he uses it to argue that there cannot be any natural beings which are infinite in magnitude, since an infinite being could not move: it could not move in a straight line, because there would be no place where it was not, into which it could move, and it could not move through rotation, because radii at infinite distances from the center would be infinitely distant also from themselves, and therefore no point on one radius would ever be able to occupy the same place as another point equidistant from the center on another radius—which is what the rotational motion of that thing would require.[12]

WHAT ARE THE NATURAL *INCLINATIONES* OF A HUMAN BEING?

Since an *inclinatio* is consequent upon form, then there are as many natural *inclinationes* in a human being as there are natural forms. Aquinas thinks that the definition of a human being, in terms of genus and species, reveals the relevant forms. A human being is defined as a rational animal: thus the genus, animal, indicates one natural form, and the species, rational, indicates another.

What is meant by *form* in this connection? A form is an intelligible structure which serves to sort something into a kind. So, to speak of the natural forms of a human being is to speak of the kinds into which a human being is sorted in virtue of what it intelligibly is by nature. Hence, another way of approaching this question of the natural forms of a human being is to ask into what kinds a human being is naturally sorted, or, alternatively, what are the main commonalities that a human being has by nature with other existing things. So, in saying that a human being is in the genus, "animal," one is saying that an aspect of what a human being intelligibly is, by nature, establishes a commonality between human beings and animals in general. Or, in saying that a human being is in the species "rational," one is saying that an aspect of what a human being intelligibly is, by nature, establishes a commonality between human beings and rational beings in general.

This way of identifying commonalities, through considering with which sort of things it is by nature grouped, implies that there is a third natural form (or grouping, and commonality), which can be attributed to human beings, namely, that which a human being has in virtue of being an existing thing within the category of substance. Aristotle's doctrine of the categories is a doctrine of highest kinds or *ultima genera*, the most general kinds into which beings are sorted in virtue of their form. Hence, besides looking to the definition of a human being, to identify its natural forms and its *inclinationes*, one may also look to the doctrine of the categories, note that a human being is a being in the category of substance, and therefore say that a human being also has a commonality with all other natural substances.

These three *inclinationes* that I have been discussing—substance (category), animal (genus), rational (species)—are exactly those that Aquinas identifies in his discussion of natural law:

> In man there is first of all an inclination to good in accordance with the nature which he has in common with all substances. . . . Secondly, there is in man an inclination to things that pertain to him more specially, according to that nature which he has in common with other animals. . . . Thirdly, there is in man an inclination to good, according to the nature of his reason, which nature is proper to him.[13]

So, not only is *inclinatio* a technical term taken from a broadly Aristotelian philosophy of nature, but also Aquinas's method of identifying *inclinationes* depends upon the Aristotelian doctrine of the categories and his conviction of the possibility of devising satisfactory definitions in envisaged within Aristotelian logic and philosophy of nature.

IS THERE AN ORDERING OF THE *INCLINATIONES* OF A HUMAN BEING?

Antecedently we would expect that Aquinas believes that there is indeed an ordering, because of his commitment to the classical doctrine of an *ergon*, or function, which he inherits from Plato and Aristotle, which may be explained as follows. The *ergon* of a thing is what it is meant to do and to achieve. Plato says that one should locate a thing's *ergon* in what is distinctive of or proper to it: the *ergon* of a kind thing is what that kind of thing alone can do or can do better than any other kind of thing.[14] The *ergon* of a thing is its characteristic or distinctive work, and everything else in a thing should be interpreted in relation to and as contributing to this *ergon*. To discover the *ergon* of a thing, Plato and Aristotle say, one should look to what sets a thing apart, or what is "proper" to it (*idion* in Greek, *proprium* in Latin). In a human being, reason is distinctive or proper, and thus Aquinas holds, following Aristotle and Plato, that the *ergon* or distinctive task of a human being is to live in accordance with reason. It would follow that *inclinationes* that are associated with aspects of human nature other than the rational aspect of human nature are subordinated to that proper and distinctive inclinatio which is consequent upon the rational nature of a human being.

Although the ordering of *inclinationes* is not a topic in his discussion of natural law, Aquinas does affirm it in his treatment of the kinds of law, in his discussion of whether and in what sense there is in human beings a "law of sin" (*fomes peccati*).[15] In that discussion, Aquinas first says that those who are under a law to that extent "receive an *inclinatio*" from the lawgiver, in the sense that their being directed and ordered by that law sets them on the path toward the common good which that law serves. Then, he says,

> under the Divine Lawgiver various creatures have various natural inclinations, so that what is, as it were, a law for one, is against the law for another: thus I might say that fierceness is, in a way, the law of a dog, but against the law of a sheep or another meek animal. And so the law of man, which, by the Divine ordinance, is allotted to him, according to his proper natural condition, is that he should act in accordance with reason: and this law was so effective in the primitive state, that nothing either beside or against reason could take man unawares.[16]

In this passage he is speaking as if there is only one *inclinatio* in a human being and only one law, clearly because he is presupposing that everything else in man is subordinated to it. Indeed, the possibility of an *inclinatio* that is distinct from this principal one, in the sense that its "law" can be at odds with the *inclinatio* of reason, is the result solely of original sin, as Aquinas goes on to say in the body of the article. But in the reply to the third objection we find the following consideration, highly relevant for our purposes. The objection is that "the law is ordained to the common good, as stated above. But the *fomes* inclines us, not to the common, but to our own private good. Therefore the *fomes* has not the nature of sin," and in reply Aquinas states,

> This argument considers the *fomes* as to its peculiar *inclinatio*, and not as to its origin. And yet if the *inclinatio* of sensuality as found in other animals is considered, there it is ordained to the common good, namely, to the preservation of nature in the species or in the individual. And this is so in human beings also, in so far as sensuality is subject to reason. But it is called *fomes* in so far as it strays from the order of reason.[17]

There are two things interesting about this reply. First, Aquinas clearly presupposes that an *inclinatio* of a natural being has as its end some common good of that natural being: this consideration is essential for any account of natural law as based upon human inclinationes, because, as indeed is said in the objection, nothing which fails to aim at a common good can be considered properly a law. Second, Aquinas is clearly interpreting the *inclinatio* which we have in common with other animals, which he calls the "*inclinatio* of sensuality," as rightly and by nature subordinated to that to which the *inclinatio* of reason inclines.

So we see that Aquinas clearly regards the more widely shared *inclinationes* of a natural thing as subordinated to that which proper to it, and that in a human being the two other *inclinationes* (in common with substances and with animals) are subordinated to the *inclinatio* associated with human reason.

IS AN *INCLINATIO* A DESIRE?

An *inclinatio* in Aquinas's sense is certainly not what we refer to as a "desire," for four reasons. First, what we call a desire is subjective, in the sense that we are conscious of it, and it is accompanied by feelings of pleasure or pain (for example, the desire which is hunger is painful, the desire for continuing to enjoy a beautiful landscape is pleasant). But an *inclinatio* can take the form simply of an adaptation or ordering of parts or elements to some end, and therefore it is not subjective. For instance, it would make sense and it would be correct to say that the *inclinatio* of a knife is to cut, but not that the knife desires to cut (except if one speaks metaphorically). Aquinas would express this point by saying that, while a desire is attributable to the soul, things without souls can have *inclinationes*, and, moreover, things with souls can have *inclinationes* that are evident in the body as well as in the soul.

Second and relatedly, what we call a desire in a living thing is always, for Aquinas, attributable to some appetitive faculty of the soul: for instance, the desire for food is attributable to the concupiscible faculty, and the desire for knowledge is attributable to rational appetite, or what is called the "will." However, the *inclinatio* of a living thing is attributable to it in virtue of its body–soul unity. So the *inclinatio* of sensuality, already mentioned, is manifested in the structure of the digestive tract and the sexual organs also, not simply in the soul. Again, the *inclinatio* of reason in human beings, which admittedly inclines toward knowledge, is manifested in the human body also, for example, in the fact that human beings walk on two feet and therefore have a head which rises above the ground, so that human beings can easily look into the distance or up at the heavens.

Third, an *inclinatio* in the sense relevant to natural law is a natural *inclinatio*, that is, it pertains to what a natural being essentially is, whereas what we call desires can be and typically are incidental to human nature and fleeting. Recall that an *inclinatio* is supposed to be an immediate consequence of what a natural being is: to be a certain kind of thing is to have an *inclinatio* of a certain kind. There is a sense, then, in which a natural being is even constituted by its *inclinationes*; however, what we call desires are tertiary, in the sense that for Aquinas they follow from faculties, which follow from the essence of the soul.

Fourth, as we saw, because an *inclinatio* belongs to something as belonging to a certain kind, it has as its object the good of that individual as belonging to that kind, which is to say that its object or end is for some common good of that kind, not a private good of an individual. In contrast, what we call desires can be and typically are for private goods, that is, the private good either of the individual or other person who is the object of that desire.

DO WE KNOW ABOUT THE HUMAN *INCLINATIONES* IN THE SAME WAY THAT WE KNOW ABOUT ANYTHING ELSE?

Aquinas holds that the basic precepts of the natural law are naturally apprehended by human beings in general. These precepts, he says, are based upon a natural apprehension of human goods, corresponding to human *inclinationes*. It can therefore seem that, for Aquinas, we have some kind of special knowledge of human *inclinationes* and special access to them. Such a view seems suggested by the following sentence, as it is translated in the commonly used Dominican Fathers translation: "Good has the nature of an end, and evil, the nature of a contrary, hence it is that all those things to which man has a natural inclination, are naturally apprehended by reason as being good, and consequently as objects of pursuit, and their contraries as evil, and objects of avoidance."[18] This sentence seems to suggest that we have knowledge of basic human goods, not from knowing about human *inclinationes*—as we know the *inclinationes* of any other kind of thing—but rather from having those *inclinationes*. It looks as though Aquinas is saying that when we "naturally apprehend" the object of an inclination, we are making explicit the object of an inclination which we experience and perhaps therefore only intuitively or implicitly grasp. However, this interpretation should be rejected for a variety of reasons. It is better to hold instead that, for Aquinas, our knowledge of human *inclinationes*, and of the human goods to which they are directed, is like our knowledge of anything else.

The first reason is that the knowledge of human *inclinationes* is bound up, as we have seen, with knowledge of "what man is," that is, with the knowledge of what sort of thing a human being is. That sort of knowledge is a familiarity with the kind, not with an individual member of the kind. As being a knowledge of the kind, it is presumably like any knowledge of any kind of thing, that is, it involves the grasp of universals which are true of any member of that kind. The universal would be grasped as the result of an induction, based on the experience of various members of the kind, and issuing in an act of abstraction. In contrast, any tendency which an individual experiences in himself could not, so far, be claimed to be an *inclinatio* belonging to the kind of thing to which he belongs.

The second reason is that two of the *inclinationes* in the above passage are identified precisely as those that human beings have in common with other kinds of things, namely, the *inclinatio* which we have in common with any natural substance, and the *inclinatio* which we have in common with other animals. It would seem, then, that our knowledge of these *inclinationes*, as they are found in ourselves, must be on a par with our knowledge of those *inclinationes*, as they are found in other things: otherwise how could it be asserted that these inclinations are shared by those other sorts of things?

Clearly, to know oneself as having these *inclinationes* is precisely to know oneself as akin to these other kinds of things. But our knowledge of these *inclinationes* as they are found in other things is like our knowledge of anything at all: it is our knowledge of those other things as having a certain kind of nature and as being inclined and ordered, as a result, to certain kinds of things. In contrast, any individual's experience of a tendency within himself could not be identified as something he has in common with those other kinds of things. What would be the basis of someone's saying that a felt tendency within himself is an inclination he has in common, for instance, with stones or fire?

A third reason is that Aquinas's examples of things that are "naturally known" are such as would be known through ordinary experience: one should expect, then, that our natural grasp of human *inclinationes* would be on a par. Consider for example the principle that "a whole is greater than its part." We know this through ordinary experience in daily life of what a whole is and what a part is. Therefore, knowledge of human *inclinationes* is presumably also acquired through ordinary experience in daily life. Indeed, it seems that, for Aquinas, naturally acquired knowledge is defined simply as knowledge which is not acquired either through any special experience or through any special inquiry: "those things which are naturally known are known in themselves, since no diligent application to inquiry is required for arriving at knowledge of them."[19] And

> some things are known right away by man from the start without diligent application or inquiry: first principles are like that, not only in speculative matters, such as that every whole is greater than its part and principles like that, but also in matters of action, such as that bad is to be avoided and principles like that. Those principles are naturally known which are principles or starting points for all knowledge which follows, which is acquired through diligent application.[20]

One might characterize naturally apprehended knowledge, then, as knowledge that we typically acquire as living in the "human condition."

A fourth reason is that, for Aquinas, it is not possible to have direct knowledge of the soul's essence or "habits." We do not even have direct knowledge of our own will, except through acts of the will, which Aquinas describes as particular *inclinationes* resulting from a prior grasped form, which is the object of the will.[21] Contrary to what Plato seems to have held, and likewise much later, Descartes, Aquinas followed Aristotle in holding that we can know the soul only through knowing its particular actualizations. Hence, on this sort of view, it would seem, it would not be the case that the having of an *inclinatio* could provide a special basis for knowledge of the soul, or any special access to what was in the soul. Knowledge of the human soul would be of a piece with knowledge about the human nature.

For all that, some misunderstandings of Aquinas's view should be avoided. That something is on his terms naturally known would not mean, of course, that people are always able to formulate, or eventually succeed in formulating, on their own, accurate assertions expressing that knowledge, or that they could not regard themselves, even, as justified in asserting the contrary. Consider the principle of noncontradiction, which Aquinas holds is naturally known: even though it is naturally known, people generally never formulate that principle until they study logic, and some philosophers—such as Heraclitus, as Aquinas interprets him in the commentary on Aristotle's *Metaphysics*, book 4—even deny the principle. Again, that something is naturally known would not mean that all human beings do arrive at knowledge of it, or that human beings invariably know it, except in some virtual or potential sense: children know the principle of noncontradiction only virtually, in the sense that there is something within them that does develop through many routes into a clearer realization of it, and severely damaged adults can be said to know it in addition potentially, in the sense that, if they were in healthy condition, then they would know it. Aquinas holds the "ends of the virtues" are like that: influenced by Augustine no doubt, he says that they are naturally known, and are virtually present in human beings from the very beginning in the manner of "seeds,"[22] which contain a principle of life, yet require culture and care—and so he also holds that whether someone, as an adult, does indeed recognize and deliberately strive for the "ends of the virtues" depends upon whether he has received a proper upbringing, because those who have acquired vices will not, as a result, have the correct ends.

The faulty interpretation—that we know about human *inclinationes* through a subjective acquaintance with them—gets some support by some inaccuracies in the familiar and widely used translation of the Dominican Fathers. The translation quoted above renders Aquinas's view thus: "All those things to which man has a natural inclination, are naturally apprehended by reason as being good, and consequently as objects of pursuit." But the clause should in fact read, "all those things to which man has a natural inclination, man's reason naturally apprehends as goods, and, as a consequence, as things to be pursued in action." The difference is slight, but the common translation gives encouragement to the idea that Aquinas is suggesting that an individual "feels" or "experiences" his inclinations and takes what they aim at therefore to be good. However, what Aquinas is actually saying is, in effect, that ordinary shared human knowledge recognizes certain things as obviously good for beings constituted such as we are.

DO WE KNOW HUMAN *INCLINATIONES* THROUGH SPECULATIVE OR PRACTICAL REASON?

For Aquinas, that natural substances have *inclinationes* as a consequence of their forms is a general truth about nature; it is a claim within "natural philosophy," or what we would call "science." Moreover, that what these *inclinationes* aim at are natural goods, for those beings which have those inclinations, is similarly a truth of natural philosophy. For Aquinas, there is nothing about the word *good* which lifts an assertion employing it out of the realm of science and into some other putatively "normative" domain of discourse. After all, for Aquinas, the natural world is teleological, that is, "nature is in the class of causes which act for the sake of an end," as Aristotle says in his *Physics*.[23]

It is a matter of "speculative" reason—that is, reason insofar as it simply tries to determine how things are and what is true—that natural substances have *inclinationes*, and that there are certain natural goods which are aimed at by these *inclinationes*. Nor is this a particularly strange idea: we are not surprised if, say, an expert on wolves is brought in to tell us how a captured wolf should best be cared for, before being released, or if an expert on a certain kind of beetle proves to be the person who can tell us what is good for beetles and, contrariwise, bad for them, if we wish to exterminate them.

For Aquinas and Aristotle, when the object of an *inclinatio* is disputable, that dispute is apparently also appropriately settled by "natural philosophy." For example, what is the correct interpretation of the *inclinatio* toward reproduction which Aquinas says we have in common with other animals? Aristotle articulates his view of the matter in his textbook on fundamental biology, *De anima*, and Aquinas follows him on it. The nature and purpose of an animal's *inclinatio* toward reproduction is that a species of animal, precisely as a species, may imitate God's immortality:

> For any living thing that has reached its normal development and which is unmutilated, and whose mode of generation is not spontaneous, the most natural act is the production of another like itself, an animal producing an animal, a plant a plant, in order that, as far as its nature allows, it may partake in the eternal and divine. That is the goal towards which all things strive, that for the sake of which they do whatsoever their nature renders possible. . . . Since then no living thing is able to partake in what is eternal and divine by uninterrupted continuance (for nothing perishable can forever remain one and the same), it tries to achieve that end in the only way possible to it, and success is possible in varying degrees; so it remains not indeed as the selfsame individual but continues its existence in something like itself—not numerically but specifically one.[24]

Again, that this is the correct interpretation of the urge toward reproduction in animals is a matter of speculative reason: the *De anima* is a book of natural philosophy, whereas practical rationality in Aristotle is found in the *Ethics* and *Politics*.

Aquinas in numerous places insists (again taking himself to be following Aristotle) that the difference between speculative and the practical reason is purely incidental.[25] One way of understanding this claim is that it is not the content of what reason holds or asserts on any occasion which makes that holding or assertion, as the case may be, either speculative or practical, but rather the purpose for which something is held or asserted: if something is held or asserted merely because it is true, and not for any direct purpose other than its truth, then that act is an act of speculative reason; otherwise it is assignable to practical reason. On this view, clearly, that human beings are a certain kind of thing (natural substances which are rational animals), which have certain *inclinationes* as a consequence of what they are, and that therefore certain things are good for beings of that kind—these would all be assertions of speculative reason.

Of course one might, in a manner, assign a statement to speculative or practical reason, on the grounds that typically and for the most part, no one would wish to hold or assert that statement, except because it was true (and so it "belonged" to speculative reason), or except in relation to some proposed action (and thus it was "practical"): thus, a truth about the solar system would (until recent times) have been assignable to speculative reason on these grounds, whereas a truth about the amount of money in someone's personal checking account would not be the sort of thing which typically someone would care to know or to assert except for some financial and therefore action-related purpose. Along these lines, one might want to distinguish and say that an observation about human *inclinationes*, as it is about already existing "forces" or "directions" in nature, is more likely to be asserted just because it is true, and so it is more assignable to speculative reason, whereas an observation about the good things which these inclinations are for, as it is about what things not yet existing best match these inclinations, is more likely to be asserted with a view to action and therefore is more assignable to practical reason.

HOW DO WE ARRIVE AT LAWLIKE PRECEPTS FROM OUR NATURAL KNOWLEDGE OF HUMAN *INCLINATIONES*?

Even precepts can be affirmed by speculative reason, in the form of statements which are nearly equivalent to the precepts, but which are about what constitutes due order: for example, "No smoking is allowed in the aircraft" may be asserted speculatively in the form of the close equivalent, "There is no smoking on the plane"—on the condition that one does not want fires in the airport. Again, "Women and children first" amounts to "Due order for evacuation is when the weaker members are first assisted in leaving by the stronger"—on the assumption that one wants everyone to get out alive, when that is attainable. Or again, "Put forks on the left" amounts to "Forks go on the left (if you please)." Note that, as these examples illustrate, if the orientation toward the goal for which the order is required can be presupposed, then there is no need to state the condition, and in that case the statement about due order is most appropriately put in the form of a precept: we address it toward someone as having or sharing that goal (or as someone we expect to have or think should have that goal). In this way there is no gap between *is* and *ought*: the big step was already taken, once we said that there are genuine *inclinationes* and goods in nature, which we can apprehend.

To say that something is good is to say also that what contributes to that thing is good—because a good is a goal, and that which is for the sake of a goal is thereby also a goal, and good. Hence, to say that something contributes to some good is to say that due order requires that someone who affirms that that good is good must affirm also that that which contributes to that good is good. This last point may be stated, for someone who takes that good as his own goal, in the form of a precept, to do what contributes to that good. Hence, anyone who is committed to the good is committed *eo ipso* to the precept; that is, he is bound by it, on pain of irrationality. In particular, then, in addressing anyone who takes those goods to which human *inclinationes* point as his own goal, it would be enough to state the precepts, to do what contributes to that good. That is how, for Aquinas, a finding about what things are naturally good for us implies precepts for us. The precepts hold for us because they command that which contributes to what we are inclined to, as members of the kind, and because we are members of the kind, we can be presupposed to have the requisite goals.

Another way of approaching this matter is to ask whether for Aquinas knowledge of human *inclinationes* can in principle be attained by any rational agent—say, by an angel looking on at human beings, or by a scientist from another planet—and, if so, whether that knowledge would also imply a law, for that observer, about how human beings are to be treated. The answer to the first question, for Aquinas, would surely be that any rational inquirer with sufficient intelligence can learn what things are good for human beings, just as we can learn what things are good for plants, wolves, or jellyfish. But, in answer to the second question, such knowledge would not imply precepts for those inquirers, or at least not imply them on the same grounds and in the same way, because these inquirers cannot be supposed themselves to have the very same *inclinationes* they have identified in us, as they are not members of the same kind.

CONCLUSION

Aquinas regards the basic precepts of natural law as true examples of law: they are precepts of reason, which bind all human beings to deal with all human beings in certain ways, for the sake of a common good, and they are set down by someone with responsibility for that common good, and promulgated.

If the human *inclinationes* which Aquinas speaks about in part 1, question 94, article 2 are interpreted as subjective feelings or felt tendencies within an individual human being, then it becomes impossible to arrive at laws having that sort of character, beginning from that sort of starting point. Laws which are universal for human beings, both in the subjects they bind and the objects they bind in relation to, must be based upon *inclinationes* which are understood as pertaining to and (in effect) constituting the kind, human beings.

Aquinas understands the natural law as based upon commonsense knowledge of what human beings are and a recognition of the natural teleology of human nature. If there is no such thing as human nature, and no natural teleology, then Aquinas's account of natural law is untenable. Similarly, any account of natural law consistent with a rejection of these premises will be sharply discontinuous with Aquinas's account.

NOTES

1. See Aquinas, *Summa theologiae*, trans. Fathers of the English Dominican Province (New York: Benzinger Bros., 1947), 2.1.94.2.
2. Aquinas, *Sth* 1.5.5.
3. Aquinas, *Sth* 1.60.1.
4. Aquinas, *Sth* 1.80.1.
5. Aquinas, *Sth* 1.8.1.
6. See Aquinas, *Sth* 1.28.1.
7. See Aquinas, *Commentaria in octo libros Physicorum* 1.10.5.
8. See Aquinas, *In Physic.* 8.8.7.
9. Aquinas, *Summa contra Gentiles* 4.26.8 (translation mine).
10. See Aquinas, *Sth* 2.1.23.4.
11. See Aquinas, *Sth* 2.1.91.6.
12. See Aquinas, *Sth* 1.7.3.
13. Aquinas, *Sth* 2.1.94.2.
14. See Plato, *Republic* 352e–53a.
15. Aquinas, *Sth* 2.1.91.6.
16. Aquinas, *Sth* 2.1.54.2.
17. Aquinas, *Sth* 2.1.91.6.
18. Aquinas, *Sth* 2.1.94.2.
19. Aquinas, *ScG* (supra) 1.10.5
20. Aquinas, *De virtutibus* 1.8 (translation mine).
21. Aquinas, *Sth* 1.87.
22. Aquinas, *Sth* 1.93.9; *Scriptum super Sententiis* 1.17.1.3 (translation mine).
23. Aristotle, *Physics* 2.8 (translation mine).
24. Aristotle, *De anima* 2.4.415a–b (translation mine).
25. See, e.g., Aquinas, *Sth* 1.79.11.

WORKS CITED

Aquinas. *Commentaria in octo libros Physicorum.*
———. *De virtutibus.*
———. *Scriptum super Sententiis.*
———. *Summa contra Gentiles.*
———. *Summa theologiae*. Translated by Fathers of the English Dominican Province. New York: Benzinger Bros., 1947.
Aristotle. *De anima.*
———. *Physics.*
Plato. *Republic.*

Chapter Three

Natural Law and Natural Right(s)

Conceptual and Terminological Clarifications

Fulvio Di Blasi

In the terms *natural law* and *natural right(s)*, the qualification *natural* specifies that the source of normativity or value is more than human.

"Natural" is opposed to "conventional" as something that does not proceed from human (contingent and historically determined) free choice, but rather precedes, grounds, and/or guides it—for example, as the natural attraction (or inclination) toward people of a different sex makes the entire sphere of human affective, familiar, and reproductive relationships possible; or as a natural inclination to live in society is supposedly the source and the limit of the agent's choice to join, here and now, any kind of cultural association or political party. What we call "conventional" always presupposes what we call "natural" precisely because it implies that nature is originally unindifferent toward certain goals or ends. If men were indifferent to women as dogs are indifferent to math textbooks or to Raffaello's paintings, we would not be here today—nor would Raffaello's paintings!

"Natural" is opposed to "conventional" also as necessity is opposed to freedom. It is necessary, for example, that human beings express themselves linguistically, but Italian, English, and Latin are freedom's children. Again, it is necessary that human beings are attracted by the "beautiful," but the *Discobolus* and *The Last Supper* are powerful and marvelous fruits of freedom. In this relationship between freedom and necessity, the former cannot exist without the latter, and from it—from nature, that is—it should be able to get, through reasoning, the meaning and the right direction. At the same time, it is also proper to say that (nature's) necessity cannot express itself but in the contingent and the conventional—there is no way to speak without using a specific language, as there is no way to feel the inclination to the beautiful independently from the existence of a piece of art we are working on or we are contemplating (even if only through our mind's eyes). "Natural" is not something that exists in and of itself in a separate world; rather it is primarily our way to understand the way of being of the existing things. The attempt to think of the "natural" as if it were a concrete (and separate?) existence is the typical mistake of rationalism of any sort.

When *natural* qualifies *law*, *right*, or *rights*, it is meant to refer the conventional aspects of human law(s) and legal systems to a necessary and noncontingent source able to shed light on their goals, structures, and limitations. All the specific contracts we have today, for example, are clearly conventional, but, at the same time, it is hard to see as "conventional" the entire structure of contract law which regulates certain areas of human relationships. And this structure—regarding, for example, the way to make the parties' will free from violence, mistakes, and deceits—can reasonably be said to be characterized by elements which are (not physically, but morally) necessary: elements that human reason, throughout history, discovers, highlights, and deepens ever more. Modern rationalism—after the long and passionate euphoria of the Enlightenment's omnipotent reason—has discredited the natural law tradition by trying, in several ways, to write down on paper the code of the natural law; and, by the same token, by generating the kind of confusion between necessity and freedom—or between the "natural" and the "conventional"—that in this field should be carefully kept in mind. On the other hand, when the idea of a natural law is freed from rationalism and from this confusion, it appears to be, not only useful, but even necessary to lawyers' correct reasoning, and to the reasoning of every refined observer of the problems and implications of moral, social, and political phenomena.

The meanings of *natural law* and *natural right(s)* partly overlap and should be traced back to close—though not identical—philosophical and theological origins. This paper aims at offering an overview of these terms' meanings. To this purpose, it is particularly important to distinguish between natural law (*lex naturalis*) and natural right (*ius naturale*); and, with respect to the latter, between its meaning which refers to the order of justice and its meanings which refer to the concepts of *facultas* and right/just action. In the last few decades, the debate on natural law theory has been especially fruitful in the English-speaking countries. However, English relevant terminology possesses a certain ambiguity with respect, for example, to Latin and Italian.

This ambiguity makes sometime more difficult the international dialogue among scholars (as well as the dialogue with Latin scholars from the past) and should be immediately addressed in the first section. This linguistic ambiguity makes it clear why we should distinguish between an objective and a subjective meaning of natural law, a distinction that provides the main architectonic or organizing principle to this essay. Thus, the second section addresses the objective meaning in general, which coincides with the (natural) order of justice, and which matches the understanding of nature in terms of regularities and teleology. Sections three and four address two more specific meanings of it, which are the natural law as claim (*facultas*) and the natural law as the just action. To be clear, in my discussion here, the subjective meaning of *claim/facultas* belongs to what I just referred to as the objective meaning of natural law.

Section five turns to what I call the subjective meaning of natural law, explaining its origins in Greek philosophy and its comprehensive treatment in St. Thomas Aquinas's *Treatise on Law*. The sixth section compares the objective and the subjective meanings, both conceptually and historically, with respect to the rationalistic and voluntaristic accounts of natural law. The last two sections provide an overview of the revival of natural law theory in the last century and in the most recent scholarly debate.

IUS NATURALE, LEX NATURALIS, AND THE AMBIGUITY OF NATURAL LAW THEORIES

Broadly speaking, we might say that *ius naturale* (natural right) does have more of an objective meaning, while *lex naturalis* (natural law) has more of a subjective meaning. *Ius naturale* points to the existence of an objective *ordo* (i.e., an organized whole which includes all things) in the universe, according to which something is due, or belongs, to something else as part of this something else's whole. *Lex naturalis*, on the other hand, refers this (natural) ordo to a divine source: namely, to a Legislator who wanted and arranged the ordo the way it objectively presents itself to the observers. By *subjective meaning*, therefore, I just mean that the semantic area of *lex naturalis*—contrary to the semantic area of *ius naturale*—cannot do without reference to a legislating God: namely, to the Subject who is responsible for the existence of the natural ordo.

In English, this sketch is made more complicated by the fact that both *ius naturale* and *lex naturalis* are commonly translated as *natural law* (*ius naturale*, sometimes, also as *natural right*). This is why H. L. A. Hart could confidently affirm that natural law has not always been associated with the existence of a divine legislator, and that the success of this expression is due precisely to this conceptual independence from human and divine authorities.[1] However, as far as Latin (or Italian) is concerned, this statement could partly hold true only for *ius naturale* (*diritto naturale*), but not for *lex naturalis* (*legge naturale*).

Moreover, talking about success might be confusing as success is unstable and too dependent on different geographical areas and historical periods. No doubt, modern time, unlike classical and medieval, is dominated by the "ethics without God" hypotheses and by the raising, ever more forceful, of practical and theoretical atheism. Modern time witnessed a stronger public success of *ius naturale* over *lex naturalis*.[2] The latter, however, has remained very much alive in those cultural milieus influenced by Christian philosophy and theology: milieus which are often quite significant both in Europe and the United States, and in which the questions of the Commandments that God gave to men and of their philosophical meaning has always been prominent and addressed by prominent and leading thinkers.

At any rate, taking this question into account, we should just point out here that the English *natural law* does have both a (more) objective meaning—which refers to the natural order and which matches better the meaning of *ius naturale* (or *diritto naturale*, for what matters)—and a (more) subjective meaning—which is more technically linked to the semantic area of *lex naturalis* (or *legge naturale*).[3]

NATURAL LAW AS NATURAL ORDER (OF JUSTICE)

The meaning of *ius naturale* (or the objective meaning of *natural law*) can be traced back to the Pythagorean idea of the universe as an ordinate whole—as *kosmos*—and to the very Greek understanding of nature (*physis*) as a dynamic, intrinsic, and intelligible (teleological) principle determining what things are, and, consequently, how they come to existence, where they come from, and how they move toward their ends. This meaning includes regularities and necessary correlations among physical events, for which it is more common to use the term *laws of nature* to better distinguish a scientific sphere from moral discourse. *Laws of nature* should be taken as more general than *natural law* insofar as it indicates all physical regularities and necessary correlations, and not only those specific to moral action. It is important, however, not to draw here too sharp of a line between scientific sphere and moral sphere, as *ius naturale* and *kosmos* include both. The objective natural law is always a matter of regularities and necessary correlations of events, whether these can be interpreted as morally relevant or not.

It is important to understand that this meaning of *ius naturale* is metaphysically all-embracing. It is a way of looking at things from the viewpoint of being due to them what their forms tend to with respect to their place and meaning in the universe. If my form inclines me to become an adult it is due to my nature to become an adult. Accordingly, it is due to me to receive all the nourishment, education, and care necessary to that purpose. In the gnoseological order, I know the forms of things through the regularities in nature. Human beings tend (regularly) to become adults. We know what lions are, not just because we see one lion chasing a prey, but because lions tend to chase their preys. Regularities in nature reveal both its forms and its teleology.

Some people may have a hard time connecting the notions of teleology with the notion of regularities in nature, especially when moral inclinations are at stake. After all, vices are regular too. This is not the right place for a detailed discussion about this point. Still, I must clarify that, according to classical natural law theory, the inclinations of even the natural moral law are the most (or the true) regular things in nature. In fact, they are present even in the devil and in the evilest human beings. The regularity of our inclination to love our children, for example, is the necessary presupposition of our possibly mistreating them. The regularity of our inclination to give people their due is the necessary presupposition of our understanding the injustice of theft, and it is the reason why human societies are regulated by justice systems. It is only in the light of the regularity of our basic inclinations that we are able to discern good from evil.

As is well known, according to St. Thomas Aquinas even our inclinations to moral virtues belong to "synderesis": that is, to the very first actualization of our practical reason. This means that these inclinations too are the most regular things that we can observe in human nature. This is more common sense–related than it may look. People are more attracted (inclined) to true friendship than to friendships of pleasure or utility. They are more attracted to love and generosity than to hate and stinginess. They appreciate the beauty of moral life more than its ugliness. The movie industry knows this very well. The happy ending is more successful than the death of the characters. True love moves more than hatred and makes cry even those who in private life behave like selfish people. Unfaithful people love to be treated faithfully. Again, it is only by observing the basic regularities of the attractions to the good that we can understand the distortion brought to them by vices. If we do not see the regularities of our primary natural inclinations (including those of the virtues) we have still a long way to go to understand classical natural law theory. At the level of secondary precepts, vices reveal both the regularity of the primary inclinations, the regularity of our sentient passions, and the regularity of our weaknesses in adjusting our sentient life to our rational life.

The intelligible character of nature is, for the Greeks, the source of natural justice and human moral action. For Socrates, who is considered the initiator of moral philosophy, men are the only beings who, due to their spiritual nature, can judge things for what they are and choose to act accordingly. What other beings do by necessity—that is, operate according to their natures—becomes normative to human beings, who should act according to the truth, or according to nature as they understand it. Human beings cannot escape the urge of their inclinations, but they can raise themselves above them by using their intellect, and, in doing so, they can judge their own inclinations and freely modulate their way to relate themselves to them.[4]

It should be noticed that the concept of truth involved in this classical view does not correspond to the rationalist image of the mirror. In the Greek view of knowledge—later developed by Christian medieval thought—truth is a certain presence of the known thing in the knower: more or less as a file about elephants is present to the computer's memory. This *presence*, however, takes place, not according to the known's nature, but according to the knower's nature: eyes, for example, know according to colors, but the known thing is actually colored only with respect to the eyes looking at it, and with respect to the kind of color(s) these eyes can see; similarly, the intellect knows according to intelligible universals, but the known thing which falls under our senses is an "intelligible universal" only potentially. For the same reason, the presence of the known thing can be more or less "intense," so to speak, according to the exposure to it, or experience of it, that the knower has, had or is having de facto. My knowledge of the tree is different from the knowledge of the tree that an expert botanist has, and it is different from the knowledge of the tree that I myself had when I was three. Also, from the distance or from some limited viewpoints, I may not even be sure if what I see is a plant, an animal, or an inanimate thing. In this sense, knowledge is often (but not necessarily accurately) said to be "intentional," because it varies, being constantly dependent on the knower's relationship with the known thing. And in the same sense, the knowledge of a thing's nature does not imply at all—pace the image of the mirror—knowing everything about one thing even from only one specific viewpoint. For example, from the limited viewpoint of my eyes I know (visually) more and better the closer I am to the known thing.[5]

Opposite to Socratic acting according to the truth is the *hybris*: that is, the (immoral) attitude of arbitrarily disregarding one's role in the universe. Against the Sophists' denial of *physis*, Plato offers the most relevant Greek account of justice as the harmony of each part with a universal order of nature. In the Republic, this harmony flows from the human soul—in which there is justice when its three parts interact harmoniously with each other—into the polis—in which there is justice when the three classes of citizens interact harmoniously with each other according to their respective functions and roles. The intelligible and normative character of nature also explains Greeks' idea of a natural right, or justice (*physikon dikaion*), which, at the same time, grounds legal justice (*nomikon dikaion*) and corrects it through equity (*epieikeia*): "the equitable is just, but not the legally just [*nomon*] but a correction of legal justice [*nomimou dikaiou*]."[6]

The meaning of *natural law* as the natural order (of justice) corresponds to a general meaning of the Latin *ius naturale* that can also be translated as "natural right." In this sense, for example, the expressions "X belongs to natural law," "X belongs to natural right," and "X belongs to *ius naturale*" have the same meaning. However, both *ius naturale* and *natural right* refer more commonly either to (1) the claim, or subjective power (*facultas*), that natural law—as the objective order of justice—attributes to someone, or to

(2) the very action that, in a certain place and time, should be done according to (natural) law/justice.

IUS NATURALE AS CLAIM OR *FACULTAS*

The meaning of *ius naturale* as claim or *facultas* admits both a generic and abstract two-term predication—as in the expressions "right to life" and "right to freedom"—and a specific and concrete three-term predication, when we say, for example, that "Tom has a right to receive tomorrow $10,000 from Jim." The three-term predication implies the conclusion of the relevant train of reasoning about what should be done, among particular subjects, according to (natural) law/justice. In the human judicial systems, this is technically known only at the end of a trial in, and through, the judge's decision.[7] The three-term predication coincides with the classical so-called (three-term) relationship of justice between (a) what is due, (b) he who owes it, and (c) he who is entitled to it.

In modern legal theory, this claim meaning becomes the primary one. The historical debate about when this happens exactly goes way beyond the limit of this essay. Many authors trace the shift back to Francisco Suárez and Hugo Grotius:

> [In] the treatise on law by the Spanish Jesuit Francisco Suárez, written c.1610, we find another analysis of the meanings of "*jus*." Here the "true, strict and proper meaning" of "*jus*" is said to be: "a kind of moral power [*facultas*] which every man has, either over his own property or with respect to that which is due to him." The meaning which for Aquinas was primary is rather vaguely mentioned by Suárez and then drops out of sight; conversely, the meaning which for Suárez is primary does not appear in Aquinas's discussion at all. Somewhere between the two men we have crossed the watershed.[8]

In modern contractualism (Hobbes, Locke, Pufendorf, Rousseau), the claim meaning defines the natural rights that people possess in the state of nature prior to, and independently of, the existence of any authority and law. These natural rights are basic powers, or freedoms, that the political community—flowing from the social contract—must take into account. However, one of the strongest criticisms to modern contractualist theories is that there is no meaningful way to characterize as rights these powers and freedoms. By definition, the state of nature is a situation, so to speak, that precedes any sort of social organization and, therefore, any rule that might possibly limit human behavior. Hence, in the state of nature, natural rights end up being no more than mere powers to do whatever one wants to do. In other words, in the state of nature I cannot claim that others respect my rights if they have enough power to do otherwise and are willing to do so.[9]

On the other hand, it should be noticed that the idea of a state of nature, as well as the concept of social contract, are already present—though with different meanings—in premodern thought. "State of nature" is a term used in the Christian theological tradition to indicate human condition before the original sin: prior, that is to say, to an event that has supposedly strongly damaged human capacities. According to Christian theology, for example, our current way to experience affections, rationality, pain, and moral tension does not perfectly match the way we would experience these things had the original sin not be committed; and our reason needs to make a strong effort to figure, in this present condition, what is natural to us, as opposed to what is just corruption and damage. In this context, thinking of the state of nature is a heuristic device helping us understand what the genuine meaning of our being and the authentic end of our actions are. As for the concept of social contract, it is already present in ancient and medieval political thought—for example, that of Aristotle, Augustine, and Aquinas—to indicate, not a real historical prepolitical condition of the human beings, but rather one of the conceptual presuppositions of human nature's political condition: namely, the agreement. The idea is that the actual existence of a kind of agreement or contract among the individuals is a necessary presupposition of their political community at any stage of its development. At the most basic level, this agreement can be seen in the tacit acceptance of a sort of political leadership (authority), or, what is the same, in the recognition by most of the individuals of one or more persons as the authority(ies) everybody refers to for solving or addressing social issues and problems.[10]

Social contract theory has been a powerful ideology that historically led to the modern state as a political system at the service of the rights of the individual. This ideology played a major role in the drafting of the bills of rights at the time of the American and French Revolutions. This was a key historical moment, when in Western societies started the important development of those fundamental rights that will be placed at the basis of all constitutional democracies and the international law. However, these rights have been mainly developed according to the claim meaning—or as basic powers and freedoms of the individual—and this meaning does not necessarily need the concept of nature. The same natural rights of early modern thought have become human rights in contemporary constitutional systems and international law. On the other hand, the current crisis concerning the basis of, and the international agreement about, human rights is a powerful reminder of the unavoidable problem of their being somehow natural or not.[11]

IUS NATURALE AS ACTION

The meaning of *ius naturale* as action goes back to Aristotle's idea of practical truth, which, having the action as its object, can only be found through the work of prudence and the moral virtues. *To dikaion* is, for Aristotle, what the virtue of justice leads the good man (the *phronimos*) to do here and now. It is the just, the *iustum*, or the (objective) right: namely, what the agent should objectively do according to justice. This Greek view of *ius* informs both Roman law and medieval thought. This is why Roman lawyers called their science *iurisprudentia* (i.e., prudential knowledge of the *ius*) and why they thought of it not as a theoretical science but as an art (*ars boni et aequi*).[12]

In the famous definition offered by Ulpian—"iustitia est constans et perpetua voluntas ius suum cuique tribuendi"[13] —justice is a virtue that makes the will constantly inclined to give everybody what is due to him: that is, his *ius*. This definition matches the famous *endoxon* (common opinion) that Aristotle uses, in the fifth book of the *Nicomachean Ethics*, to begin his inquiry on what kind of human act relates to the virtue of justice:

> With regard to justice and injustice we must consider what kind of actions they are concerned with, what sort of mean justice is, and between what extremes the just act is intermediate. Our investigation shall follow the same course as the preceding discussions. We see that all men mean by justice that kind of state which makes people disposed to do what is just and makes them act justly and wish for what is just; and similarly by injustice that state which makes them act unjustly and wish for what is unjust. Let us too, then, first lay this down as a rough sketch.[14]

The action meaning of *ius/right* overlaps the claim meaning and can also be used—in abstract talk about *iura*/rights—according to a two-term predication. However, the action meaning is objective and, unlike the claim meaning, cannot be detached from an external normative source as the ground of the relationship of justice; or, in other words, it cannot be detached from a measure of the just action that the agent must look at and follow. On the other hand, when natural rights are interpreted only according to the claim meaning (as in modern social contract theories) they do not necessarily involve a universal order of justice but only the idea or the semantic of basic subjective powers and freedoms—which are potentially unlimited, and which belong primordially to the individuals.

As far as the action meaning is concerned, a key historical text is Thomas Aquinas's *Treatise on Justice*,[15] where *ius* is introduced (following the Aristotelian and Roman law view) as the (practical) object of the virtue of justice. Aquinas explains that it is proper to justice to order man with respect to those things that relate him to others (ordinet hominem in his quae sunt ad alterum), and he adds that this order depends on a certain equality; that is to say, *ius* depends on a rule, or a law, that determines what is due to each person in the relationship of justice.

This external source of the *ius*, which makes it objective, determines the special status of justice among the virtues, whose objects, unlike *ius*, depend also on the subjective conditions of the agent:

> And so a thing is said to be just [*iustum*] . . . when it is the term of an act of justice, without taking into account the way in which it is done by the agent: whereas in the other virtues nothing is declared to be right [*rectum*] unless it is done in a certain way by the agent. For this reason justice has its own special proper object over and above the other virtues, and this object is called the just [*iustum*], which is the same as right [*ius*].[16]

The point Aquinas wants to make here is that, in the case of the other virtues, say temperance, the subjective condition(s) of the agents are part of the measure we must use to judge the morality of the action—we cannot say, for example, that eating three ice creams is temperate/intemperate without evaluating each time who is eating them, when he is eating them, where he is eating them, etc. (whether, e.g., it is a big 120-kilo man who is starving to death or a full five years old child after a Thanksgiving dinner). In the case of justice, on the other hand, once a certain legal relationship among two or more subjects is established, the action must be evaluated as just/unjust only on the basis of the terms of that relationship. This objective and external character of *ius* is similar to Kant's distinction between moral law, as an interior law that cannot be externally enforced by human authority, and positive law.

LEX NATURALIS

The idea of a *lex naturalis*—the more subjective, or legal, meaning of *natural law*—already appears in Sophocles's *Antigone* as the need to obey the laws of God before human laws. Moreover, there are several suggestions, in pre-Socratic thought, about the existence of a natural teleology caused by an ordering Love-Intelligence, which Aristotle interprets as the discovery of the principle of movement and the final cause:

> When one man said, then, that [intelligence] was present—as in animals, so throughout nature—as the cause of the world and of all its order, he seemed like a sober man in contrast with the random talk of all his predecessors. We know that Anaxagoras certainly adopted these views, but Hermotimus of Clazomenae is credited with expressing them earlier. Those who thought thus stated that there is a principle of things which is at the same time the cause of beauty, and that sort of cause from which things acquire movement.[17]

Before Aristotle, there is also a strong doctrine of divine providence in both Socrates and Plato. And the idea of a higher (divine) law as the ultimate norm of moral action becomes crucial for the Stoics in the context of their deterministic and cyclical theory of the universe. Stoic natural law is a divine logos immanent in nature, which necessarily moves everything (even the gods) to its proper end.

Christian thought gave to the Greek final-cause-ordering-Intelligence the further connotations of being a transcendent, efficient, and creative free cause of the natural order. The Latin *lex naturalis* expresses the relationship between this cause and the *ius naturale*'s order. Thus, after early reflections by authors like Theophilus of Antioch, Minucius Felix, Origen, and the Cappadocians, Augustine could offer a clear notion of an eternal law (*lex aeterna*) regulating the entire universe and existing in the mind of God.

The scholastic tradition, then, reached its highest refinement in the scholastic tradition with the famous *Treatise on Law* by Thomas Aquinas.[18] Aquinas defines law (*lex*) as "an ordinance of reason, for the common good, made by one who is in charge of the community, and promulgated" (rationis ordinatio ad bonum commune, ab eo qui curam communitatis habet, promulgata),[19] and analogically applies this concept to four kinds of law: eternal, natural, divine (old and new), and human.[20]

Ordinatio rationis means here a commanding act of practical knowledge, which is truly a rational plan meant to "order" (i.e., to create an *ordo* between) a plurality of things in view of the good common to them. This is why Aquinas sees law primarily as an act of reason, and secondarily of the will: the act of ordering things with respect to an end belongs as such to reason. This view seems to be close enough to the idea, quite common in contemporary legal theory and philosophy, that the end of the law is the coordination of actions.

The most important and innovative concept, perhaps, which allows Aquinas to arrange the subject matter is the relation, intrinsic to the concept of law, between the legislator and the community of his subjects/citizens that he has to order by means of his command. Aquinas explains several times, starting with the first article of his *Treatise*, that there are "two ways in which" law "is said to exist in something": first "in that which measures and regulates" (i.e., the legislator), and second "in that which is regulated and measured" (i.e., the subject or citizen).[21] Law makes sense if it orderly moves or directs the subjects toward the common good. Accordingly, if a law exists, it is (1) an act of reason in the legislator, and (2) an inclination to the common good—according to the order commanded by the legislator—in the subjects. The concept of inclination as the way in which law exists in the subject(s) is subtle and it relates closely to Aristotle's concept of practical rationality. In rational *subditi*—as human beings are—what is inclined is the very knowledge of the law, which, as such, becomes the principle of the citizen's rational/free movement. In other words, the inclination as a way in which law exists in the subjects, coincides with the citizen's act of practical knowledge.[22]

The inherent relationship between the two ways in which law exists is, at the same time, a relationship of causality and subordination between, on the one hand, the legislator's act of practical rationality and, on the other, the subject's inclination, which, by its movement, participates in the disposing act of the legislator. The concept of participation expresses precisely this relationship of causality and subordination. Nature, as dynamic principle of movement inherent to every being, is therefore participation in God's eternal law as the rational plan according to which everything has been created. And human reason, as knowledge inclined to the good proper to the human being, is a special way of participating in the eternal law. This is why Aquinas defines natural law as "participation in eternal law on the part of a rational creature" (participatio legis aeternae in rationali creatura).[23] The essential difference between eternal law and natural law, on the one hand, and human law, on the other, is that human law cannot generate in the subjects any inclination inherent to their nature. Therefore, in order to be effective, human law must rely upon natural inclinations: for example, in case of recalcitrant and unreasonable citizens, the inclinations to flee punishments and pains; and in case of good citizens, the inclination to care for one's children and relatives. Generally speaking, the more human law is based on natural inclinations the more it is true and effective. It is according to this main meaning that, in the classical tradition, it has always been said that the morality of human law depends on its conformity to natural law.

LEX NATURALIS AND *IUS NATURALE*

The philosophical reflection on *lex naturalis* and *ius naturale* has always faced the need to harmonize the (more) legal meaning of the former—according to which moral goodness depends on obedience, or conformity, to God's plan—with the (more) objective meaning of the latter—according to which the principle of moral action cannot be just an extrinsic command but should rather be intrinsic to the natural order. Aquinas reaches this harmony by distinguishing the two ways in which *lex* exists that we have already mentioned above: namely, "in that which measures and rules" (the legislator) as a mental object, and "in that which is measured and ruled" (the subject) as an inclination to do what the legislator aims at in view of the common good. God (and his thoughts) entirely transcends the world, but his law exists also inside the world as the (intelligible) inclinations of nature toward the ends of each thing.

After Aquinas, the two meanings are carried to opposite extremes by the nominalist school, originating with William of Ockham, and the antinominalist reaction, led by Gregory of Rimini. The nominalists, following John Duns Scotus's voluntarism, reduce the source of morality to mere obedience to the will of God. The antinominalists remove all value from the will of God, and conceive morality as simply conforming oneself to the intrinsic truth of human nature. This is the view that has become dominant in the modern age. The so-called "modern school of natural law"—from which, through the American and French Revolutions, the first declarations of universal natural/human rights stem—builds upon Grotius's famous *etiamsi daremus non esse Deum* principle.[24] It is common to say that modern tradition is no longer religious but secular; no longer heteronymous but autonomous. However, both voluntarism and rationalism will keep being coexistent traits of modern and contemporary legal theory. Worth noticing, from this viewpoint, is the utilitarian and rationalistic natural law theory offered by John Austin in the context of his voluntaristic theory of law.[25]

THE RECENT REVIVAL OF NATURAL LAW THEORIES

In the last century, as far as I can tell, there have been two major moments of revival in natural law theory: the first in the first half of the century (until, more or less, the 1960s), and the second (still going on) in the 1980s. In addition, there have been important debates, theoretical proposals, and schools of thought that, in one way or another, can be related to natural law theory. For example, Hart's minimal content of natural law, Rawls's deontological neocontractualism, Lon L. Fuller's procedural natural law proposal (and his lively debate with Hart), and even Dworkin's theory of legal reasoning and justification. Overall, I believe that the last century (up to our day) can be seen as an extremely fruitful period for natural law theory, a period in which some of the most interesting books on the subject have been written.

In the first half of the twentieth century, a key role has been played, in the natural law field, by the tragic political events associated with the world wars. In this context, natural law has become the natural and most plausible ground to appeal to objective ethical values—beyond each particular and concrete legal system—to be used to refuse the atrocities and the risks of wars, and as the basis of a long-lasting and stable peace. Reference to natural law has been in the background of the strong judgments against the wars and against those accountable for them (think of the Nuremberg trial), not to mention the drafting of the 1948 Universal Declaration of Human Rights. In this part of the century, we can locate the work of prominent natural law theorists like Heinrich Rommen, Jacques Maritain, Leo Strauss, Yves Simon, and Alessandro Passerin D'Entrèves.

The second important moment, starting with the 1980s, is almost entirely characterized by the debate raised by the so-called "new natural law theory," or "new classical theory of natural law." The landmark here is the publication of John Finnis's *Natural Law and Natural Rights*. After 1980, this new natural law proposal stimulated, and got involved in the relevant debate, significant theorists whose specific reflections on the issue might otherwise have remained merely potential. I'm thinking above all of Ralph McInerny and Russell Hittinger. Moreover, in the 1980s, there emerged forcefully the Aristotelian natural law proposal of Henry Veatch, who soon became as well an important voice in the debate generated by the new classical authors. This debate is still alive in our day, and its subject deserves, at the end of this conceptual and historical sketch, a more specific consideration.

THE NEOCLASSICAL THEORY OF NATURAL LAW

The neoclassical theory is grounded on a peculiar rereading of Thomas Aquinas's *lex naturalis*, which openly contradicts other interpretations of Aquinas described as the common leading interpretations, and generically defined as neoscholastic or conventional. The founder of the neoclassical school is Germain Grisez; the most important author is certainly John Finnis; another remarkable name is that of Robert George.

Generally speaking, the neoclassicists originally belong to the environment of analytic philosophy, and their main concern is to provide a reasonable defense of natural law against the objection known as the naturalistic fallacy, or Hume's law. The neoclassicists welcome the progress achieved in analytic philosophy in the study of moral reasoning, insofar as it discloses the existence of some objectivity in the reasoning that leads to action, and it highlights that moral reasoning is intrinsically characterized by values in the form of good reasons for action. Those very values that, according to Hume's law, cannot be derived from nature, are indeed already present in moral reasoning since the beginning.

By remaining cognitively in the order of practical reason, the neoclassicists believe they can escape the objection of the naturalistic fallacy, and recover for ethics an adequate objectivity, showing that every man's practical reason rests on some first premises—in the form of evaluative judgments about what constitutes a good reason for action. Such evaluative judgments, precisely because they are primary, are not known by the agent deductively but with an original intuition, and they cannot be strictly demonstrated, but only identified. These premises are therefore the basic values, or the ultimate ends, of human existence, and anyone capable of reflecting on them with sufficient attention, can find them in himself as well as in others. This way of viewing the problem is reflected above all in the distinction between objectivity and nature: the natural law of the neoclassicists wants to be an objective ethics but one that does not in any way derive values from the knowledge of human nature.

The link with Aquinas's thought here is to be found in his distinction between practical and theoretical reason, on the one hand, and in his thesis that the first practical principles are self-evident and not deduced by speculative knowledge, on the other. These first principles coincide with the first precepts of natural law, or, in other words, with the basic human values, or goods (or basic reasons for action), that guide every rational agent's practical reasoning.

In the most developed elaboration of their theory, the neoclassicists identify the following seven categories of basic human goods: (1) life, health, and safety; (2) knowledge and aesthetic experience; (3) some degree of excellence in work and play; (4) living at peace with others, neighborliness, friendship; (5) inner peace; (6) peace of conscience and consistency between one's self and its expression; (7) peace with God, or the gods, or some nontheistic but more-than-human source of meaning and value.[26]

When man, either as an individual or in his social interactions with others, pursues with full reasonableness these ultimate values, he fulfills himself and is morally good. However, the basic values or goods, of themselves, do not indicate what is the good or just action to be done: in this sense, they are premoral. Morality obtains only in the concrete choices, when one pursues the basic values within different contexts in a reasonable manner, that is to say, based upon the following first principle of the moral order: "In voluntarily acting for human goods and avoiding what is opposed to them, one ought to choose and otherwise will those and only those possibilities whose willing is compatible with integral human fulfillment."[27] The interaction of this principle with the different contexts of human choice allows one to make some specifications of the principle that can logically be called "intermediate principles," and which correspond to the moral principles of common sense. Examples of intermediate principles are the golden rule (do not do to others what you would not want done to yourself) and the rule whereby one cannot do evil that good may come of it.

Neoclassical theory ends up taking a position that distances itself decisively from Aquinas, rejecting two essential elements of his concept and of the entire classical tradition of natural law: the existence of an ultimate end for man, and an objective hierarchy of good or values. From the point of view of an analysis of practical reasoning, the basic values are those good reasons for action to which any possible reason for action can be analytically traced back: irreducibility, as an essential feature of ultimate values or ends, not only excludes the possibility of a single further good which would trump all others, but renders all values logically incommensurable, and thus prevents one from situating them in any form of hierarchy.[28]

Viewed from another perspective, the neoclassical theory of natural law wants to propose an ethical foundation for human rights which is opposed to utilitarianism, neocontractualism, and, in general, to minimalist liberal positions. In *Natural Law and Natural Rights*, Finnis explains that these basic values correspond perfectly to human or natural rights. The modern language of rights is, in fact, a way of expressing virtually all the demands of practical reasonableness insofar as they bear on relations of justice; and the language of human rights is a useful way of pointing to all the basic aspects of the human good as the primary objective of the political community. "When we survey" the rights proclaimed in the Universal Declaration,

> we realize what the modern "manifesto" conception of human rights amounts to. It is simply a way of sketching the outlines of the common good, the various aspects of individual well-being in the community. What the reference to rights contributes in this sketch is simply a pointed expression of what is implicit in the term "common good," namely, that each and everyone's well-being, in each of its basic aspects, must be considered and treated favorably at all times by those responsible for co-ordinating the common life.[29]

Neoclassical theory's fundamental criticism of Rawls's neocontractualism—and of deontological liberalism in general—is that it is arbitrary, "in selecting the principles of justice," to consider as primary only goods such as "liberty, opportunity, wealth and self-respect," refusing to confer intrinsic value upon goods "such as truth, or play, or art, or friendship."[30] On the other hand, its fundamental criticism of utilitarianism is that the basic values, which form the basis of individual as well as political action, are mutually incommensurable, and consequently it is not possible to instrumentalize them and treat them as the object of a calculation for the greater overall good or the lesser overall evil. Given that the basic values have this status, they are to be respected in all circumstances, and it is thus possible that there are actions in which it is never licit to engage. In other words, it is possible to speak of absolute human rights; as the Universal Declaration does about slavery and torture, which, precisely for this reason, according to a careful exegesis of the text, seem to escape the limitations envisaged in article 29.[31]

Neoclassical authors and their critics represent a big part of contemporary natural law literature. In the context of the debate mostly raised by the neoclassicists, other interesting and promising positions have emerged. For example, Russell Hittinger and myself have been particularly focusing on the meaning of natural law as "law": that is to say, on the subjective meaning of natural law I mentioned above, and, therefore, on the relationship between natural law and the concept of God both from a philosophical viewpoint and from a theological viewpoint. Ralph McInerny has focused on implicit (or spontaneous) knowledge of the first moral principles, or first natural law precepts. It is also worth mentioning the increasing interest that many scholars show for the relationship between natural law and the concept of narrative, which is meant to underline the dynamism of ethical knowledge involved in natural law theory as opposed to the static and absolute (or anti-historical) reason we all inherited from the Enlightenment. The idea of a narrative natural law is probably linked at first to students of Alasdair MacIntyre, but it relates more in general to the contemporary revival of the so-called "virtue ethics": namely, of those approaches to ethical theory that underline the importance of considering the personal story of the moral agent.[32]

NOTES

1. H. L. A. Hart, *The Concept of Law* (Oxford: Clarendon Press, 1961), sec. 9.
2. See, e.g., F. Di Blasi, *From Aristotle to Thomas Aquinas: Natural Law, Practical Knowledge, and the Person* (South Bend: St. Augustine's Press, 2018), chap. 9.
3. I have explained more in detail the meanings and the translation problems of *law*, *natural law*, and *rights* in my introductory essay to the Italian edition of Yves Simon, *The Tradition of Natural Law* [*La tradizione del diritto natural: Le riflessioni di un filosofo*, trad. F. Di Blasi (Palermo: *Phronesis*, 2004)].
4. On the different kinds of inclinations which operate in the human being, and on the way in which they affect human rational choice, see Di Blasi, *God and the Natural Law* (South Bend: St. Augustine's Press, 2006), 198–201. On the ethical subjectivity of the human being, see Di Blasi, *From Aristotle to Thomas Aquinas*, 4.2 ("Discovering the Concept of Person") and 7.2 ("Ethics and Natural Law").
5. See Di Blasi, *God and the Natural Law*, chap. 2. On the concept of intention, see Di Blasi, "Intentions," in *Encyclopedia of British Philosophy*, eds. A. C. Graylings and A. Pyle, (Bristol: Thoemmes Continuum, 2006).
6. Aristotle, *Nicomachean Ethics*, trans. W. D. Ross, 5.1137b7–12.
7. On the specification of rights and on the two and three-term predication, see J. M. Finnis, *Natural Law and Natural Rights* (Oxford: Clarendon Press, 1980), chap. 8, sec. 5.
8. Finnis, *NLNR*, 207.
9. H. B. Veatch describes affectively this criticism in his *Human Rights: Fact or Fancy?* (Baton Rouge, LA: Louisiana State University Press, 1985). See also the first chapter of my *God and the Natural Law*.
10. Aristotle, e.g., writes, "[Friendships] of fellow-citizens . . . are more like mere friendships of association; for they seem to rest on a sort of compact" (*Nicomachean Ethics* 8.1161b13–16); and Augustine, "But those offences which are contrary to the customs of men are to be avoided according to the customs severally prevailing; so that an agreement made, and confirmed by custom or law of any city or nation, may not be violated at the lawless pleasure of any, whether citizen or stranger" (*The Confessions*, trans. J.G. Pilkington, from *Nicene and Post-Nicene Fathers, First Series*, vol. 1, ed. Philip Schaff [Buffalo, NY: Christian Literature Publishing Co., 1887], rev. and ed. for New Advent by Kevin Knight, New Advent, http://www.newadvent.org/fathers/110103.htm.)
11. See Di Blasi, *From Aristotle to Thomas Aquinas*, chap. 9.
12. Publius Juventius Celsus, *Digest* 1.1.1.
13. Ulpian, *Digest* 1.1.10.
14. Aristotle, *Nicomachean Ethics* 5.1129a1–11.
15. Aquinas, *Summa theologiae* 2.2.57ff.

16. Aquinas, *Sth*, trans. Fathers of the English Dominican Province (1920), 2.2.57.1.
17. Aristotle, *Metaphysics*, rev. ed. (Oxford), 1.984b15ff.
18. Aquinas, *Sth* 2.1.90–108.
19. Aquinas, *Sth*, trans. A. J. Freddoso, 2.1.90.4.
20. On the conceptual components of Aquinas's concept of law and its analogical nature, see Di Blasi, "Law as 'Act of Reason' and 'Command,'" *New Things & Old Things* 3 (2006): 515–28; and Di Blasi, *From Aristotle to Thomas Aquinas*, chap. 7 ("Natural Law as Inclination to God").
21. Aquinas, *Sth* 2.1.90.1.
22. I explained in detail the relationship between Aquinas's concept of natural law and Aristotelian practical rationality in "Practical Syllogism, *Proairesis*, and the Virtues: Toward a Reconciliation of Virtue Ethics and Natural Law Ethics," *New Things & Old Things* 1 (2004): 21–41.
23. Aquinas, *Sth* 2.1.91.2.
24. H. Grotius, *De iure belli ac pacis* (1625), *prolegomena* 11.
25. J. Austin, *The Province of Jurisprudence Determined and the Uses of the Study of Jurisprudence* (London: Weidenfeld and Nicolson, 1971).
26. See J. Finnis, G. Grisez, and J. Boyle Jr., *Nuclear Deterrence, Morality and Realism*, (Oxford: Clarendon Press, 1987), 278–80; "Practical Principles, Moral Truth, and Ultimate Ends," *American Journal of Jurisprudence* 32 (1987): 107–8.
27. See Finnis, Grisez, and Boyle, *Nuclear Deterrence*, 283.
28. For criticisms of these features of neoclassical theory, see Di Blasi, *John Finnis* (Palermo: *Phronesis*, 2008); Di Blasi, *God and the Natural Law*; Di Blasi, "I valori fondamentali nella teoria neoclassica della legge naturale," *Riv. Int. di Filosofia del Diritto* 2 (1999); R. McInerny, "The Principles of Natural Law," *The American Journal of Jurisprudence* 25 (1980); H. B. Veatch, *Swimming Against the Current in Contemporary Philosophy* (Washington, DC: The Catholic University of America Press, 1981); and H. B. Veatch, *Human Rights: Fact or Fancy?* (Baton Rouge, LA: Louisiana State University Press, 1985).
29. Finnis, *Natural Law and Natural Rights* (supra), 214.
30. Finnis, *Natural Law and Natural Rights*, 106.
31. Finnis, *Natural Law and Natural Rights*, 210–18.
32. See, e.g., P. M. Hall, *Narrative and the Natural Law: An Interpretation of Thomistic Ethics* (Notre Dame: University of Notre Dame Press, 1994); R. A. Gahl, "From the Virtue of a Fragile Good to a Narrative Account of Natural Law," *International Philosophical Quarterly* 37, no. 4 (1997); B. A. Craig, *A Shared Morality: A Narrative Defense of Natural-Law Ethics* (Grand Rapids, MI: Brazos, 2007).

WORKS CITED

Aquinas. *Summa theologiae*.
———. *Summa theologiae*. Translated by A. J. Freddoso.
———. *Summa theologiae*. Translated by the Fathers of the English Dominican Province.
Aristotle. *Nicomachean Ethics*. Translated by W. D. Ross.
———. *Metaphysics.* Revised Oxford translation.
Augustine. *The Confessions*. New Advent translation.
Austin, J. *The Province of Jurisprudence Determined and the Uses of the Study of Jurisprudence*. London: Weidenfeld and Nicolson, 1971.
Celsus, Publius Juventius. *Digest*.
Craig, B. A. *A Shared Morality: A Narrative Defense of Natural-Law Ethics*. Grand Rapids, MI: Brazos, 2007.
Di Blasi, F. *From Aristotle to Thomas Aquinas: Natural Law, Practical Knowledge, and the Person*. South Bend: St. Augustine's Press, 2018.
———. *God and the Natural Law*. South Bend: St. Augustine's Press, 2006.
———. "Intentions." In *Encyclopedia of British Philosophy*, edited by A. C. Graylings and A. Pyle. Bristol: Thoemmes Continuum, 2006.

———. "I valori fondamentali nella teoria neoclassica della legge naturale." *Riv. Int. di Filosofia del Diritto* 2 (1999).
———. *John Finnis*. Palermo: *Phronesis*, 2008.
———. "Law as 'Act of Reason' and 'Command.'" *New Things and Old Things* 3 (2006): 515–28.
———. "Practical Syllogism, *Proairesis*, and the Virtues: Toward a Reconciliation of Virtue Ethics and Natural Law Ethics." *New Things and Old Things* 1 (2004): 21–41.
Finnis, J. M. *Natural Law and Natural Rights*. Oxford: Clarendon Press, 1980.
Finnis, J., G. Grisez, and J. Boyle Jr. *Nuclear Deterrence, Morality and Realism*. Oxford: Clarendon Press, 1987.
———. "Practical Principles, Moral Truth, and Ultimate Ends." *American Journal of Jurisprudence* 32 (1987): 107–8.
Gahl, R. A. "From the Virtue of a Fragile Good to a Narrative Account of Natural Law." *International Philosophical Quarterly* 37, no. 4 (1997).
Grotius, H. *De iure belli ac pacis*. 1625.
Hall, P. M. *Narrative and the Natural Law: An Interpretation of Thomistic Ethics*. Notre Dame: University of Notre Dame Press, 1994.
Hart, H. L. A. *The Concept of Law*. Oxford: Clarendon Press, 1961.
McInerny, R. "The Principles of Natural Law." *The American Journal of Jurisprudence* 25 (1980).
Simon, Yves. *La tradizione del diritto naturale: L e riflessioni di un filosofo*. Palermo: *Phronesis*, 2004.
Ulpian. *Digest*.
Veatch, H. B. *Human Rights: Fact or Fancy?* Baton Rouge, LA: Louisiana State University Press, 1985.
———. *Swimming Against the Current in Contemporary Philosophy*. Washington, DC: The Catholic University of America Press, 1981.
———. *Human Rights: Fact or Fancy?* Baton Rouge, LA: Louisiana State University Press, 1985.

Chapter Four

"The Same as to Knowledge"

J. Budziszewski

Considering that natural law is *natural*, it is amazing how it scandalizes people—even some scholars of natural law. We are continually told that some offensive part of the theory must be "bracketed" because it is too much to take. For example, we are urged to bracket theology and say nothing about God; or to bracket philosophy so that natural law is *just* theology and has nothing to say to nonbelievers; or to bracket natural teleology so that natural law is hardly natural; or to bracket conscience so that natural law is hardly law.

The classical tradition insisted on keeping all those things in. The problem with natural law is not that it speaks too implausibly but that it speaks all too plausibly, telling us more than we want to hear. Our actual inclinations are at war with our natural inclinations; our hearts are riddled with desires that oppose their deepest longings; we demand to have happiness on terms that make happiness impossible.

One article cannot take on all of the protests, but I do want to defend what the classical tradition says about conscience.[1]

In the *Summa theologiae*, St. Thomas Aquinas—asking whether the natural moral law is the same for all men—makes the very strong claim that "the natural law, as to general principles, is the same for all, both as to rectitude and as to knowledge."[2] Let's unpack this statement to see why it is so astonishing.

To say that the general principles of the natural law are the same "as to rectitude" means that they are *right* for everyone. For example, just as it would be wrong for me to murder, so it would be wrong for you to murder. This claim is already quite strong, and a good many people in our time consider it pretty dubious. We hear every day that "what's right for you may not be right for me," and that this is why we must not "judge" anyone else's acts by our own standards.

But St. Thomas makes this already-strong claim stronger still. For to say that the general principles are the same for all "as to knowledge" means that everyone *knows* them. For example, not only is it the case that theft is wrong for everyone, but *everyone knows* that theft is wrong, even thieves. I take this to mean not only that everyone knows that theft is wrong for him, but that everyone knows that theft is wrong for everyone. Of course we are not speaking of persons incapable of reason: "all men" means everyone with an undamaged adult mind. Nor are we speaking of the remote, detailed implications of the general principles: I may understand the wrong of theft in general, yet be confused about whether it would always be theft to refuse to return property entrusted to me at the time it is demanded. Notice, too, that we are speaking of knowledge of the natural law itself, not the knowledge of the *theory* of natural law. For example, people in general may not know that "do not steal" is a natural law; they may not even know that there is such a thing as natural law. They may, in fact, steal. *Nevertheless, they know that they ought not steal.* This is the claim.

If St. Thomas is correct, then no matter which kind of denier we are speaking of—whether the universal denier, who denies that there are any true moral universals, or the particular denier, who denies particular true moral universals such as the wrong of adultery or murder—the denier *knows better*. Though he may give seemingly rational accounts of his objections, he is unreasonably resistant to solutions, because the obstacles that prevent him from acknowledging true moral universals lie less in the realm of the intellect than in the realm of the will. He may even desire to concoct intellectual obstacles, because they give him a pretext for refusing to admit to himself that he knows what he does, in some sense, know.

And if this in turn is true, then we have an enormous problem. It implies that a good portion of contemporary ethical and metaethical debate is not carried on in good faith.

But we are getting ahead of ourselves. Here I am worrying about the implications of the proposition that persons who deny true moral universals know better, when I have not even presented any reasons to think that they do, in fact, know better. Some people would say that I am even further ahead of myself than that, because I have not established that St. Thomas really means what I say he means when he *states* that the general principles of the natural law are the same for all as to knowledge.

Here then is what I propose. First I will reply to possible arguments against my interpretation of St. Thomas's claim; then I will present objections to his view and offer replies; then a more general argument for thinking that he is right; then why it is so important that he is right. Finally I will return to the question of what to do about all of this.

IS THIS REALLY WHAT ST. THOMAS MEANS?

Does St. Thomas really mean what I say he means? Someone might suggest that when he says that the general principles of the natural law are the same *for all* as to knowledge, he really means the same for *almost* all. As C. S. Lewis suggested, those thinkers who said that everyone knew the natural law "did not mean, of course, that you might not find an odd individual here and there who did not know it, just as you find a few people who are color-blind or have no ear for a tune. But taking the race as a whole, they thought that the human idea of decent behavior was obvious to everyone."[3] And no doubt some natural law thinkers did think this way about the race as a whole. But St. Thomas didn't. In the following passage he clearly distinguishes between principles that are the same for all in every case, and principles that are the same for all with rare exceptions:

> Consequently we must say that the natural law, as to general principles, is the same for all, both as to rectitude and as to knowledge. But as to certain matters of detail, which are conclusions, as it were, of those general principles, it is the same for all in the majority of cases, both as to rectitude and as to knowledge; and yet in some few cases it may fail, both as to rectitude, by reason of certain obstacles (just as natures subject to generation and corruption fail in some few cases on account of some obstacle), and as to knowledge, since in some the reason is perverted by passion, or evil habit, or an evil disposition of nature. . . .[4]

So although St. Thomas agreed that you might find an odd individual here and there who does not know one of the detailed precepts of the natural law, he really did believe that everyone knows the general principles of the natural law.

Someone might also propose that when St. Thomas says the general principles of the natural law are the same for all as to knowledge, he is speaking only of the first, indemonstrable principle of practical reason. In its ontological form, this may be expressed, "Good is that which all things seek after." In its preceptive form, it may be expressed, "Good is to be done and pursued, and evil is to be avoided." So the only thing that is the same for all as to knowledge—the only thing that each of us really knows—is that he ought, in fact, to pursue those things which are such as to draw his pursuit, and avoid those things which are such as to repel it. The knowledge of what these things are is *not* the same for all as to knowledge, so I am entirely mistaken in thinking that it includes such details as "Honor thy father and thy mother," "Thou shalt not kill," and "Thou shalt not steal."

The difficulty with this interpretation is that St. Thomas explicitly contradicts it. For in a later section of the *Summa*, where he is explaining the relation between the natural law and the moral precepts of Old Testament law, he remarks, "there are certain things which the natural reason of every man, of its own accord and at once, judges to be done or not to be done: e.g. 'Honor thy father and thy mother,' and 'Thou shalt not kill,' 'Thou shalt not steal': and these belong to the law of nature absolutely."[5] He makes much the same point in his commentary on Aristotle's *Nicomachean Ethics*, where he remarks that "in practical matters there are some principles naturally known as it were, indemonstrable principles and truths related to them, as evil is to be avoided, no one is to be unjustly injured, *theft must not be committed and so on.*"[6] St. Thomas speaks here of first indemonstrable principles of practical reason in the plural—there are more than one. He says that the things naturally known include not only such first indemonstrable principles, but also truths related to them—this probably means proximately derived from them—such as "Theft must not be committed." Although he is explaining a point in Aristotle about the meaning of the natural just, the illustration about theft is his own, not Aristotle's. The upshot is that yes, he does think we all know we must not steal.

Am I being hasty? For someone might suggest that St. Thomas explicitly contradicts my own interpretation too. In a later article in the same question, he writes that "some precepts are more detailed, the reason of which even an uneducated man can easily grasp; *and yet they need to be promulgated, because human judgment, in a few instances, happens to be led astray concerning them: these are the precepts of the decalogue.*"[7] If the possibility of being "led astray" concerning these precepts means that from time to time a person might be altogether ignorant of their truth, then St. Thomas is admitting that they are *not* the same for all as to knowledge. And at first it seems that this conclusion must be right, for back in question 94, article 4, following the Dominican Fathers translation of the *Summa*, widely accepted as the gold standard, St. Thomas famously remarks that "theft, although it is expressly contrary to the natural law, was not considered wrong among the Germans."[8]

This time the problem with the objector's interpretation is that it seems to make St. Thomas contradict himself. In dealing with a thinker of St. Thomas's stature, we should always investigate whether an apparent inconsistency can be resolved. This one can be, for there it is far from obvious that the expression "led astray" refers to moral ignorance, and as to that troubling passage about the Germans, the translation has slipped badly. Read properly, St. Thomas is not in any way suggesting that the Germans were ignorant of the wrong of theft.

What do I mean by the proper reading? Here is what St. Thomas actually says: "Thus formerly, *latrocinium*, although it is expressly contrary to the natural law, was not considered wrong among the Germans." Although the Dominican Fathers translation renders *latrocinium* as "theft," actually the term *latrocinium* does not refer to theft. St. Thomas carefully distinguishes *furtum* (theft), which is unjustly taking another's property by stealth, from *rapina* (robbery), which is unjustly taking another's property by coercion or violence.[9] It turns out that latrocinium is neither theft in general, nor robbery in general, nor even a particular kind of theft, but a particular kind of robbery. The term is best translated "banditry" or "piracy." A *latro*, in Roman law, was an armed bandit or raider.

If we turn to St. Thomas's source, the sixth book of Julius Caesar's *Commentaries on the Gallic Wars*, we find right away that the Germans were very much aware of the wrong of both furtum and latrocinium. In fact, Julius remarks that the Germans considered such crimes as theft and banditry so detestable that on those occasions when they burned victims to propitiate their gods, they preferred to burn the perpetrators of such crimes: as he put it, "they consider that the oblation of such as have been taken in *furto*, or in *latrocinio*, or any other offence, is more acceptable to the immortal gods."[10]

But if the Germans did know the wrong of *latrocinium*, then what can St. Thomas be thinking? We don't have to look far for the answer. When he claims Julian authority for the statement that *latrocinium* "was not considered wrong among the Germans," what he doubtless has in mind is a somewhat later passage in the *Commentaries*, where Julius explains that the Germans approved not of banditry as such, but only of a particular kind of banditry, raiding *against other tribes*. Here is what Julius says:

> *Latrocinia* which are committed beyond the boundaries of each state bear no infamy, and they [the Germans] avow that these are committed for the purpose of disciplining their youth and of preventing sloth. And when any of their chiefs has said in an assembly "that he will be their leader, let those who are willing to follow, give in their names;" they who approve of both the enterprise and the man arise and promise their assistance and are applauded by the people; such of them as have not followed him are accounted in the number of deserters and traitors, and confidence in all matters is afterward refused them.[11]

The manner in which the judgment of these barbarians was "led astray," then, was not that they were ignorant of the wrong of theft, or the wrong or robbery, or even of the wrong of banditry, but that they refused to draw one of the detailed corollaries of these precepts. They knew the wrong of plundering their neighbors, but they failed to acknowledge the members of other tribes as neighbors. Consequently they classified raiding them not as banditry, but as something like justified war. It is as though they said, "I know people who commit banditry deserve to be burned, but come on, raiding doesn't count as banditry." We do much the same thing. "I know theft is wrong, but come on, inflating the currency to finance expenditures the government can't pay for doesn't count as theft."

OBJECTIONS AND REPLIES

Even if one concedes that St. Thomas means what I say he means, it might be argued that his claim is simply wrong. Let us consider a few of the most likely objections.

> *Objection 1*
> *Perhaps in a manner of speaking everyone does "know" general moral principles such as "Don't murder," but these principles are mere tautologies. For example,* murder *means merely "wrongful killing," so "Don't murder" means merely, "Killing is wrong when it is wrong to kill." All that we are really being told is that it is wrong to do what it is wrong to do. Concerning when it is wrong to do it, there is not even an approximate agreement.* [12]

I suggest that the premise is untrue: there *is* an approximate agreement. People of widely diverse cultures more or less agree that the prohibition of murder is about the avoidance of deliberately taking innocent human life. This is the central tendency, to which the codes of particular cultures are better or worse approximations. Probably not even the cannibal thinks it is all right to deliberately take innocent human life. It is much more likely that he concedes the point but denies that the people in the other tribe are human (or perhaps that they are innocent).

The objector might now claim that I have merely substituted an elaborate tautology for a simple one. He might say that *human* means merely, "a being who is such that deliberately taking his life, when he is innocent, is wrong." Therefore, my so-called agreement means no more than "it is wrong to deliberately take the lives of innocent beings whose lives, when they are innocent, it is wrong to take." Yet this is not the case, for we also share implicit understandings about what counts as human. If we did not, then it would be impossible to argue with cannibals that their moral codes are defective. Yet experience shows that we can: various cannibal tribes have yielded to the persuasion of missionaries and other outsiders and given up their cannibalism. Consider, too, that unless the cannibal knows deep down that the people in the other tribe are human, it is difficult to explain why he performs rituals for the expiation of guilt before taking their lives. Yet he does.

> *Objection 2*
> *If it were really true that everyone knows the general precepts of the moral law, then they would be more faithfully observed. Consider the Holocaust. Surely the Nazis did not know the wrong of deliberately taking innocent human life.*

I would address the objector directly: Haven't you ever had the experience of doing something wrong even though you knew it was wrong? The monstrosity of the Nazis is not that they didn't know the wrong of deliberately taking innocent human life, but that they knew it and rationalized it anyway. Nazi propaganda went to great lengths to depict Jews as bestial (not human) and criminal (not innocent). And even here the Nazis knew better. Robert Jay Lifton reports on an interview with a former Wehrmacht neuropsychiatrist who had treated large numbers of death camp soldiers for psychological disorders. Their symptoms were much like those of combat troops, but they were worse and lasted longer. The men had the hardest time shooting women and children, especially children, and many of them had nightmares of punishment or retribution.[13] In our own country we find similar symptoms among people who practice our own "final solution," the abortion trade.

> *Objection 3*
> *If it were really true that everyone knows the general precepts of the moral law, then everyone who violated them would feel the pangs of conscience. But psychologists report that sociopaths and psychopaths have no conscience. To much the same effect, anthropologists commonly distinguish between guilt cultures, shame cultures, and fear cultures. Remorseful feelings are prominent only in guilt cultures.*

Psychologists who hold that sociopaths and psychopaths lack conscience are confusing the *judgment* of conscience, an intellectual event, with the *feeling* of remorse, an emotional event. Again I would address the objector: Have you never had the experience of doing something you knew to be wrong, *but not feeling bad about it*? Sociopaths and psychopaths are not people who do not know their acts are wrong, but people who *never* feel bad about it. Even without guilty feelings, by the way, they do show signs of guilty knowledge. One young murderer who had been described by police as having no conscience confirmed to a reporter that he didn't feel bad for what he had done. But after a moment he added, "There must be something wrong with me, don't you think? Because I should."

The same point applies to the distinction between so-called "shame" and "fear" cultures. There may be a great deal of cultural variation in the emotional reaction to guilty knowledge. We are not discussing whether everyone feels the same when he violates a known moral law, but whether everyone knows the moral law.

> *Objection 4*
> *If St. Thomas is right, then anyone who denies knowledge of the general principles of the natural law must be self-deceived. But the notion of self-deception is incoherent, because it conceives of a single person as two persons, one of whom knows something, though the other is in the dark. It is as though I were to say that I am thinking about something, and at the same time that I am not thinking about it.*

Yes, the suggestion that one and the same mind can both know and not know something in the same sense at the same time is incoherent. However, the hypothesis that the denier really does know what he claims not to know can be developed without this dubious notion. St. Thomas would suggest,

> "Don't say that you are both thinking and yet not thinking about something, or thinking about it in what both is and yet is not your real mind. Rather say that you have *one* mind, but its operations are subtle and complex. Even when you are not actually thinking about something, you may be apt to think of it at any moment. To put it differently, even when the knowledge is not actualized in present awareness, you may possess it habitually. In the meantime, your mind may continue to be dispositionally influenced by it."

If this analysis is correct, then the distinction between unconscious and conscious knowledge which is so common today is perhaps best viewed as an unsuccessful attempt to get at something that St. Thomas's own distinction, between habitual and actualized knowledge, gets at more successfully. Expressions like *self-deception* are best used in a figurative rather than in a literal sense. To be self-deceived does not mean that there are two of me. It means that although I have a dispositional tendency to be aware of something—a "natural habit," as St. Thomas says—I am resisting it; I am trying not to think about this something.

Trying not to think about something is rather difficult. If that my aim, then I must school myself in the arts of self-distraction. In fact, in order to avoid thinking about one thing, I must regiment myself not to think of a large number of things which act as triggers for thinking about it. And let us not forget that the ever-increasing effort required to *resist* my dispositional tendency has dispositional consequences of its own—a point to which we will return.

> *Objection 5*
> *Even if we do all know the general moral principles, the only reason we all know them is that we are all taught them. If you could find someone who had not been taught them, you would find that he didn't know them either.*

There is a grain of truth in this objection, for teaching the moral rules helps. Yet isn't it curious that the world over, the young are taught pretty much the same ones? It isn't as though in Canada they are taught the good of gratitude, but in France they are taught the good of ingratitude. It is also curious how often even adulterers admit the wrong of adultery, thieves the wrong of theft, and murderers the wrong of murder. The murderer does not usually excuse himself by claiming that it is right to deliberately take innocent human life, but by claiming that he couldn't help it (so it wasn't deliberate), that the victim would have died anyway (so it wasn't taking), that he deserved it (he wasn't innocent), that he was garbage (he wasn't human), or that he "didn't have a life."

The reason for these facts should be plain, for consider how teaching works. At a certain stage of mental development, when the teacher says, "Johnnie, two plus two is four," Johnnie can see for himself that two plus two is four; otherwise the words would be meaningless to him. At a certain stage of development, when Mother says, "Johnnie! Stop pulling your sister's hair! How would you like it if someone pulled your hair?" Johnnie can see for himself that he should not treat another person as he would not wish to be treated himself; otherwise the command would seem arbitrary to him. Such knowledge can't be simply *pumped in.* There has to be soil, or the seed cannot take root.

WHAT DOES ST. THOMAS'S CLAIM EXPLAIN?

But why, in the end, should we *believe* that everyone really knows the general moral principles? I suggest an argument to the best explanation. If the hypothesis of moral denial provides a better explanation of how people at odds with moral basics act than the alternative hypothesis of moral ignorance provides, then the hypothesis of moral denial is probably true, and we are justified in accepting it.

I think denial does provide a better explanation than moral ignorance. I rest this judgment on the observation that people who are at odds with the moral basics tend to "act guilty." So strong is this tendency that many guilty people expend enormous energy in the effort *not* to act guilty. Although some guilty people are better at this than others are, the strain shows.

Please notice what I am *not* suggesting. I am not suggesting that the guilty person is necessarily thinking to himself "I am guilty." But according to St. Thomas he does have a natural dispositional tendency to be aware of the first principles of natural law and their proximate, general corollaries, and I am suggesting that he also has a natural dispositional tendency to judge his behavior as wrong when it obviously violates these principles. He can resist these dispositional tendencies—for example, he can try not to think of certain subjects, or try to find ways of viewing the obvious as not obvious—but if he does, then he is also going to have to fight the dispositional tendency to be aware that he is resisting. Three sets of intellectual "habits" are therefore in conflict: first, all those associated with the natural *habitus* of the knowledge of the general principles of the natural law; second, all those associated with what I consider a natural *habitus* of knowing when I have violated them; and third, all those associated with the acquired *habitus* to resist the actualization of this knowledge.

Second, I am not suggesting that a dispositional tendency to act guilty proves that the person manifesting it must really be guilty of something; it only proves that he has a dispositional tendency to believe that he is guilty. Such belief may be unwarranted and false. For example, I may blame myself because I survived an automobile crash that killed everyone else, even though I was not driving and was not at fault. *However*, when my belief in my guilt is warranted and true, it is knowledge. So consider a person who has murdered, who claims to believe that murder is no big deal, and yet who acts guilty. I say that although he claims not to view murder as wrong, he knows better.

Third, when I speak of acting guilty I am not suggesting that it is always easy to tell precisely what guilty knowledge is being betrayed. To be sure, sometimes it is easy to tell, for example, when a person displays a compulsion to tell everyone about what he did even though he insists that his behavior was innocent. But sometimes it isn't at all easy to tell: a person may engage in behavior strongly which is suggestive of self-punishment, but which does not advertise what he is punishing himself for.

Fourth, I am not suggesting that people who are at odds with the general principles of natural law always *feel* guilty. Guilty feelings—sorrowful pangs of remorse—are probably the least reliable sign of guilty knowledge. No one always feels remorse for doing wrong; some people never do. Yet even when remorse is absent, guilty knowledge generates other telltales.

I believe that the reason guilty knowledge leaves telltales is that the violation of the conscience of a moral being generates certain objective needs, including confession, reconciliation, atonement, and justification. These are the greater sisters of remorse; elsewhere, borrowing from Greek mythology, I have called them the Furies. Now if I straightforwardly repent of my deed, then I make an honest effort to satisfy these avengers of guilt. I respond to the need for confession by admitting that I have done wrong; I respond to the need for reconciliation by repairing broken bonds with those whom I have hurt or betrayed; I respond to the need for atonement by paying the price of a contrite and broken heart; and I respond to the need for justification by getting back into justice. But what happens if I am in denial? The Furies do not go away just because I want them to. What happens is that I try to pay them off in counterfeit coin. I try to pay off the need for confession by compulsively admitting every sordid detail of my disreputable deed except that it was wrong; I try to pay off the need for reconciliation by seeking substitute companions who are as guilty as I am; I try to pay off the need for atonement by paying pain after pain, price after price, all except the one price demanded; and I try to pay off the need for justification by diverting enormous energy into rationalizing my unjust deeds as just.

Such behaviors are matters of everyday observation. To be sure, they are difficult to study systematically. Even so, much of the data about the psychological effects of abortion, from both law and the social sciences, are strongly suggestive, though of course, as one would expect in such a case, they are disputed.[14]

Someone might suggest that all these supposed telltales are imaginary, that the behavior I call "acting guilty" is more naturally explained in other ways. If I think my behavior has been blameless, why *not* talk about it? There is no need to think that I am engaging in some sort of displaced confessional urge. If my friends unreasonably subject me to moral criticism, why *shouldn't* I drop them and make new ones? There is no need to think that I am trying to find a substitute for supposedly having hurt them. If I am doing things that aren't good for me, why *shouldn't* we write my behavior as bad judgment? There is no need to think that I am punishing myself. If some people view my behavior as wrong, but I disagree with them, why *shouldn't* I defend myself? If you say that I'm making excuses, your argument is circular: it assumes what it sets out to prove.

But when I speak of displaced confession, reconciliation, atonement, and justification, I have in mind cases in which these other explanations seem to fall short—cases like the following. All of them are drawn from the annals of a single hot button issue in our culture, abortion, which is rather obviously the deliberate taking of innocent human life, but which many claim to view as entirely blameless.

- The pro-life young woman who gets pregnant, has an abortion, suddenly reverses her views and becomes pro-abortion, looks for opportunities to tell everyone how her abortion solved her problems, but falls into depression around the time the baby would have been born.[15]
- The abortion clinic operator and head nurse who write an article about the psychological burdens of doing such work in an article revealingly titled, "What About Us?"[16]
- The clinic workers mentioned in the article who have dreams of vomiting up fetuses.[17]
- The ones who report suffering from an obsessive need to talk about their experience.[18]
- The ones who refuse to look at the fetus.[19]
- The one who reports increasing resentment because some of the clients don't seem to feel as bad as she does.[20]
- The women in the clinical trials of the abortion pill who seem glad to submit to the protracted bleeding and cramping of this method of abortion because it makes them feel that they are accepting punishment for what they are doing.[21]
- Other women in the trial, as well as some members of the clinical staff, who refuse to use the term *abortion* and call what is happening a "miscarriage."[22]

- The pro-abortion counselor, quoted by a pro-abortion journalist, who is frustrated by clients who have had abortions and subsequently feel guilty *about not feeling guilty*.[23]
- The abortion clinic operator who publishes the bizarre proposal that pregnancy be socially redefined as an "illness" which "may be treated by evacuation of the uterine contents"—a suggestion one finds hard not to view as desperate.[24]
- The pro-abortion activist who insists that the act is not wrong and yet proposes that feminists "hold candlelight vigils at abortion clinics, standing shoulder to shoulder with the doctors who work there, commemorating and saying goodbye to the dead."[25]

Do such phenomena provide airtight proof that everyone who claims to consider abortion blameless knows better? No. However, I think most reasonable persons would agree that the hypothesis of moral denial explains them much better than the hypothesis of moral ignorance does.

Worth noting is the fact that many pro-abortion writers come very close to agreeing with me. One pro-abortion journalist quotes a pro-abortion counselor as commenting, "I am not confident even now, with abortion so widely used, that women feel it's OK to want an abortion without feeling guilty. They say, 'Am I some sort of monster that I feel all right about this?'" The counselor's statement is very revealing. Plainly, if a woman has guilty feelings for *not* having guilty feelings about deliberately taking innocent human life, sheer moral ignorance is not a good explanation.

In fact, the phenomenon of moral denial is taken for granted even by many people who commerce in abortion. However—chillingly—they regard denial as *good*. One of the physicians involved in the clinical trials of the abortion pill remarked, "I think there are people who want to be in denial about whether it's really an abortion or not. I think that's fine. . . . For some people that's a very useful denial and more power to them if they have to use that not to have an unwanted child." The authors of the article, who are strongly pro-abortion, seem to agree: "Indeed, denial may be considered a form of agency," they write, "in that it enables women who are troubled about abortion to get through the experience more easily."[26]

Needless to say, even if everyone really does know that deliberately taking innocent human life is wrong, it does not follow that everyone knows the rest of the general moral principles as well. So I do not claim to have *proven* St. Thomas's claim that the general moral principles are all "the same for all as to knowledge." But I think I have made it plausible.

WHY IS THE MATTER SO GRAVE?

Why is moral denial such a serious matter? Right at the beginning of the essay I mentioned one reason: it vitiates moral conversation and degrades the practice of philosophy. But there is another reason too.

Consider the driver of an automobile. Ordinarily, the threat of civil punishments like traffic fines and the deprivation of license discourage people from driving recklessly. But they only have this effect up to a certain point of corruption in the will. For consider someone who drives recklessly anyway. After a certain number of punishments, his license is taken away. After a certain number of punishments for driving without a license, his vehicle is in danger of impoundment. The risk of losing his vehicle may excite a person like this to drive even faster and more recklessly than before, just to keep the policeman from catching him. Paradoxically, the threatened penalty crosses the line from inhibiting violation to encouraging it.

I suggest that something like this happens with the penalties of conscience too. You would think that the terror of having to live with oneself afterward would deter everyone from involvement in abortion. But one who will not face conscience as a teacher must face it as an accuser, and in this way it urges him to yet further wrong. Consider the woman who told her counselor, "I couldn't be a good parent," amended her remark to "I don't deserve to have any children," and still later revealingly added, "If it hadn't been for my last abortion, I don't think I'd be pregnant now."[27] The hieroglyph is not hard to decipher. When she says she could not be a good mother, what she means is that good mothers do not kill their children. She keeps getting pregnant to replace the children she has killed; but she keeps having abortions to punish herself for having killed them. With each abortion the cams of guilt make another revolution, setting her up to have another. She can never stop until she admits what is going on.

What this shows is that if we do not authentically repent and carry out the movements of confession, reconciliation, atonement, and justification in good faith, we may actually be driven to plunge deeper into wrongdoing instead of backing off from it. The examples I have just given arise from trying to atone the wrong way, but the same dreadful dynamism operates when we confess, seek reconciliation, or try to justify ourselves the wrong way. Confessing the wrong way becomes a strategy for recruiting to the Movement. Reconciling the wrong way means that instead of giving up the wrongdoing that separates me from man and God, I demand that man and God approve of it. Justifying myself the wrong way drives me toward new evils that it was no part of my original intention to excuse—if in order to make abortion seem right I must commit myself to premises which also justify infanticide, then so be it! In such ways, not only does moral conversation become dishonest, but the whole society may be thrust out of moral equilibrium.

WHAT IS TO BE DONE?

If Thomas Aquinas is right in thinking that the most general moral principles are the same for all as to knowledge, then whenever one does deny them, *he knows better*. This fact makes it crucial to distinguish between honest objections and smokescreens. Honest objections are brought by persons who are in real perplexity and want to get out of it; smokescreens by persons who are in fictitious perplexity, and in whom the essential ordering of the human being toward knowing the truth is at sword's point with the accidental motive not to know it.

The hypothesis that those who deny general moral principles are self-deceived makes many people who take philosophy seriously deeply uncomfortable, for it seems to them to spell an end to philosophy. After all, even if the statement "You are self-deceived" is true, it does not refute the proposition "There are no true moral universals." So what do you do with someone who is in denial? And how do you make sure that you yourself are not in denial? It sounds like a problem not for a philosopher but for a psychological therapist. Unfortunately, therapists are even more helpless here than the rest of us. In the first place, a therapist can treat a person only if the person recognizes that he has a problem and submits himself for treatment. The persons we are talking about don't; no one says, "Help me, doctor, I'm a selective relativist."

Curiously, such persons often do say, "Help me, doctor, my life has no meaning," but although they complain of meaninglessness in general, when it comes to meaninglessness in morals they are more likely to boast than to complain. Besides, the theories of psychological therapy prevalent in our day tend to be just as deeply immersed in nonjudgmentalism and the rejection of moral universals as the rest of the culture is, if not even more. So I think the ball is in our court.

If it is really true that the obstacles that prevent intelligent persons from recognizing true moral universals lie not mainly in the realm of the intellect, but mainly in the realm of the will, how can such persons be reached? Perhaps by a mode of conversation that addresses not just their intellects but also their wills; say, by conversational moves that somehow help them to become aware that they are, in fact, in denial. But does that kind of conversation even belong to philosophy?

It certainly belongs to the teaching of philosophy. A student said to me once, "Morality is all relative anyway. How do we even know that murder is wrong?" Once upon a time I would have tried to convince him that murder is wrong, but one cannot convince someone of something he already knows. So I asked, "Are you at this moment in real doubt about murder being wrong for everyone?" After a long pause and a little hemming and hawing, he said, "No, I guess I'm not." I replied, "Then you aren't really perplexed about whether morality is relative after all; you only thought you were. Can you suggest something you are perplexed about?"

On another occasion, I remarked to a student, "Did you realize that you've just taken an incoherent position? You say truth can't be known, all the while supposing that you know it to be true that you can't." "I guess I am being incoherent," he replied. After thinking for a moment, he added, "But that's all right, because the universe is incoherent, and I don't need to have meaning in my life." I thought he knew better than that. So I said, "I don't believe you. You know as well as I do that the longing for meaning and coherency is deep-set in every mind. So the real question is this: What is it that is so important to you that you are willing to give up even meaning and coherency to have it?"

If such conversations are part of the teaching of philosophy, why shouldn't they be part of philosophy? Socrates, the ancestor of all philosophers, thought they were. If we strip out the dialogue from his dialogues, boiling away the spiritual combat and leaving only a dusty residue of syllogisms, then we miss much of their point. Figuring out what their point is requires a philosophical analysis of something we might have preferred not to consider a philosophical problem at all. We find this to be true of some of the conversations in the New Testament as well, such as the dialogue between Christ and the woman at the well in the fourth chapter of the Gospel of John. On the surface it seems like a series of non sequiturs, but really it is a duel of feints, thrusts, and ripostes.

Such conversations are likely to be full of paradoxes. For example, getting through to the denier will sometimes require a great deal more than presenting a sound argument to him. But on the other hand, sometimes it may require presenting *less*. The mere tender of arguments to someone who is determined to remain self-deceived is more likely to provoke him to cleverness than to stir him to wisdom. Just because he is still talking, we may think we are getting somewhere, but he is merely generating objections for their own sake. For him, the conversation is not so much a means of attaining truth as a sophisticated means of avoiding it.

One thing this suggests is that what might be called the purely professional way of doing philosophy is a mistake. By the purely professional way, I mean the attitude which separates the intellectual from the moral virtues, which separates what I am doing from what kind of person I am. Philosophy is only accidentally a profession. It is essentially a vocation. Characteristic of any vocation is that in order to pursue it I must do more than acquire a certain set of abilities; I must try to become a certain kind of person. If I do not practice the moral virtues, then I acquire an interest in justifying myself without being just. This is a disincentive to discovering the truth. So I must either try to be a better man, or stop pretending that I want to know the truth.

The hypothesis of moral denial also underscores the importance to *both* sides—both deniers and anti-deniers—of reaching the young first. Virtue has a reason for reaching them first because if they develop vicious dispositions, they will probably become deniers themselves. But vice has a reason for reaching them first because it *cannot have* them thinking straight. For the denier has an interest in converting others into deniers. If he allowed the new generation to think straight, they might join his unmaskers. His troubled conscience therefore defends itself against exposure by surrounding itself with a ring of recruits.

And what of my own conscience? It is one thing to have such a conversation with a self-deceived student. It is harder to have it with a self-deceived colleague. More difficult still is to have it with a self-deceived public, with whom one must carry it out in sound bites. The most difficult thing of all—ah, that it were not—is to have such a conversation with myself.

To know truth, I must be converted into truth. I think this is what Socrates had in mind. But alas, I resist.

NOTES

1. For years, beginning with "The Revenge of Conscience," *First Things* 84 (June/July 1998): 21–27, I have written about various aspects of this theme. In this article, however, I try to pull all the diverse parts of the analysis into one piece. I have adapted, and augmented, some of my previous comments about the Furies in *What We Can't Not Know: A Guide* (San Francisco: Ignatius Publisher, 2011) and about the ancient German tribes in *The Line Through the Heart: Natural Law as Fact, Theory, and Sign of Contradiction* (Wilmington, DE: ISI Books, 2009) and in *Commentary on Thomas Aquinas's Treatise on Law* (New York: Cambridge University Press, 2014). Gratitude to these publishers is rendered gladly.

2. Aquinas, *Summa theologiae*, trans. Fathers of the Dominican Province, 2nd rev. ed. (1920; public domain), 2.1.94.4.

3. C. S. Lewis, *Mere Christianity*, rev. ed. (New York: HarperCollins, 1982), 5.

4. Aquinas, *Sth* 2.1.94.4. I have omitted the final clause from this quotation, but only in order to return to it later.

5. Aquinas, *Sth* 2.1.100.1. Cf. art. 8, *ad* 3, where St. Thomas explains that although exceptions may be made to "determinations" adapted to particular circumstances, "as to the essence of justice they contain" the precepts of the Decalogue are unchanging.

6. Aquinas, *Commentary on Aristotle's Nicomachean Ethics*, trans. C. J. Litzinger, OP, rev. ed. (Notre Dame, IN: Dumb Ox Books, 1993), 5.12, 325 (emphasis added).

7. Aquinas, *Sth* 2.1.100.11.

8. Aquinas, *Sth* 2.1.94.4.

9. Aquinas, *Sth* 2.1.66.3–4.

10. Julius Caesar, *The War in Gaul,* trans. W. A. MacDevitt, in *"De Bellico Gallico" and Other Commentaries of Caius Julius Caesar,* 6.16, http://classics.mit.edu/Caesar/gallic.html (public domain). For *furto* and *latrocinio*, MacDevitt has "theft" and "robbery." Though Julius does not mention other, more routine Germanic penalties for theft, such as compensation, these double the proof that they knew theft was wrong.

11. Caesar, *War* 6.23.

12. See, e.g., the argument of Richard A. Posner in "The Problematics of Moral and Legal Theory," *Harvard Law Review* 111 (1998): 1637–709.

13. Robert Jay Lifton, *The Nazi Doctors: Medical Killing and the Psychology of Genocide* (New York: Basic Books, 1986), 15.

14. As to the law, see for example *Sandra Cano v. Thurbert E. Baker, Attorney General of Georgia, et al., on Petition for Writ of Certiorari to the United States Court of Appeals for the Eleventh Circuit*, brief of Amicus Curiae J. Budziszewski in Support of Petitioner, sec. 6, "The Affidavits of Post-Abortive Woman Submitted to the District Court in This Case Confirm that the Violation of Conscience Has Destructive Consequences." (This was in support of a petition for reconsideration of *Roe v. Wade* and *Doe v. Bolton*.) As to the social sciences, see, e.g., David M. Fergusson, L. John Horwood, and Joseph M. Boden, "Abortion and Mental Health Disorders: Evidence from a 30-year Longitudinal Study," *British Journal of Psychiatry* 193 (2008): 444–51.

15. Anecdote passed on by the young woman's college chaplain.

16. Warren M. Hern, MD, MPH, and Billie Corrigan, RN, MS, "What About Us? Staff Reactions to D & E," *Advances in Planned Parenthood* 15, no. 1 (1980): 3–8.

17. Hern and Corrigan, "What About Us?"

18. Hern and Corrigan, "What About Us?"

19. Hern and Corrigan, "What About Us?"

20. Hern and Corrigan, "What About Us?"

21. Wendy Simonds et al., "Abortion, Revised: Participants in the U.S. Clinical Trials Evaluate Mifepristone," *Social Science and Medicine* 46, no. 10 (1998): 1316.

22. Simonds et al., "Abortion, Revised."

23. Nicci Gerrard, with Kim Bunce and Kirsty Buttfield, "Damned If You Do . . .," *The Observer* (Apr. 22, 2001), http://www.observer.co.uk/review/story/0,6903,476313,00.html.

24. Hern, "Is Pregnancy Really Normal?" *Family Planning Perspectives* 3, no. 1 (Jan. 1971): 9.

25. Naomi Wolf, "Our Bodies, Our Souls," *The New Republic* 233, no. 16 (Oct. 16, 1995): 26–35.

26. Simonds et al., "Abortion, Revised," 1318–19.

27. Other anecdotes passed on to me by crisis pregnancy counselors follow much the same pattern.

WORKS CITED

Aquinas. *Commentary on Aristotle's Nicomachean Ethics*. Translated by C. J. Litzinger, OP. Rev. ed. Notre Dame, IN: Dumb Ox Books, 1993.

———. *Summa theologiae*. Translated by the Fathers of the Dominican Province. 2nd rev. ed. 1920.

Budziszewski, J. *Commentary on Thomas Aquinas's Treatise on Law*. New York: Cambridge University Press, 2014.

———. *The Line Through the Heart: Natural Law as Fact, Theory, and Sign of Contradiction*. Wilmington, Delaware: ISI Books, 2009.

———. "The Revenge of Conscience." *First Things* 84 (June/July 1998): 21–27.

———. *What We Can't Not Know: A Guide*. San Francisco: Ignatius Publisher, 2011.

Fergusson, David M., L. John Horwood, and Joseph M. Boden. "Abortion and Mental Health Disorders: Evidence from a 30-year Longitudinal Study." *British Journal of Psychiatry* 193 (2008): 444–51.

Gerrard, Nicci, with Kim Bunce and Kirsty Buttfield. "Damned If You Do . . . ." *The Observer* (Apr. 22, 2001). http://www.observer.co.uk/review/story/0,6903,476313,00.html.

Hern, Warren M. "Is Pregnancy Really Normal?" *Family Planning Perspectives* 3, no. 1 (Jan. 1971): 9.

Hern, Warren M., MD, MPH, and Billie Corrigan, RN, MS. "What About Us? Staff Reactions to D and E." *Advances in Planned Parenthood* 15, no. 1 (1980): 3–8.

Julius Caesar. *The War in Gaul.* Translated by W. A. MacDevitt. In *"De Bellico Gallico" and Other Commentaries of Caius Julius Caesar,* 6.16. http://classics.mit.edu/Caesar/gallic.html (public domain).
Lewis, C. S. *Mere Christianity*. Rev. ed. New York: HarperCollins, 1982.
Lifton, Robert Jay. *The Nazi Doctors: Medical Killing and the Psychology of Genocide*. New York: Basic Books, 1986.
Posner, Richard A. "The Problematics of Moral and Legal Theory/" *Harvard Law Review* 111 (1998): 1637–709.
Sandra Cano v. Thurbert E. Baker, Attorney General of Georgia, et al., on Petition for Writ of Certiorari to the United States Court of Appeals for the Eleventh Circuit. Brief of Amicus Curiae J. Budziszewski in Support of Petitioner. S ec. 6, "The Affidavits of Post-Abortive Woman Submitted to the District Court in This Case Confirm that the Violation of Conscience Has Destructive Consequences."
Simonds, Wendy, Charlotte Ellertson, Kimberly Springer, and Beverley Winikoff. "Abortion, Revised: Participants in the U.S. Clinical Trials Evaluate Mifepristone." *Social Science and Medicine* 46, no. 10 (1998): 1316.
Wolf, Naomi. "Our Bodies, Our Souls." *The New Republic* 233, no. 16 (Oct. 16, 1995): 26–35.

Chapter Five

Aquinas's Second Reason for the Necessity of Divine Law

Certainty of Knowledge with Respect to Particular and Contingent Moral Actions

Steven Brust

Most contemporary commentators and writers on Thomistic natural law (and natural law in general), focus primarily on the "natural" aspect in Aquinas's *Treatise on Law*: that it is a law of reason and can therefore be known by reason alone, without the aid of divine revelation.[1] Yet, in question 91—which presents the four reasons for the necessity of divine law—there is one passage which suggests that this emphasis on natural reason should be re-evaluated and moderated.[2] In what follows, I intend to contribute to a renewed attention on what Aquinas has to say about the necessity and importance of the divine law for knowledge of the natural law, and to briefly explore its consequences for our contemporary circumstances.

In the *Treatise on Law* (the locus classicus for Aquinas's natural law), Aquinas presents the natural law as principles of practical reason, some of which are self-evident to all, and some of which are not.[3] Many scholarly treatments concerning knowledge of natural law principles focus on reason—unaided by divine revelation—as the means by which one comes to know these principles. And for most, there is the usual discussion about the relation between natural law and eternal law—that natural law is man's participation in the eternal law, which emanates from the eternal reason of God.[4] This reference to God however, is still one based on human reason, and comes under the heading of natural (philosophical) theology: one can know by reason alone that there is a God who governs his creation by a law of reason.[5] As a result, knowledge of the natural law by natural/human reason alone is still the primary consideration and emphasis. The main reason is to underscore that although Aquinas associates man's reason and the natural law as a participation in the eternal law (which is the eternal reason and will of God), this does not mean it is ipso facto not natural or not known by reason—and thus known only through a special divine revelation. Most commentators on the natural law thus focus on man's reason participating in God's eternal reason with respect to reason's natural powers—thereby making a clear distinction between reason and revelation/faith.[6] It is precisely this emphasis and clear distinction that should be rethought in light of what Aquinas has to say about the relationship between particular and contingent moral actions and divine positive law—that is, actions known through a specific divine revelation, and not merely between natural law and eternal law, that is, known only by a natural theology. What then is this relationship between knowing the natural law with reference to moral actions by human reason *and* the knowledge that comes from supernatural (divine) revelation?

In article 4 of question 91, concerning the different types of law, Aquinas asks whether human beings need a divine law—law which is specifically posited (set down) by God through an act of divine revelation to human beings. He gives four reasons for why they do, the second of which is most relevant for our purposes:

> Second, because of the uncertainty of human judgment, especially regarding *contingent and particular* matters, different persons may judge differently about various human actions, and so even different and contrary laws result. Therefore, in order that human beings can know beyond any doubt what they should do or should not do, a divinely revealed law, regarding which error is impossible, was needed to direct human beings in their actions.[7]

Thus, divine law is needed because of the uncertainty of human judgment—that we could be wrong about what is morally good or bad to do in particular matters.[8] Exactly what is meant by "contingent and particular" matters will be considered below. For now, one notes that divine law cannot err, because Aquinas assumes as a premise (and argues elsewhere) that the divine source—God—cannot err, and thus does not promulgate laws and precepts which would direct persons to commit particular morally evil actions.

In this passage, Aquinas doesn't explain why human judgment is uncertain and therefore could err in moral judgment, just that it is de facto the case. In question 94, article 6, one discovers why human judgment is capable of and does fall into error. There, Aquinas claims that, although in the abstract the general principles of the natural law cannot be blotted out in men, they can be blotted out with regard to applying the general principles to particular actions on account of "concupiscence or some other passion." And the secondary principles can be blotted out from the hearts of men because of "evil opinions, vicious customs, or corrupt habits."[9] So, our intellect is affected by these influences, leading us to make erroneous judgments regarding particular and contingent actions—even to the point of whole cultures thinking vices are not vices.[10]

The more I reflect on these passages, the more I think that perhaps the natural law as known by the light of human reason alone is not as well known after all—at least in "contingent and particular" human actions.[11] This necessity of divine law—that which is positively revealed by God in a special way—for knowledge of the natural law in particular matters is not something out of the ordinary for Aquinas; rather, it comports well with his understanding of the relationship between reason and revelation. As seen at the beginning of the *Summa*, divine revelation is needed not only to obtain knowledge of things which man's reason can't come to know on its own power, but also because even if man could know things about God from reason, he would still need divine revelation because his reason is capable of making many erroneous judgments.[12] This is also reinforced in the *Treatise on Law*, where Aquinas, in responding to the objection that man's reason is sufficient for knowledge of the natural law precepts, remarks that divine revelation rescues man because his reason has been impeded or obscured by sin.[13] Due to sin, man's reason is deficient and the Old Law is a remedy for this sin-induced ignorance.[14] Of course, it is of utmost importance for Aquinas that we be certain about divine matters (both speculative and practical-moral), so that we might attain eternal life with God. Thus, it seems that we should take seriously what Aquinas says about the necessity of divine law for knowledge of particular human actions. But if we are, what does it entail?

DIVINE LAW

To answer this, we must look more at what specifically divine law can tell us, especially regarding the "contingent and particular matters" of moral actions to which Aquinas refers. For Aquinas, divine law is twofold, the Old and New Law. I will explore each law in turn.

The Old Law

The Old Law consists of ceremonial, judicial, and moral precepts. The ceremonial precepts pertain to the specific ways the Jewish nation was to worship God, as well as those judicial precepts that pertained to the specific ways in which the Jews were to direct their actions in relation to each other. The ceremonial precepts were binding on the Jews alone.[15] For Aquinas, the ceremonial precepts are more specific determinations of those moral precepts regarding the worship of God.[16] Thus, in a strict sense, the ceremonial law of the Old Testament appears to provide for knowledge of particular and contingent moral actions—but only those concerning worship. Since they are specific to the Jews, they are not binding on others, and ultimately they will cease with Christ, who will provide new ways of worship.[17]

The judicial precepts, on the other hand, have to do with "the relation of man with man" within the Jewish community in particular, but also in general.[18] These precepts are instituted by God in the case of the people of Israel, or are instituted by men for other political communities. Since they primarily concern relations among men in a community, it primarily rests with the rulers of the respective (non-Israelite) communities to determine these precepts.[19] Since the judicial precepts of the Old Law were instituted by God for Israel, they are no longer binding and were annulled due to the coming of Christ and full establishment of the New Law.[20] However, the judicial precepts of other communities come and go with their respective forms of government. In one sense, Aquinas does consider judicial precepts to be moral precepts, because "the act of justice, in general, belongs to the moral precepts." Nonetheless, with respect to the Old Law, he differentiates them from the moral precepts.[21] Therefore, one can safely conclude that, in the strict sense, the Old Law did help in knowing particular and contingent matters regarding legal relations among the Israelites. However, from a Judeo-Christian perspective, judicial precepts are not divinely instituted for other communities; rather, they are instituted by men. Consequently, they do not provide help to know particular and contingent matters with certainty qua divine law.[22] Since the ceremonial and judicial precepts are no longer binding in their respective ways as divine laws, given their application to the Israelites alone, we need to focus on the moral precepts, particularly those with universal and timeless application.

Aquinas considers the moral precepts of the Old Law to "show forth the precepts of the natural law,"[23] and that all of the moral precepts are contained within the Decalogue.[24] Since the Decalogue is part of the natural law, why was it necessary to be revealed by God? Aquinas states that a primary reason why the Old Law was not given immediately after the first sin is "because as yet the dictate of the natural law was not darkened by habitual sinning,"[25] and that it was provided during the time of Moses; because "with regard to good men, the Law was given . . . as a help; which was most needed by the people, at the time when the natural law began to be obscured on account of the exuberance of sin."[26] Even though he doesn't use the terms "contingent and particular matters," we see here that the Old Law is specifically given to aid human reason's knowledge of the natural law which obviously pertains to particular moral actions.

Randall Smith demonstrates more precisely how the Old Law contains the written precepts of the natural law—general to more specific, and those that are invariable and variable.[27] These precepts do provide some moral guidance on particular matters on at least three levels: primary and common, secondary, and tertiary—all of which have different degrees of knowability.

The primary and common precepts such as the two great commandments, "Love God" and "Love your neighbor," according to Smith's analysis, are self-evident to human reason and are known by all. The second level of precepts, such as "Thou shalt not kill" and "Thou shalt not steal," can be known by everyone—but nonetheless need to be divinely revealed because man's judgment can be corrupted. For Aquinas, these secondary principles are the precepts of the Decalogue. This second level would fall into the practical and contingent matters which Aquinas deems are in need of the divinely revealed Decalogue in order to know them with certainty. However, it is the third level of precepts—which concern many particular and contingent moral actions that especially need further specification. Aquinas provides some specification by "adding" to the Decalogue other third-level precepts that spring from the second-level ones explicitly referenced in the Decalogue.[28] For instance, the sixth commandment, "Thou shalt not commit adultery," does not specifically mention fornication, masturbation, prostitution, homosexual sex, etc. More precise principles are needed to express a more complete understanding of how to act according to human sexuality and its purposes. These more precise principles are generally encompassed by the sixth commandment, but need to be drawn out and specified. Thus, for Aquinas, another precept which prohibits prostitution is said to be "added"[29] to the sixth commandment. In "adding" this precept prohibiting prostitution, Aquinas cites Scripture (Deut. 23:17) as his source. This could be seen as an example of one of those "particular matters" about which Aquinas mentions is in need of divine law for its immorality to be known for certain. Indeed, he states that God gives these precepts through Moses and Aaron (those chosen to reveal God's law). The point Aquinas wants to make is that these other precepts are divinely revealed, and are themselves derived from the original divinely revealed commandments, and in this way are added to the Decalogue. Thus, in light of the second reason for the necessity of divine law found in question 91, article 4, it appears that the Old Law brings certainty to at least some of the second- and third-level precepts (i.e., to additional "particular" moral actions).[30]

However, Aquinas also states that the third-level precepts are known by the wise through the exercise of the virtue of prudence. It would seem that the Old Testament could not mention every practical conclusion within the third level precepts, and so an appeal to the prudential judgments of the wise seems fitting.[31] Indeed, it is the virtue of prudence which allows one to make the right judgments in the right circumstances, at the right time, going from the more general precepts to the third-level conclusions.[32] In accord with this, Aquinas elsewhere states that the immorality of prostitution could be known by reason alone.[33] But appealing to the wise for knowledge of these more specific precepts seems to put in doubt the necessity of revealed divine law, at least regarding the Old Law, as the means to provide certainty in *every* particular and contingent matter. Yet, as we have seen in various matters, the Old Law does and can act as an affirmation of what could, in principle, be known by reason.

The New Law

We now turn to see what the New Law's relationship is to obtaining certain knowledge of particular and contingent matters. In question 106, article 2, where Aquinas asks whether the New Law is a written law, he responds that the "New Law is in the first place a law that is inscribed on our hearts, but that secondarily it is a written law."[34] It is inscribed on our hearts because it "is chiefly the grace itself of the Holy Ghost, which is given to those who believe in Christ." It is the divine law in our hearts.[35] The New Law, as the grace of the Holy Spirit, provides the *power to fulfill* the precepts of the Decalogue and those moral precepts added to it.[36] Even the letter would kill without the efficacious grace. Consequently, the New Law does not primarily concern knowledge of the law but the efficacy of fulfilling it. Recall that Aquinas's second reason for the divine law concerns providing the certain knowledge of what to do in contingent and particular matters and does not mention supplying the grace to fulfill those moral actions. Thus, I turn to the New Law in relation to knowledge of human actions.

For Aquinas, the New Law instructs the faithful concerning things that dispose persons to receive grace, and to use that grace. These instructions are given by word and writing both as to what is to be believed (faith) and what should be done (commandments).[37] The New Testament writings "exhort men in diverse ways."[38] How does the New Law instruct? For Aquinas, Christ "added very few precepts to those of the natural law."[39] Rather, in the New Law, Christ shows the "true sense of the Law" by showing that external acts are "extended also to interior acts of sins." For instance, the prohibition of the act of murder includes the interior act of "the wicked impulse to hurt our brother."[40]

In question 108, article 2, Aquinas asks if the New Law prohibits or prescribes externals acts. He responds that the New Law forbids and prescribes certain external acts: "Accordingly the New Law had no other external works to determine, by prescribing or forbidding, except the sacraments, and those moral precepts which have a necessary connection with virtue, for instance, that one must not kill, or steal, and so forth."[41] These moral actions that connect to virtue are part of the natural law. Therefore, "there was no need [in the New Law] for any precepts to be given besides the moral precepts of the [Old] Law [of the Decalogue and those added to it], which proceed from the dictate of reason."[42] Thus, it appears the New Law does not add anything to the natural laws of reason, as found in the moral precepts of the Old Law—but this lack of new knowledge appears to apply only with respect to external actions. In question 108, article 3, Aquinas emphasizes that the Lord:

> directs man's will in respect of the various precepts of the Law: by prescribing that man should refrain not merely from those external works that are evil in themselves, but also from internal acts, and from the occasions of evil deeds. In the second place He directs man's intention, by teaching that in our good works, we should seek neither human praise, nor worldly riches, which is to lay up treasures on earth.[43]

Aquinas also states that Christ "directs man's interior movement in respect of his neighbor, by forbidding us, on the one hand, to judge him rashly, unjustly, or presumptuously; and, on the other, to entrust him too readily with sacred things if he be unworthy."[44]

What is the takeaway from all of this about the New Law regarding its helping us know how to act in contingent and particular matters? Primarily it appears that help comes in the way of prohibiting interior actions that foster prohibited external actions. But as far as external actions themselves, Aquinas appears to say that the moral precepts of the New Law are those of the Old Law, the Decalogue and its additions, which are laws of reason. So the New Law, like the Old Law, affirms with certainty the natural law precepts known by reason—that is, it is a divine aid due to the darkening of the intellect. Thus, as expressed in the New Testament, divine law does provide some certitude about some specific behaviors.[45] However, the New Law does not address many specific moral actions for which one needs to have certainty, or rather, it does not reference many particular and contingent behaviors that might fall under the more general (primary and secondary) precepts.

At this point, it is helpful to distinguish between types of "contingent and particular" moral matters about which divine law can or cannot provide certitude. It seems safe to say that *every* particular and contingent moral matter does not lend itself to obtaining the certitude of a true moral judgment. That is, it appears to be human experience that. for many moral decisions, one might not have the certitude of their rightness or wrongness. For instance, whether I should visit a friend in the hospital or attend the baptism of another friend's child that occur at the same time is a matter of prudential judgment for which moral certitude about the "morally correct decision" might not ever come. Yet, there are other prudential judgments for which one can and must have certitude, especially judgments which pertain to morally grave actions. These come in the application of the immutable, universal moral precepts of the natural law, found in the Old and New Testaments, especially the Decalogue, and those additions to the Decalogue. Furthermore, knowing whether some particular action is morally wrong might also depend on whether it falls under a precept which is unchangeable and applicable to all persons and all circumstances. For example, the intentional killing of an innocent person is always morally wrong, but there might be cases where determining that a particular action is indeed the intentional killing of an innocent person (applying the principle to the circumstance) may be difficult for some to know.[46] Additionally, one might need to determine if an action is indeed always and everywhere a morally evil action.

These distinctions, I think, allow us to affirm Aquinas's claim about the necessity of divine law for knowledge of the natural law, but also think that it might be insufficient. It appears that the kinds of particular and contingent matters about which divine law can help to achieve moral certitude are those which directly implicate universal moral principles, especially the negative moral norms. It doesn't seem that it includes the myriad of actions of daily life determined by the virtue of prudence. These are just too numerous and contingent for the divine law—both the Old and New Law in the form of the written and nonbiblical teachings—to be of any direct help regarding very particular actions (although the divine law, again, is undoubtedly helpful regarding other particular actions, including those involving general precepts of the natural law).

CONTEMPORARY CIRCUMSTANCES

Today, we face many moral challenges which the Old and New Laws do not explicitly mention. For instance, with respect to contemporary bioethical issues such as embryo-destructive research or physician-assisted suicide or removing food and water from a medical patient (specific and contingent behaviors), there are no explicit references in Scripture or Tradition regarding these behaviors. Although certain parts of revelation (e.g., Psalm 139:13) can help to reaffirm human life as beginning in the womb, and the sacredness of each human life given by God, additional moral reasoning is needed to help demonstrate why embryo-destructive research is always wrong. Now, the natural law tradition would (rightly) claim that our powers to think—reason—can help us morally sort through these issues based on other natural law precepts rooted in the nature of the human person, and thereby come to a true and certain moral judgment. Indeed, reason can help us ascertain the moral truth with respect to these behaviors. Be that as it may, it is Aquinas's contention that due to the influence of sin and the passions on our reason, we need the unerring divine law to provide certainty about some of our moral judgments—especially those pertaining to more particular actions. But if divine law as found, for example, in the Bible—both Old and New Testaments—does not include references to these (and other) specific matters, then how can it be said that divine law is needed for knowledge of these types of particular and contingent matters which pertain to grave moral matters, and not just everyday moral decisions which don't involve universal moral norms? It appears that Aquinas's claim about the necessity of the divine law cannot be affirmed with respect to some grave moral matters.[47] Does this mean, then, that we are left with our fallible reason, throwing up our arms in a state of skepticism and thus never knowing for certain what is the right way to act in these particular and contingent actions?

One might look to Aquinas's "wise men" for assistance in making correct judgments on more particular moral actions, both the ones relating to the determination of whether a certain action does indeed fall under a particular precept, and those relating to the determination of whether a particular action is always prohibited by a moral precept.[48] But, of course, we must not forget that as men, they are still fallible. Thus we need to look elsewhere for a source of this certainty. Or perhaps we must conclude that Aquinas is just mistaken on this claim.[49]

Perhaps human reason, in all its fallibility due to man's fallen and sinful nature, needs to be purified by grace. Since grace, in addition to divine revelation (here meaning what is written law), is mentioned, I will briefly explore this. Grace comes to dwell in persons through the Holy Spirit by means of the theological virtues of faith, hope, and love. As we recall from Aquinas, the New Law is the grace of the Holy Spirit by faith in Christ, and is a law "inscribed on our hearts."[50] Grace heals the effects that sin and the passions have on reason, enabling one more likely to know the natural law principles and to make correct moral judgments. The more one participates in the life of divine grace, the more one will be able to know this law in one's heart (conscience) and make morally right judgments in specific circumstances. How grace operates upon an individual is ultimately a mystery, but the important point is that Aquinas argues it is necessary for a more complete and certain knowledge of the natural law. Indeed, it could not only help with grave moral challenges, but also the myriad of daily particular decisions.

How much of the natural law can be known both in general and in more specific matters is the fundamental question. In looking at the United States today, there is reason to be pessimistic about how much of the moral law is known by a majority of the populace mostly regarding some very grave matters. For instance, basic natural law understandings of human sexuality, marriage, and the family are being rejected as false. And in more particular issues such as in vitro fertilization, embryo-destructive research, and other bioethical issues, there exists even more confusion and erroneous judgment. Or, put a different way, many human actions that traditional natural law principles—involving both general and particular moral precepts—have judged to be morally evil are now judged by many to be morally good, and vice versa. Perhaps one can say that when the more general principles are denied, erroneous judgments regarding the more specific principles tend to follow. This, of course, is consistent with what Aquinas said regarding subsidiary precepts of the Decalogue. When the general principles (or more precisely, those ethical understandings of human nature which underlie those principles) are misunderstood or rejected, one will end up distorting or rejecting principles that follow upon them.[51]

Why does this widespread rejection and inversion of natural law in these important matters exist today? Could it be that reason has been steadily shorn from revelation and grace, so that it falls into more and more error? To elaborate on this, I refer to Cardinal Joseph Ratzinger's (now Emeritus Pope Benedict XVI) thought on the relationship between reason and revelation. He has consistently written about the need for reason to be purified by faith and revelation, going so far as to claim that ethics can't "supply its own rational basis," and that "reason needs revelation in order to be able to function as reason."[52] This is quite a statement—which appears to mean that reason can't be itself unless it is aided by revelation.[53]

Perhaps a way to understand how revelation purifies or allows reason to be itself is to see that there is never an "abstract" reason. Rather, reason is always historically situated and operating amidst the customs, ways of life, and institutions of the whole society. Ratzinger writes of reason needing to be purified by faith/revelation so that it not become distorted and truncated, limiting its horizons and rejecting metaphysical truths.[54] Thus, when reason is separated from a historical culture and society formed by Christian revelation, or rather, when the culture and society become less and less imbued in its customs, ways of life, manners, institutions, etc., with Christian revelation and the related way of life penetrated by grace, it becomes a "naked reason" which is prone more and more to erroneous judgments. It is not purified, but rather becomes less pure and darker, especially as immoral behavior increases. This, I agree with Ratzinger, is supported by the historical evidence.[55] As the West has become more and more de-Christianized in its culture, knowledge of the natural law has become less and less known—at least in the form of knowing what is good and evil (at times reversing the judgments of good and evil). To return to a previous example above, the basic natural moral laws pertaining to marriage and human sexuality that have been acknowledged for two millennia have been disregarded, distorted, and/or rejected. Without revelatory truth and grace penetrating the historical existence of the culture—customs, institutions, ways of life—then reason itself becomes increasingly impoverished. The efficacy of revelation rests on its contribution to the "purification of reason and to the reawakening of those moral forces without which just structures are neither established nor prove effective in the long run."[56] Pope Benedict XVI (as we saw when he was Cardinal Ratzinger) also claimed that faith can purify reason so that it can be itself in order to attain justice in the political order.[57] He emphasized the purification of reason by revelation, encouraging reason to be open to its full potential and accept metaphysical and moral truths.

In conclusion, I think it imperative, especially given the state of modern culture, that adherents to the natural law tradition take seriously what Aquinas claims, namely, that the revelation of the divine law is needed to help man know for certain the natural moral law in particular and contingent matters, whether these are associated with the moral precepts of the Decalogue and those added to it regarding external matters or related inner moral dispositions. Yet, the divine law, as a written law, is not helpful with respect to the many of the new actions, because they don't explicitly address them.[58] Nevertheless, divine law does provide us with some of the principles from which to reason. Furthermore, while divine law—as a written law[59]—does not specifically help us with the myriad decisions individuals are faced with on an everyday basis, the precepts of the divine law can help us in evaluating our various decisions, and the divine law as the grace of the Holy Spirit working in persons and the culture can help us successfully live them out. The more the divine and natural law are instantiated in institutions, ways of life, customs, habits, of persons and the culture, the more certitude of the rightness and wrongness of particular and contingent moral actions will be attained. The focus on "unaided" reason, while necessary, is not sufficient, and a neglect of divine law leaves society (and the individual) in an inadequate state.

NOTES

1. Aquinas, *Summa theologiae*, 2nd rev. ed., trans. Fathers of the English Dominican Province (1920; New Advent, 2008), 2.1.90–108, esp. 94, http://www.newadvent.org/summa/. However, in more recent years, there has been an increase in a reappropriation of the relationship of divine revelation (and divine law) to natural law by some scholars. Most notable is Matthew Levering's *Biblical Natural Law* (Oxford: Oxford University Press, 2006), esp. 219, where he affirms, "Bracketing the eternal and divine law [with respect to knowledge of the natural law] does not work, then." This paper is, I hope, a contribution to this much needed reappropriation.

2. Aquinas, *Sth* 2.1.91.4.

3. Aquinas, *Sth*. Aquinas does not specifically and precisely state all of the principles which are self-evidently known, and which are not; rather, he says that the primary precepts are known by all and the secondary ones are not.

4. Aquinas, *Sth* 2.1.91.2, 94.2.

5. Aquinas, *Sth* 2.1.91.1, 93.1.

6. Or philosophy and revealed theology.

7. Aquinas, *Sth* 2.1.91.4 (my emphasis); Secundo, quia propter incertitudinem humani iudicii, praecipue de *rebus contingentibus et particularibus*, contingit de actibus humanis diversorum esse diversa iudicia, ex quibus etiam diversae et contrariae leges procedunt. Ut ergo homo absque omni dubitatione scire possit quid ei sit agendum et quid vitandum, necessarium fuit ut in actibus propriis dirigeretur per legem divinitus datam, de qua constat quod non potest errare.

He also mentions in 2.1.100.11 that some moral precepts (the commandments of the Decalogue), even though known by uneducated men who can easily grasp them, need to be promulgated because human reason in a few instances may be led astray regarding them. "Few instances" is not exactly equivalent to "particular and contingent moral matters"; nonetheless, the fallibility of human reason and necessity of divine revelation is confirmed.

8. See Levering, *Biblical Natural Law*, 210. For Aquinas, "divine law is a unity of the Torah and Gospel of Christ from whom flows the Holy Spirit."

9. Aquinas, *Sth* 2.1.94.6. "Blotted out" appears to mean "no knowledge of," which in turn leads to making erroneous judgments. After all, the natural law is a law of reason which is the knowing faculty, and his response begins with reference to knowledge of the natural law. All these human conditions are facts, and the original reason why our intellects are somewhat darkened (to knowing) is because of Original Sin (*Sth* 2.1.77.3–4). Further sins and disordered passions increase this darkening effect.

10. Aquinas, *Sth* 2.1.94.6. This last point regarding the moral blindness of cultures will be touched upon below with reference to contemporary moral issues.

11. Or as we shall see below, perhaps it is known by the light of reason, when that reason is purified by revelation.

12. Aquinas, *Sth* 1.1.1.

13. Aquinas, *Sth* 2.1.99.2. See also Randall Smith, "What the Old Law Reveals About the Natural Law According to Thomas Aquinas," *The Thomist* 75, no. 1 (2011): 95–139. This will be addressed below.

14. Aquinas, *Sth* 2.1.98.6.

15. Aquinas, *Sth* 2.1.98.5.

16. Aquinas, *Sth* 2.1.99.3.

17. Aquinas, *Sth* 2.1.107.2.

18. Aquinas, *Sth* 2.1.99.4, 104.1, 105.2.

19. Aquinas, *Sth* 2.1.105.1.

20. Aquinas, *Sth* 3.104.3. Orthodox Jews—and other Jews to one extent or another—still consider them binding.

21. Aquinas, *Sth* 2.1.99.4.

22. Aquinas, *Sth* 2.1.108.3. Aquinas states, "Whereas the judicial precepts did not necessarily continue to bind in exactly the same way as had been fixed by the Law: this was left to man to decide in one way or another."

23. Aquinas, *Sth* 2.1.100.1.

24. Aquinas, *Sth* 2.1.100.3.

25. Aquinas, *Sth* 2.1.98.6.

26. Aquinas, *Sth*.

27. See Randall Smith, "What the Old Law Reveals," esp. 114–17. I draw upon his classifications in this and the next paragraph.

28. Aquinas, *Sth* 2.1.100.1.

29. Aquinas, *Sth*. Perhaps one could say it is subsumed under or contained within the sixth commandment. Also, it is worth noting that some of these immoral acts were punished before the Old Law was given (Gen. 19, 38). So perhaps St. Thomas apparently means that the culture was not yet pervasively dark for God's people until the time of God's giving of the Old Law, and those prior to its promulgation were still held accountable.

30. Aquinas, *Sth* 2.1.91.4.

31. Although, no doubt, Moses and Aaron would be considered wise men, nonetheless, appealing to them as providing additional precepts is not the same as appealing to wise men who after experience and training know these more specific natural law precepts and can therefore teach them to others.

32. Aquinas, *Sth* 2.2.47.2–3.

33. Aquinas, *Sth* 2.2.154.2.

34. Aquinas, *Sth* 2.1.106.2.

35. Aquinas, *Sth* 2.1.106.1. One should note that even the unbaptized are provided for by God, as via their human nature, including their conscience, in that they have the law of God written on their heart. See Rom. 2:13–16 (New American Bible Revised Edition).

36. Aquinas, *Sth* 2.1.106.1, 107.2. The New Law is perfect in relation to the imperfect Old Law because it enables the Old Law to be fulfilled. Levering, *Biblical Natural Law*, 213: Levering does say that "the New Law contains written teachings that are requisite to the life of

grace" but that Aquinas says these teachings could not "serve as an efficacious 'rule and measure of acts.'" I follow Levering's discussion (209–13) on the relation between the Old Law and the necessity of the grace of the Holy Spirit which is given in Christ to fulfill the Old Law.

37. Aquinas, *Sth* 2.1.106.1–2.
38. Aquinas, *Sth.*
39. Aquinas, *Sth* 2.1.107.4.
40. Aquinas, *Sth* 2.1.107.3; 2, 4. See also 91.5: the Old Law motivated one to observe the Commandments through fear, while the New Law primarily motivates through love (although the fear factor endures in the New Law as well, as we see in Matt. 25:31–46 and 1 Cor. 6:9–10.)
41. Aquinas, *Sth* 2.1.108.2.
42. Aquinas, *Sth* 2.1.108.2. See also 107.3: The substance itself of the precepts of the New Testament, they are all contained in the Old. Hence Augustine says (Contra Faust. xix, 23,28) that "nearly all Our Lord's admonitions or precepts, where He expressed Himself by saying: 'But I say unto you,' are to be found also in those ancient books. Yet, since they thought that murder was only the slaying of the human body, Our Lord declared to them that every wicked impulse to hurt our brother is to be looked on as a kind of murder.' "
43. Aquinas, *Sth* 2.1.108.3.
44. Aquinas, *Sth.*
45. In some books of the New Testament, we do find lists of some behaviors (vices) that are prohibited, in order to guide us to live a morally good life, e.g., Rom. 1:18–28; 1 Cor. 6; Gal. 5:19–21; Eph. 4:25–31; 1 Thess. 1.
46. For instance, embryo-destructive research.
47. One response to this is that certainty of knowledge on these "newer" moral matters comes from the institution which God established to provide the certitude of divine and natural law on these issues: the Catholic Church, which through the Magisterium has been the teacher and final arbiter of the divine and natural law over 2,000 years. In other words, God has established his church to properly interpret and teach what is found in the Old and New Law (in Scripture and Tradition). Aquinas would no doubt appeal to the Magisterium as well. *How* the Church's Magisterium relates to Aquinas's thought as presented here is the subject for another paper.
48. And perhaps the variety of difficult prudential moral decisions one might face, although in these the wise man might still not be able to give the certitude needed.
49. See n. 47 above.
50. Aquinas, *Sth* 2.1.106.1.
51. This also can go in the other direction whereby if more particular moral matters are rejected, then the more general principles can be rejected as well. For example, if contraception is accepted, then sexual relations outside of marriage are more likely to be excepted, and then other nonmarital sexual acts are more likely to be accepted. So we see that interconnectedness of the different moral principles is quite profound.
52. Cardinal Ratzinger, "A Christian Orientation in a Pluralistic Democracy? On the Indispensability of Christianity in the Modern World," in *Church, Ecumenism, and Politics* (San Francisco: Ignatius Press, 2007), 205–6.
53. In another chapter of the book, "Europe: A Heritage with Obligations for Christians," 218, Ratzinger writes of an emancipation of a kind of reason which "contradicts the nature of human reason" and destroys its own foundations.
54. Cardinal Ratzinger, "What Is Truth? The Significance of Ethical and Religious Values in a Pluralistic Society," in *Values in a Time of Upheaval* (San Francisco: Ignatius Press, 2005) 65–66.
55. As Ratzinger observes, "What Is Truth?" 66–67.
56. Pope Benedict XVI, *Deus Caritas Est*, Vatican website, Dec. 25, 2005, sec. 28, http://w2.vatican.va/content/benedict-xvi/en/encyclicals/documents/hf_ben-xvi_enc_20051225_deus-caritas-est.html.
57. Benedict XVI, *Deus Caritas Est*, sec. 28a.
58. Again, I refer the reader to n. 47 above mentioning the Church's Magisterium (Tradition) as a source of Divine Law complementary to the written Old and New Law in the Bible.

59. Again, see n. 47.

WORKS CITED

Aquinas. *Summa theologiae*. 2nd rev. ed. Translated by the Fathers of the English Dominican Province. 1920; New Advent, 2008. http://www.newadvent.org/summa/.

Benedict XVI, Pope. *Deus Caritas Est*. Vatican website. Dec. 25, 2005. http://w2.vatican.va/content/benedict-xvi/en/encyclicals/documents/hf_ben-xvi_enc_20051225_deus-caritas-est.html.

Levering, Matthew. *Biblical Natural Law*. Oxford: Oxford University Press, 2006.

Ratzinger, Cardinal Joseph. *Church, Ecumenism, and Politics*. San Francisco: Ignatius Press, 2007.

———. "What Is Truth? The Significance of Ethical and Religious Values in a Pluralistic Society." In *Values in a Time of Upheaval*, 65–66. San Francisco: Ignatius Press, 2005.

Smith, Randall. "What the Old Law Reveals About the Natural Law According to Thomas Aquinas." *The Thomist* 75, no. 1 (2011): 95–139.

II

Natural Law Past and Present

Chapter Six

Burying the Wrong Corpse

Second Thoughts on the Protestant Prejudice toward Natural Law Thinking

J. Daryl Charles

INTRODUCTION: CULTURAL AND THEOLOGICAL UNDERPINNINGS OF THE PROTESTANT BIAS

Of the many things that are striking about Protestant theology in our day, perhaps most significant for the culture is that people who otherwise have very little in common theologically find common ground—almost inexplicably so—in their opposition to the natural law as a metaphysical notion rooted in divine revelation.[1] This "consensus" is mirrored in the fact that one is hard pressed to identify a single major figure in Protestant theological ethics since the eighteenth century who has developed and defended a theory of natural law.

Observing this neglect in the 1970s, James Gustafson classified Protestant opposition to natural law in the modern era according to two notable philosophical tendencies—historicism and existentialism. Gustafson understood this neglect in the light of rationalism and fideism as theological responses to the modernist spirit since Hume and Kant. Surely, with Gustafson, we may detect historicist and existentialist thinking in the broader rejection of natural law thinking.[2] To these two tendencies we might as well adduce the pietistic strain in much of Protestant thought-life. More recently, J. Budziszewski has identified wider cultural factors that have undermined the natural law in our day—among these are therapeutic culture, the eclipse of tradition in general, an intractable resistance to wisdom and common sense (what Budziszewski calls the "cult of the expert"), postmodern sophistry, and the removal of shame that has characterized our society's moral desensitization.[3]

While theologically revisionist objections to the natural law are part of the story, blame for Protestant neglect of the natural law cannot merely be laid at the doorstep of secular fundamentalists, even when they, more than any cultural "player," determine the tenor of moral discourse in the public square. More significant, and even more tragic, is the rejection of natural law thinking among confessionally orthodox thinkers, for whom the chief objection takes several forms. Natural law thinking, it is alleged, places misguided trust in the powers of human reason, which has been debilitated by the Fall, and thus fails to take seriously the reality of sin and the condition of human depravity. It is, therefore, thought to be insufficiently Christocentric and to engender a form of works-righteousness through its detracting from the work of grace in Christ. These critics of the natural law remain skeptical out of a concern that it is autonomous and somehow external to the center of theological ethics and God's providential care of the world.

Because much of the bias against natural law thinking is rooted in theological conviction, objections to the natural law must be taken seriously. Such is the focus of the discussion that follows.

THE MAGISTERIAL REFORMERS AND THE NATURAL LAW: ETHICAL CONTINUITY

Luther

To the surprise of many, the notion of the natural law is resolutely affirmed in the writings of the Protestant Reformers. However deeply entrenched the bias against natural law thinking seems to be among Protestant thinkers, it cannot be attributed to the sixteenth-century Reformers themselves. While it is undeniable that they sought to champion a particular understanding of grace and faith that in their estimation was utterly lacking,[4] their emphasis was *not* to the exclusion of other modes of divine agency. It is accurate to insist that the Reformation controversies with the Catholic Church were foremost *theological and not ethical* insofar as the Reformers assumed the natural law as a moral-theological bedrock in their system and therein maintained continuity with their Catholic counterparts.

Natural law thinking, for example, is firmly embedded in Luther's thought, as a cursory reading of treatises such as *Against the Heavenly Prophets* (1525), *Against the Sabbatarians* (1538), *Against the Antinomians* (1539), and *On the Jews and Their Lies* (1543) makes abundantly clear. In *How Christians Should Regard Moses* (1525), Luther distinguishes between the Law of Moses, with its historically conditioned components, stipulations, and illustrations for theocratic Israel, and the natural law.[5] "If the Ten Commandments are to be regarded as Moses' law, then Moses came too late," Luther can quip somewhat wryly, for "Moses agrees exactly with nature" and "what Moses commands is nothing new."[6] And, he adds, Moses also addressed himself to far too few people, because the Ten Commandments had spread over the whole world not only before Moses but even before Abraham and all the patriarchs. For even if a Moses had never appeared and Abraham had never been born, the Ten Commandments would have had to rule in all men from the very beginning, *as they indeed did and still do.*[7]

The law that stands behind the Ten Commandments, according to Luther, "was in force prior to Moses from the beginning of the world and also among all the Gentiles."[8] So far as the Ten Commandments are concerned, Luther believes, there is no difference between Jews and Gentiles.

Lest he be misunderstood, Luther clarifies his position: "We will regard Moses as a teacher, but we will not regard him as our lawgiver—unless he agrees with both the New Testament and the natural law."[9] "Where . . . the Mosaic law and the natural law are one, there the law remains and is not abrogated externally."[10] While faith, for Luther, fulfills the law, those aspects of the Mosaic code that were temporal and confined to theocratic Israel are said to be "null and void" and "not supported by the natural law."[11] Luther's position is unambiguous: the moral norms that apply to all people, Christians and non-Christians, are the same. There are no two ethical standards that exist within the realm of divine revelation.

Everyone, Luther insists, is compelled to acknowledge that what the natural law dictates in the human heart is right and true, and there is no one who does not sense the effects of the natural law. If men would only pay attention to it, they would have no need of any other law, since they carry along with them in the depth of their hearts a living witness as to right and wrong, acceptable and unacceptable behavior, and how they ought to judge.

While acknowledging a basic moral sense in all people, Luther is mindful of a common misperception among religiously minded people, namely, that "natural law" is presupposed by—and therefore the common fund of—only "Christian" societies. To the contrary, he insists; human experience demonstrates that all nations, all cultures and people-groups possess this rudimentary knowledge. The natural law "is written in the depth of the heart and cannot be erased."[12] In fact, people bring this awareness, this natural moral sense, with them when they enter the world, since the moral realities expressed in the Decalogue antedate Israel.[13]

But what about situations in which Christians must participate intelligibly with unbelievers in the public square? In his treatise *Temporal Authority*, Luther deliberates over two relevant scenarios that might involve believer and unbeliever—the unlawful seizure of private property and resolving financial debts. Luther exhorts his readers to use both "the law of love" and "the natural law." However, when love has no observable effect, the latter is to be our guide, since natural law is rooted in reason, by which societies order themselves and intuit justice.

Against the popular stereotype, it needs reiteration that Luther is perfectly content to allow the natural law and righteousness that comes by faith to stand side by side. Luther is representative of the Protestant Reformers as a whole: general revelation does not cancel out or undermine faith. Herein the Reformers witness against their spiritual offspring of the present day, for the natural law was presumed to be at work within all people and thus is lodged at the core of Christian social ethics. Were this not the case, Luther reasons, one could not appeal to conscience at all.

Luther understands the purpose of law as being a concrete provision of divine love by the Creator for humankind. In fact, Luther associates the provision of divine law with Adam's worship. The law is not, as many Protestants tend to assume, some postlapsarian device or makeshift reparation made necessary by the Fall. To the contrary, it belongs to Adam's original righteousness and as such accords with St. Paul's statement that the law is "holy and just and good" (Rom. 7:12, New Revised Standard Version). Luther believes, then, that the concept of law, properly understood, presupposes not sin but grace. And even the Fall itself does not eliminate in Luther's view the law's original function and identity.[14]

Calvin

Over against his Catholic counterparts, Calvin might be thought to have a dim view of the natural law, given the place in his theological system of divine sovereignty and human depravity. But this is not the case. Notwithstanding the ravages of sin, Calvin is cognizant of the Pauline argument that Gentiles "show the work of the law written on their hearts" (Rom. 2:14, my translation). And as with Luther, his distinction between various categories of law—ceremonial, judicial, and moral—mirrors the conviction that there are aspects of human law that are both binding and nonbinding.[15]

In addition, Calvin maintains continuity with the Thomist assumption that "by nature man is a social animal." Because of this anthropological reality, man is disposed "from natural instinct, to preserve society," the result of which is that "human societies must be regulated by law," without which there would be no civil order. The seeds of these just laws, insists Calvin, are "implanted in the breasts of all without a lawgiver." Moreover, they remain unaffected by the vicissitudes of life; neither war nor catastrophe nor theft nor human disagreement can alter these moral intuitions.

In light of the accent on divine sovereignty in Calvin's theology, how is it precisely that the world is ordered and sustained? The divine law, which directs all things, expresses itself in the natural law, thus forming the basis for all of morality. And because man is by nature a social animal, he is disposed, from natural instinct, to preserve society; for this reason, the minds of all people have impressions of civil order implanted on them.

There is no missing the emphasis in Calvin's theology on human depravity, and particularly the effects of sin on the human mind: man is "so shrouded in the darkness of errors" that he "hardly begins to grasp through this natural law what worship is acceptable to God"; surely he is "very far removed" from its actualization. Pride, ambition, and self-love, furthermore, have so blinded him as to prevent him from humbling himself and confessing his own miserable condition.

Yet, this is not the whole story. Even when the human heart is thoroughly corrupt and no realm of human experience has gone untouched by sin, to acknowledge sin's pervasiveness is *not* to obliterate the rudimentary moral sense in each person. One cannot say that Gentiles are "altogether blind" as to the rule of life; all possess sufficient light through the natural law, and this we call "conscience."[16] The natural law is "that apprehension of the conscience which distinguishes sufficiently between just and unjust, and which deprives men of the excuse of ignorance while it proves them guilty by their own testimony." And despite "man's perverted and degenerate nature," the image of God is not "totally annihilated and destroyed"; rather, "some sparks still shine" in human creation.[17]

In Calvin's theological system, the natural law operates as an extension of divine providence, linking a morally ordered universe to the human order, so that in human interpersonal relationships and in the role of government justice is both presupposed and maintained. In its character, it both restrains and directs human beings.

Zwingli and Bullinger

Both the restraining as well as the directing functions of the natural law are presupposed by the Swiss Reformers. Additionally, the threefold use of the law—ceremonial, judicial, and moral—for which the Protestant Reformers are well known finds a supplement use—belonging to the judicial realm—in the Swiss Reformational emphasis on covenant. Covenant not only provides a theological basis for understanding divine work in history, but conjoined to the natural it furnishes the basis for communal and civil (i.e., moral) obligations that are thought to be binding on all human beings and all societies.

In the thought of Huldrich Zwingli (1484–1531), the natural law serves as a bulwark and primary vehicle by which to resist injustice and political oppression. Zwingli is in agreement with the other Reformers that all human laws should conform to the natural law, which has been implanted in the hearts of all men, although he goes beyond Luther in asserting that the natural law is the equivalent of "true religion, to wit the knowledge, worship, and fear of the supreme deity."[18] The "law of nature," as Zwingli understands it, is implanted by God on the heart of man and is confirmed by the grace of God through Christ. This internal light is owing to the work of God's Spirit in every person, and only strengthened after conversion to Christ. In contrast to the Lutheran position but mirroring the Swiss Reformational distinctive, Zwingli believes that due to the imperfection of reason, only those rulers and magistrates who are God-fearers properly know the natural law.

Heinrich Bullinger (1504–75), perhaps best known for his role in drafting the Second Helvetic Confession of 1566, in even more pronounced ways affirms the "law of nature" as "an instruction of the conscience, and as it were, a certain direction placed by God himself in the mind and hearts of men, to teach them what they have to do and what to eschew."[19] This capacity to engage in moral intuition derives from the Creator, who "both prompteth and writeth his judgments in the hearts and minds of men." Thus, even the Gentiles possess a basic discernment between good and evil, so that the natural law functions in the same way as the written law, teaching us "justice, equity, and goodness" and having as its source God himself.[20]

Have moral norms—and thus the requirements of human societies—changed at all in the period of the New Covenant? Bullinger answers emphatically in the negative. We are still to regard basic moral truth, respect parents, live out the golden rule, and keep the Ten Commandments, for the natural law reminds us that there exists an objective moral order in which human laws are said to inhere.[21]

In an important book titled *Rediscovering the Natural Law in Reformed Theological Ethics*,[22] Stephen Grabill has profiled the theological substructure of Calvin, Peter Martyr Vermigli, Johannes Althusius, and Francis Turretin, who are representative of both the magisterial Reformation period as well as Protestant orthodoxy up to the mid–eighteenth century, in order to demonstrate, without ambiguity, that the Protestant Reformers' disagreement with the Church was fundamentally *theological and not ethical* in nature. As to ethics, they maintained *full continuity* with their Catholic counterparts. Thus, the contention of Roman Catholic theologian Romanus Cessario that "the sixteenth-century Protestant Reform championed grace and faith to the practical exclusion of all other instruments of divine agency" needs moderation.[23] While the Reformers protested what they believed to be an absence of grace and faith, they uniformly affirmed the role of general revelation and the natural law, even when the accent of their teaching was faith and grace. They were, however, one in their conviction that Christian ethics presupposes—and stands on the bedrock of—the natural law.

RECENT PROTESTANT THINKERS AND THE NATURAL LAW: ETHICAL DISCONTINUITY

While Protestant theology has retained, in varying degrees, its Christocentrism, unlike the sixteenth-century Reformers, Protestant protestations to the natural law over the last sixty years have been characterized—wittingly or unwittingly—by a marked ethical discontinuity in their understanding of Scripture. Few have argued more vehemently for a rejection of natural law thinking than Karl Barth.

Karl Barth

The teaching of this Swiss theologian in the decade before Hitler's rise to power, to his great credit, paved the way for the resistance that took the form of the Confessing Church. This group, emergent within the official state (Lutheran) Church, "confessed with fresh devotion historic Christian commitments in the light of their immediate political situation."[24] One year after Hitler's accession to power, a conference of Confession Church leaders, meeting at Barmen, drew up the brief declaration consisting of six points that became the theological foundation for resistance to Nazi hegemony. Barth played a key role in the Barmen declaration, with its rejection of the Nazification of German culture and affirmation that a Christian's ultimate allegiance could not be given to an earthly *Führer*. Not for nothing would Barth be removed from his university teaching post in the year following the Barmen synod.

Barth's very astute cultural criticism deserves our consideration. His examination of the eighteenth and nineteenth centuries led him to conclude that modern society, at least at its higher levels, had very close ties with nature, and that these ties were "far from being simply of the kind which lead man to study nature scientifically."[25] The "idealized" and "humanized" understanding of nature, as Barth viewed it, would have serous implications for German thought. *Inter alia* it would mean "an attitude of detachment towards the view of history held in earlier times, which had been dictated by church dogma."[26] The increasing secularization of European culture, coupled with a romantic view of "nature," as Barth saw it, blended easily into the core assumptions of Enlightenment thinking and the new humanism of the eighteenth century.[27]

This theological emptying of Christianity's theistic, Christological, and anthropological core constituted for Barth the creation of an entirely different religion, and thus a departure from Christianity, which is revealed through Christ the Living Word of God and Scripture as the mediator of the Word of God. The result is that authority, divine command, and the sacraments all are undermined by an emphasis on "nature" and "reason." The preoccupation with "nature" and "reason" in much eighteenth- and nineteenth-century thinking, as Barth understands it, has pernicious consequences. It prepares the soil for a secularized humanism that empties Christian faith of its substance and undermines or denies the absolute lordship of Christ. Correlatively, it facilitates the emergence of a "natural religion" and "natural theology" that becomes a substitute for authentic faith that is Christocentric and based on the "word of God."[28]

"Natural theology," Barth concluded, functions as a Trojan horse inside the walls of Christendom, producing a sort of latent deism. The God of natural law cannot be the God of the Bible. Natural law theory, he worried, "creates an autonomous locus of moral reflection completely separate from the revelation of God in Jesus Christ. It does not take sin seriously and is overly optimistic about the human condition."[29]

How might Protestants respond to this Barthian challenge? On the surface this warning seems not only plausible but commendable, given the character of political and cultural fascism of his day. But we must raise questions. To be faithful to Christ's lordship is not to deny the challenge—or the necessity—of communicating truth to the nonbeliever, whose worldview and language are devoid of biblical and Christological understanding. How do we as Christians communicate in a non-Christian world? How do we hold conversation with nonbelievers? How does Christian faith clothe itself in pluralistic society, wherein few people, relatively speaking, know what "the Bible says" or acknowledge "the Word of God"? Our point of contact with nonbelievers is established by God himself. That reference point, that place of entry into the thinking of nonbelievers, is general revelation, which, despite humanity's rebellion against the Creator, nevertheless permeates the conscience of the unbeliever, so that all people are, in Pauline terms, "without excuse." Through the natural law all people possess this basic awareness. Without the natural law, there is no common ground, no point of connection, no meaningful engagement between Christians and nonbelievers.[30]

In times of cultural crisis, when social, legal, and political institutions are crumbling and rendered incapable of making basic moral judgments, it then becomes necessary to inquire anew into moral-philosophical first things. The crisis of Nazi Germany rendered necessary a response by the Confessing Church, to which Karl Barth belonged.

But Barth, it should be remembered, was not the only Christian mind at this time to have grappled with the dilemma of National Socialism and the totalitarian state. Heinrich Rommen, Jacques Maritain, Yves Simon, and Eric Voeglin were among European émigrés of note who arrived in the United States in the 1930s and early 1940s and contributed substantially to a renewal of natural law thinking, notably in the context of political and legal theory. And not coincidently, the leading thinkers who contributed to this renewal were Catholic. What all of these individuals shared in common, in contrast to

Barth, was the conviction that a traditional metaphysics of natural law, consistent with mainstream Christian political and moral thinking, might be advanced *without* capitulating to modernist, secularist, positivist, or fascist *Zeitgeist*. They were convinced that the orders of creation, to which the natural law belongs, are part of biblical theology. Both the creational and the salvific belong to the divine economy; both are confessed by Christians creedally. They are simply, to use Luther's metaphor, the left and right hands of God.

Jacques Ellul

While not particularly known for his theological writings, Jacques Ellul nonetheless warrants a brief critique in light of his strident rejection of natural law on expressly theological and specifically Christological grounds. In his 1946 work *The Theological Foundation of Law*,[31] the French social and legal critic concedes the renewal of natural law thinking that was occurring in his day. Ellul grants that a response to the disastrous consequences of positivism is needed. However, the state of modern culture and the emergence of numerous and unprecedented domains of law—for example, laws addressing liability, labor, and social legislation—constitute for him barriers that are insurmountable. The natural law, as he perceives it, cannot address these realms.

Ellul is suspicious of the constant attempt on the part of theologians and natural lawyers to find common ground between Christians and non-Christians. Such an aim, he believes, is misguided, since it reveals a wrongheaded wish to ignore or circumvent "the tragic separation created by revelation and grace."[32] The common humanity that we all share, Ellul insists, is not subject to modification by grace. Thus, to emphasize "nature" in his view is to abandon grace and the "supranatural" and collapse any distinction between grace and what is merely human.[33] Natural law, then, as Ellul construes it, becomes part of a major humanist project to bring about reconciliation apart from grace. Even *the very desire* to create a universally binding law on the basis of the law of God, for Ellul, is "undeniably heretical,"[34] since it presupposes the possibility of non-Christians accepting the will of God.[35]

Additionally, Ellul's Christocentric rejection of the natural law is further buttressed by his peculiar reading of the early chapters of Genesis. Through the Fall, man loses any resemblance to Adam that he may have otherwise had. Man's perversion by sin is radical; hence, "we cannot admit the idea of the *imago Dei* being preserved in man as the foundation of natural law. . . . To identify natural law with the *imago Dei* means either to admit that man has not totally fallen, or to rob human law of all its value."[36]

Precisely on this point, Ellul is emphatic, which should give us pause, both on theological and ethical grounds: "In scripture, there is no possible knowledge of the good apart from a living and personal relationship with Jesus Christ."[37] Ellul does not offer an account of how Noah or Abraham or Melchizedek knew right from wrong. For him, there is no "normative ethics of the good," only an "ethics of grace."[38] Ellul is adamant in his contention that natural knowledge of the good does not derive from a knowledge of the will of God but rather is in competition with it, producing what he believes to be an antithetical standard of morality.[39] Thus, unregenerate man is thought to be incapable of doing what is authentically good; one can only perform what is good as a result of radical conversion. For him there is no innate, pre-conversion voice of conscience that leads one to an awareness of the need for repentance and conversion.

It is here that we perceive with utmost clarity the extreme pessimism of Protestant thought. Morality, Ellul believes, is born of disobedience, not *the divine image*, and "whatever it is of the *imago Dei* which survives [original sin], that cannot in any case be the moral sense."[40] What humans call the "moral conscience," Ellul contends, "cannot be a reflection of God, a remainder from man's initial integrity."[41] Rather, the "image of God" is to be understood in the sense of humans' ultimate destiny, not a sacred quality of divine essence at the moment of creation.

In the end, our interest in Ellul, it should be emphasized, is due not to his broader influence but rather to the extent that he typifies and amplifies the "Protestant error"—the error of ethical discontinuity not only between the Old and New Covenants but also between creational and salvific orders. While he is partly correct in arguing for "the impossibility of the Christian ethic" apart from divine grace, he is mistaken to deny the *imago Dei* within all human beings based on creation. This flawed view, it goes without saying, has profound theological and ethical implications.

John Howard Yoder

Another species of opposition to natural law thinking grounds itself in what it believes to be "radical obedience" to the biblical witness to Jesus. Perhaps the most persuasive representative of this view is Anabaptist theologian John Howard Yoder, whose well-known work *The Politics of Jesus*[42] sets forth the argument that the authentic Christian social ethic is rooted in a radical understanding of Jesus's teaching—and a particular reading of the so-called Sermon on the Mount.

In his theological interpretation of the political order, Yoder laments the two dominant interpretations that, in his view, have clouded our thinking historically. One rests on the "'catholic' concept of natural law," which is questionable because it presumes an optimistic view of human nature and capacity for divine revelation. But the other is even more regrettable, namely, the "Augustinian-reformed" version of "necessary compromise or order of preservation." Both of these, Yoder insists, are "unacceptable."[43]

There is a baseline assumption that pervades all of Yoder's work. Yoder believes that the early Church, in time, wrongly absorbed pagan philosophical influence—for example, the Stoic emphasis on reason and the law of nature—which played a significant role in permitting it, by Ambrose's and Augustine's day, to be "compromised" by the political powers. Christian ethics, according to Yoder, evolved in such a way as to justify Christian presence and participation in Roman imperium; hence, Yoder's unrelenting "radical critique of Constantinianism." The history of the Church, for Yoder, is one long, unrelenting road of apostasy and cultural idolatry—that is, until the period of the "radical Reformation" in the sixteenth century. Christian ethics, as Yoder conceives it, is located neither in human "nature" nor in rational notions of justice or the common good. Rather, it subsists in our radical obedience to what Yoder understands as Jesus's ethics of nonviolent resistance to political and social oppression.

Additionally, a deep pessimism toward the political powers characterizes Yoderian thought. The powers are always and irrevocably fallen; they stand inevitably opposed to the purposes of God, so that Revelation 13, not Romans 13, represents the state as normative for all time. Yoder writes, "The divine mandate of the state consists in using evil means to keep evil from getting out of hand."[44] Because political power is inherently evil, according to Yoder's reading of the New Testament, any cooperation with or working through political power represents nothing less than compromise of the Christian. In fact, because the state is "a pagan institution in which Christians would not normally hold a position,"[45] it follows that participation by the Christian in the affairs of the state constitutes ethical compromise. Yoder believes that as Christians we have failed to understand the Cross with its implications. If our understanding were properly formed, we would be ever-vigilant to the triumphalist temptation and assume our place, with the crucified Lamb, in opposition to the powers in whatever form they might appear. And, of course, we would be "nonviolent."

In his writings Yoder champions what he understands to be Jesus's prophetic stance over against other standard models of ethical decision-making, which he believes have distracted us over the last several centuries. One "distraction" is that Roman Catholics keep reminding us that nature and grace do not stand in opposition. The Catholic emphasis, Yoder believes, has "foreshortened" the vision of the Kingdom of God by its focus on "the nature of things" in this fallen world. The result, he worries, is national idolatry and patriarchy. Yoder, as it turns out, proves himself to be a child of his time.[46]

As a product of the "radical Reformation," Yoder is supremely pessimistic about any moral education that predates the "radical Anabaptism" to which he belongs. And given the genesis of sixteenth-century Anabaptism, with persecution coming from both the Catholic and the Protestant side, this pessimism is certainly understandable. The tenor of Yoder's writings consistently reveals his belief that he stands within the prophetic tradition. To be sure, Yoder is at his best when he is critiquing the Christian community's tendency toward cultural idolatry. And it is here that he is also at his worst, to the extent that Yoder is unwilling to submit his notion of moral formation—and Christian social ethics—to the collective wisdom of the historic Christian tradition. While Yoder is fluent in his critique of twentieth-century idolatries, he is simplistic, when he is not silent, in his understanding of Christian ethics as *the cumulative wisdom of the fathers of the Church*—be they ancient, medieval, or modern. Given his overarching commitment to ideological pacifism, Yoder's rejection of the natural law, then, might be viewed as a by-product, not a cause, of his pacifist ethics. And like Barth, Yoder believes that the natural law is "an addition" to the Word of God as divine revelation. In this regard, he believes, "the warning of the Barmen confessor is still needed."[47]

Stanley Hauerwas

Extending a similar vision of "Christian social ethics" and the antipathy of Yoderian Anabaptism toward natural law thinking is the Methodist theologian Stanley Hauerwas. Explicit in his rejection of the natural law,[48] Hauerwas, like Yoder, is suspicious of natural law thinking because of the Church's purported compromise with "Constantinianism." Accordingly, we learn that "the alleged transparency of the natural law norms reflects more the consensus within the Church than the universality of the natural law itself."[49] This is substantiated for Hauerwas by "the fact that the power of natural law as a systematic idea was developed in and for the Roman imperium and then for 'Christendom.'"[50]

The natural law tradition, then, as interpreted by Hauerwas, rather than offering an account of moral principles that are "the same for all, both as to rectitude and as to knowledge,"[51] and that are known to all because they are inscribed on the heart (St. Paul in Rom. 1–2), is a "culturally assimilationist" attempt at "Christian ethics" that mirrors the Church's cultural captivity. Thus understood, "moral theology" gave expression to "an unquestioned ecclesial assumption" rather than to the practice of Christian virtue.[52]

Hauerwas believes that the "abstractions" of "nature and grace" have "distorted how ethics has been undertaken in the Catholic tradition."[53] Looking at human "nature" apart from Christian discipleship in the strictest sense, Hauerwas believes, is mistaken: "While the way of life taught by Christ is meant to be an ethic for all people, it does not follow that we can know what such an ethic involves objectively by looking at the human."[54]

Hauerwas is not inattentive to charges, such as that of ethicist James Gustafson, that his ethical approach is sectarian. Here he reasons in a manner that has characterized so many Protestant thinkers, mistakenly placing nature and grace, natural morality and Christ's lordship, creation and Christology, in diametrical opposition: "I certainly have never denied the Christian affirmation of God as Creator; rather, I have refused to use that affirmation to underwrite an autonomous realm of morality separate from Christ's lordship."[55] Sadly, the presumption of "autonomy" that worries Hauerwas, whereby nature and grace are presumed to stand in opposition, erects a false dualism that finds no place in historic Christian theology, as Oliver O'Donovan, to his credit, has reminded us.[56] In truth, this cleavage is a fairly late development, found predominately in Protestant theology.

In the end, Hauerwas believes that "Christian ethics theologically does not have a stake in 'natural law,'" which he believes to be a "primitive metaphysics" that is a reflection of the Constantinian era.[57] Like Yoder, he worries that affirming the natural law tradition offers justification for war, violence, or military conflict. And he would seem to have a point when he writes that if just war is based on natural law, which is "a law written in the conscience of all men and women by God, then it seems that war must be understood as the outgrowth of legitimate moral commitments."[58] For Hauerwas, the use of force and reluctantly going to war for justified purposes are necessarily, and therefore *always*, "the compromises we make with sin" and "cooperating with sin," and hence always unjust.[59] This ideologically absolutist stance on coercive force, however, does not represent the mainstream of the Christian moral tradition. Theologian John Courtney Murray's basic distinction between "violence" and "force," by contrast, does: "Force is the measure of power necessary and sufficient to uphold . . . law and politics. What exceeds this measure is violence, which destroys the order of both law and politics. . . . As an instrument, force is morally neutral in itself."[60] Murray's distinction between force and violence undergirds a response to Hauerwas's natural law objections that is both theologically faithful to the Christian moral tradition and ethically responsible. In truth, far from preparing society for violence, as Hauerwas contends, the natural law *preserves* social bonds and *guards* basic freedoms rather than threatening them.

Not only is it the grammar of a common moral discourse that Christians must utilize with nonbelievers, it is part of divine revelation—and not antithetical to a genuinely "Christian" social ethics that Hauerwas is so concerned to defend—by which the public square *must* be preserved (if, that is, it is to remain *public*). Thus, Hauerwas is mistaken to suggest that "Christian ethics" narrowly construed must be that which all people embrace. *Not all will embrace a Christian ethic*, since *not all will embrace Christian religion.* Ultimately, the Christian is *not* "compromising" by seeking to work for justice in the public square based on the natural law and shared humanity.

H. Richard Niebuhr

A further debilitating factor in Protestant thinking might be measured, indirectly, by the influence of theologians and thinkers who do not reject natural law thinking outright but rather proceed from a faulty understanding thereof. The work of H. Richard Niebuhr provides a useful illustration. Extending his own discussion in *Christ and Culture* of the five models to show how faith and culture interact, Niebuhr, in a previously unpublished essay, subsumes his treatment of the natural law under the rubric of "Christ of Culture; The Accommodationist Type."[61] In this discussion, Niebuhr equates the natural law with what he calls the "cultural type," that is, the "Christ of Culture" model.[62] His use of this categorization lies in the conviction that "nature is known only through culture." Those Christians, according to Niebuhr, who belong to this model are characterized by the fact that "they tend to interpret the revelation of values and imperatives . . . from the standpoint of the common reason of their culture." Moreover, "they assimilate the church to culture, identify cultural good and law with Christian good and law, yet seek also to interpret the cultural ends and imperatives in Christian fashion."[63]

For Niebuhr, then, those Christians who affirm the place of the natural law are "accommodationist" to the extent that they assimilate the injunctions and values of the Gospel to those of the society at large. Christian values are religious equivalents of the culture's best values; that is to say, those elements that are most intelligible to culture are taken to be primary and understood in the context of culture. And because natural law thinking, in Niebuhr's view, is characterized by a quest for harmony, the strategy of Christians who affirm the natural law is to ameliorate rather than separate or alienate the culture.

Rather remarkably, in his treatment of the "Christ of Culture" model Niebuhr lumps together natural law advocates with what he calls "Christian liberalism." This association raises a host of questions and is regrettable to the extent that "Christian liberalism" constitutes in *Christ and Culture* the chief example of the accommodationist model. With its "slurring over the end-terms of the gospel imperative," Christian liberalism, in its method, is noted by Niebuhr "to adopt the value judgment of modern society."[64]

These baseline assumptions, it goes without saying, would surprise most natural lawyers. Much might be said in response to Niebuhr's critique of the natural law.[65] But what *does* need to be said is that through his conflation of the natural law and cultural accommodationism, Niebuhr establishes false premises upon which to proceed. Those who affirm the natural law in the Church's history—for example, Justin, Ambrose, Augustine, Aquinas, the Protestant Reformers, Francisco de Vitoria, Francisco Suárez, Hugo Grotius, not to mention Catholic social ethics through John Paul II to the present—locate themselves within the mainstream of Christian moral thinking, yet they do not illustrate, according to Niebuhr's typology, the "Christ of Culture" model.[66] The result of Niebuhr's misconstrual of the natural law is an erroneous critique that confuses the necessity of bridge-building between Christians and non-Christians with cultural accommodation and "compromise." Natural lawyers would not recognize themselves in this critique—a critique that is constructed on a false understanding of natural law from the start.

CONCLUDING (ECUMENICAL) REFLECTIONS ON THE NATURAL LAW: REAFFIRMING THE PERMANENT THINGS

In this essay, it should be noted, we have not attempted an understanding of "natural law" thinking as it surfaces in Plato, Aristotle, or in Stoic philosophy, even when the ancients readily distinguish between what is *naturally* and *legally* just. But perhaps we assume too much. *Whence comes this basic distinction?* What "law" lies behind and transcends human law? Not only the ancients, but Christian moral thinkers from Aquinas to C. S. Lewis to John Paul II have argued for a *philosophia perennis*, a fund of basic metaphysical truths that are perennial, enduring, permanent, and eternal—what previous generations understood to be the "permanent things." Moreover, they have contended for the application of natural law thinking in the realm of public discourse, cognizant of the need to argue for moral first principles on the basis of human nature. To do such in a pluralistic environment is *not* to capitulate to the culture, as some might suggest. One of the most important lessons we Protestants might learn from those who championed the "permanent things" is that public morality must rest upon public principles—principles that are rooted in the fabric of creation. What unites these champions of the permanent things is that they affirmed the time-honored idea of the natural law—out of the conviction that basic moral principles are accessible to all people by virtue of God-given reason.

For this reason, the argument of C. S. Lewis regarding the Tao in both *Mere Christianity* and *The Abolition of Man* remains ever-relevant. Lewis, of course, was well aware that Christians—and Protestants in particular—object to the natural law precisely because they are convinced that it detracts from Christianity. But Lewis rejected this view as mistaken.[67] Far from contradicting Christian social ethics, the natural law is indeed presupposed by it, as Lewis insists in *Christian Reflections*:

> The idea that Christianity brought an entirely new ethical code into the world is a grave error. If it had done so, then we should have to conclude that all who first preached it wholly misunderstood their own message: for all of them, its Founder, His precursor, His apostles, came demanding repentance and offer-

> ing forgiveness, a demand and an offer both meaningless except on the assumption of a moral law *already known* and *already broken.*[68]

It is no more possible, Lewis argues, "to invent a new ethics than to place a new sun in the sky. Some precept from traditional morality always has to be presumed. We never start from a *tabula rasa*: if we did, we should end, ethically speaking, with a *tabula rasa*."[69] There is, I think, a resident wisdom in Lewis's ethical orientation that is necessary to counter the arrogance, autonomy, and misguided (when well-meaning) Christocentrism of much contemporary Protestant ethics.

While much of Protestants' reluctance to acknowledge the natural law might be thought to derive from a virulent strain of anti-Catholic bigotry that has dogged Protestant fundamentalism for the last hundred years, this should not be overstated, given the increasing (and encouraging) common-cause cooperation between conservative Protestants and Roman Catholics on significant cultural fronts. In the main, at the heart of Protestant social ethics' broader rejection of the natural law is the erection of a false dichotomy between nature and grace, leading to the mistaken assumption that the natural law is autonomous from "Christian social ethics." Those who labor under this misconception fail to take into consideration the role that our common human nature plays in moral theory and moral discourse. In consequence, this failure undermines any attempts to enter the public square and engage in ethical discourse with non–like-minded people when and where critical ethical and bioethical issues are at stake.[70] In practice, this posture prevents us—and those falling under our influence—from entering into responsible and heartfelt dialogue with nonbelievers. There remains for those who are so predisposed no language of ethical "transmission" that is intelligible to the nonbeliever and to which the nonbeliever might respond. In the end, apart from the natural law, we appear to lose any basis upon which to build a moral apologetic and to contribute meaningfully to civil society.

A related fallacy in the thinking of natural law opponents is their aversion to—indeed, a seemingly fundamental misunderstanding of—law. For many Protestant theologians, "law" can only be explained in terms of Christ, "the Spirit's leading," and a concept of grace that is confined to a reading of the New Testament presupposing ethical *discontinuity* with the Old Testament.[71] But law is not merely a "Christian" question, though it is indeed that. It is rather a *human* question—indeed, an anthropological and biblical-theological question of the first order.[72] Therefore, law is not some creative luxury or a sort of second-tier theological speculation; nor is it solely the domain of "grace-denying" Catholics. Rather, it is of the order of necessity and consequently must be at the heart of Christian theological reflection. Human beings cannot avoid or deny their true nature, which due to the *imago Dei* seeks order. Natural theology, then, properly understood, concerns cosmic reality, not human autonomy.[73]

In response to the mistaken and widespread belief that the natural law is "autonomous" and that it serves to undermine grace and a distinctly "Christian" ethics, Aquinas answers that virtue—that is, the good—is rooted in the natural obligations of all human beings to God. There is no dualism in Aquinas's thinking between the natural law and "Christian social ethics." And Jesus would seem to confirm the argument of Aquinas: the Ten Commandments, which express the contours of the natural law, are *summed up* in—not abrogated or eclipsed by—the "Christian social ethic" embodied and advanced by Jesus himself. John Courtney Murray expresses it well, observing that the natural law, "which preserves humanity, still exists at the interior of the Gospel."[74] Thus, those Protestants who reject the natural law, for whatever reason, surely are seeking to bury the wrong corpse.

Undergirding these renegade "Protestant" reflections is the fundamental conviction that ecumenical dialogue on the place of the natural law in Christian ethics is both necessary and timely, especially given the wholesale deconstruction of metaphysical foundations going on in our culture—a deconstruction that has moral, social, and political implications.[75] What was true in Murray's day—"as a metaphysical idea . . . natural law is timeless, and for that reason timely"[76]—is hence all the more true in our own.

NOTES

1. Such, of course, might be argued of both Protestants and Catholics, even when the latter are characterized by a greater degree of theological control than the former.This chapter draws on chapter four of *Retrieving the Natural Law* (Grand Rapids, MI: Eerdmans' Publishing Co., 2008) and is adapted by permission of the publisher.

2. While Catholic and Protestant theologians both have drunk deeply from the wells of modernism, the absence of theological authority, it goes without saying, has made Protestant thinkers much more susceptible to heterodox currents as well as to opposition to the natural law.

3. J. Budziszewski, *What We Can't Not Know: A Guide* (Dallas: Spence, 2003), 161–81.

4. See in this regard Alister E. McGrath, *Iustitia Dei: A History of the Christian Doctrine of Justification*, 2 vols. (Cambridge: Cambridge University Press, 1986).

5. In the development of his argument, Luther adopts the basic definition of natural law that had been set forth in Philip Melanchthon's commentary on Rom. 2:15: the natural law is "a common judgment to which all men alike assent, and therefore one which God has inscribed upon the soul of each man." See Charles L. Hill, ed. and tr., *The "Loci Communes" of Philip Melanchthon* (Boston: Meador, 1944), 112.

6. Luther, *Against the Sabbatarians*, in *Luther's Works*, vol. 47, ed. F. Sherman (Philadelphia: Fortress Press, 1971), 89; and *How Christians Should Regard Moses*, in *Luther's Works*, vol. 35, ed. E. T. Bachmann (Philadelphia: Muhlenberg Press, 1960), 168.

7. Luther, *Against the Sabbatarians*, 89 (emphasis added).

8. Luther, *Against the Sabbatarians*, 54; cf. *How Christians Should Regard Moses*, 166–69.

9. Luther, *How Christians Should Regard Moses*, 165.

10. Luther, *Against the Heavenly Prophets*, in *Luther's Works*, vol. 40, ed. C. Bergendorff (Philadelphia: Fortress Press, 1958), 97.

11. Luther, *Against the Heavenly Prophets*.

12. Luther, *How Christians Should Regard Moses*, 168; *Against the Sabbatarians*, 90.

13. Luther, *Against the Sabbatarians*, 94–110.

14. Given the standard "law-versus-Gospel" antinomy for which Luther is well known, Luther's theology of law has frequently been less than fully understood. Properly viewed, however, this antinomy is located within the context of *salvation*, not ethics. Moreover, it is not an all-encompassing rubric in Luther's theological system that absorbs every other theological topic. And yet the Protestant tendency since Luther has been precisely that, as Bernd Wannenwetsch correctly points out. The narrow focus on this antimony as the formal principle of modern Protestantism has led to a variety of antinomian accounts of law's fundamental opposition to grace and gospel, in which law is either flatly rejected as altogether "heteronomous" or, by way of a second-order antimony, reduced to its (formally) negative impact as a mirror of sin or a barrier against anarchy. . . . Apart from the soteriological language game, in which the most extreme contrast of law to gospel is required to convey the radical nature of grace, when it comes to moral theology, the law [in Luther] plays a more complex role. (Bernd Wannenwetsch, "Luther's Moral Theology," in *The Cambridge Companion to Martin Luther*, ed. Donald K. McKim [Cambridge: Cambridge University Press, 2003], 124–25; emphasis added)

15. Calvin, John. *Institutes of the Christian Religion*, ed. John T. McNeill, Trans. F. L. Battles (Louisville: Westminster John Knox, 2006), 2.7.6–13.

16. Calvin, *Institutes* 2.2.22, 8.1.

17. Calvin, *Institutes* 1.15.4, 2.2.12, 2.2.2.

18. Zwingli, *Zwinglis sämtliche Werke*, eds. Melchior Schuler and Johann Schulthess (Zürich: Schulthess, 1828–42), 4.243 (my translation).

19. T. Harding, ed., *The Decades of Heinrich Bullinger*, 4 vols. (Cambridge: The Parker Society, 1849), 2.194, sermon 1.

20. Harding, *Decades of Bullinger*, 2.195.

21. Harding, *Decades of Bullinger*, 2.340. "Among all men, at all times and of all ages," he writes, "the meaning and substances of the laws touching honesty, justice, and public peace, is kept inviolable." What distinguishes Bullinger from Zwingli, despite the affirmation by both of the "law of nature" as a means of divine restraint, is the ability to avoid the theocratic tendency. For Bullinger, the ministry and oversight of the Church is not to be conflated with the magistrate of Romans 13, which bespeaks all political office. The priest is not called "to sit in the judgment seat, and to give judgment against a murderer, or by pronouncing sentence to take up matters in strife," just as the calling of the magistrate is not to teach, baptize and administer the sacraments.

22. Stephen J. Grabill, "Rediscovering the Natural Law in Reformed Theological Ethics," in *Emory University Studies in Law and Religion* (Grand Rapids/Cambridge, UK: Eerdmans, 2006).

23. Romanus Cessario, *Introduction to Moral Theology* (Washington, DC: Catholic University of America, 2001), 69.

24. Karl Barth, *The Church and the War* (New York: Macmillan, 1944), v.

25. Karl Barth, *Protestant Theology in the Nineteenth Century: Its Background and History*, rev. ed. (London: SCM Press, 2001), 41.

26. Barth, *Protestant Theology*, 45.

27. Barth, *Protestant Theology*, 91. Not lost on Barth was what Enlightenment thinking, as it mirrored the theology and politics of the eighteenth and nineteenth centuries, meant for the ordering of society. The great desire, notes Barth, was a more "natural" and more "reasonable" religion, over against the dogma of a revealed or miraculous Christianity. The dominant spirit of the time understood "nature" as the embodiment of what was at the disposal of himself, his spirit, his understanding, his will and his feeling, what was left for him to shape, what could be reached by his will for form. And . . . reason was the embodiment of his capacity, his superiority over matter, his ability to comprehend it and appropriate it for himself. Thus *natural* Christianity simply means a Christianity that presents itself to man in a manner appropriate to

his capacity, and *reasonable* Christianity means a Christianity that is understood and affirmed by man in accordance with his capacity.

28. Thus, any theological or philosophical concept that is rooted in "nature" is viewed by Barth as not merely deficient but rather heretical and, therefore, a radical departure from Christian—which is to say, Christ-centered—faith. Any moral theology, according to Barth, that "tries to deny or obscure its derivation from God's command" and "set up independent principles in the face of autonomies and heteronomies," and which aims "to undertake the replacement of the command of the grace of God by a sovereign humanism or even barbarism," is to be utterly rejected (Barth, *Church Dogmatics*, trans. G. W. Bromiley [Edinburgh: T. & T. Clark, 1961], 2.1.527).

29. In this regard, see the critique of Barth's views by Carl E. Braaten, which appears as a response to Russell Hittinger's "Natural Law and Catholic Moral Theology," in Michael Cromartie, ed., *A Preserving Grace: Protestants, Catholics and Natural Law* (Washington, DC/ Grand Rapids: Ethics and Public Policy Center/Eerdmans, 1997), 31–40.

30. In this context it is helpful to keep in mind the heated debate between Barth and Emil Brunner during the mid-1940s that centered around natural law. At the heart of this controversy lay the epistemological question of whether fallen humans possess a natural knowledge of God. Brunner represented the position that nature is normative insofar as "nature teaches" or "nature dictates." The difference between Barth and Brunner is illustrative, for it captures the fundamental disagreement between Roman Catholics and Protestants over the natural law to the present day. The critical question is whether human reasoning and human apprehension of basic moral truth are universal, present, and operative within fallen human beings by nature, and thus, whether human beings can be held accountable for their actions. The historic Christian tradition, without equivocation, answers affirmatively to both questions. Ever since the Barth–Brunner controversy Protestant theology has been riddled with suspicion and skepticism vis-à-vis natural law. It would appear that the influence of Barth has been dominant. With few exceptions, it is difficult to identify any Protestant theologian or ethicist of note to this day who has robustly championed the natural law.

31. Jacques Ellul, *The Theological Foundation of Law*, trans. M. Wiesner (New York: Seabury, 1969).

32. Ellul, *Foundation*, 10.

33. Ellul, *Foundation*.

34. Ellul, *Foundation*, 13.

35. But, while it is a major player, natural law is not the lone culprit: "It is just one aspect of this [misguided] effort," he notes, "along with natural theology and Gnosticism, natural morality, and the absolute value of reason." Each of these is "designed to permit man to escape from the radical necessity of receiving revelation." As Protestant Christians, Ellul asserts, "we are called upon to confront the fact of natural law with the teaching of the Scriptures, the rule of our faith." While Ellul is concerned to guard the Christian deposit against autonomous "revelation," his bias against the natural law is buoyed by another dimension. At the most elementary level, Ellul insists that the Scriptures "do not know of law in the proper sense of the term." "There is no place in biblical revelation," he avers, "for a legal concept, an idea, or law governing all human laws and measuring all human law." And because all justice and judgment in Scripture are understood by Ellul within the context of redemption, we cannot therefore understand law without the cross of Christ at the center; only at the Cross do we understand God's will. A Christocentric view of justice, as Ellul sees it, "radically destroys the ideas of objective law and of eternal justice" (*Foundation*, 11, 25, 49).

36. Ellul, *Foundation*, 61. Remarkably, Ellul insists that prior to the Fall, "there is no moral conscience [in Adam]; there are [sic] no ethics" (*To Will and To Do*, trans. C. E. Hopkin [Philadelphia/Boston: Pilgrim Press, 1969], 6). Adam has knowledge of the good and of evil only *after* the Fall: "before the alienation, Adam had no *knowledge* of the good" (*To Will and To Do*, 14; emphasis his). Ellul is forced, then, to side with Barth on this theological point. If one adopts a strictly biblical perspective, he writes, "then it would seem that one could hardly do otherwise than to follow Karl Barth on the subject of the impossibility of the natural knowledge of God by man, which leads to the same impossibility for the knowledge of the good" (*To Will and To Do*, 16).

37. Ellul, *Foundation.*
38. Ellul, *Foundation*, 43.
39. Ellul, *Foundation*, 73–110.
40. Ellul, *Foundation*, 24.
41. Ellul, *Foundation*, 43.
42. John Howard Yoder, *The Politics of Jesus*, rev. ed. (Grand Rapids: Eerdmans, 1994).
43. Yoder, *Karl Barth and the Problem of War* (Nashville/New York: Abingdon, 1970), 120. This book is part of the "Studies in Christian Ethics" series.
44. Yoder, *Discipleship as Political Responsibility* (Scottdale/Waterloo: Herald Press, 2003), 18.
45. Yoder, *Discipleship*, 25.
46. For a most insightful commentary on the theological and ethical contours of Yoder's life and thought, see Jorge Garcia, "A Public Prophet?" *First Things* 90 (Feb. 1999): 49–53. Correlatively, of interest is the commentary by Mark Thiessen Nation regarding the end of Yoder's career, in "John Howard Yoder: Mennonite, Evangelical, Catholic," *The Mennonite Quarterly* (July 2003): 3–14. This is fully aside from recent revelations of Yoder's sexual deviancy.
47. Yoder, "Discerning the Kingdom of God in the World," in *For the Nations: Essays Public and Evangelical* (Grand Rapids/Cambridge, UK: Eerdmans, 1997), 245. That a Barthian cast can be detected in Yoder's writings should not be surprising, since Yoder studied under Barth. He writes in the preface of his work *Karl Barth and the Problem of War* (see n. 43), "To Karl Barth, who taught me to rethink my faith in the light of the Word of God" (7).
48. See, e.g., Stanley Hauerwas, *The Peaceable Kingdom: A Primer in Christian Ethics* (Notre Dame/London: University of Notre Dame Press, 1983); and *Truthfulness and Tragedy: Further Investigations in Christian Ethics* (South Bend: University of Notre Dame, 1983).
49. Hauerwas, *Peaceable Kingdom*, 51.
50. Hauerwas, *Peaceable Kingdom.*
51. Aquinas, *Summa theologiae*, trans. Fathers of the English Dominican Province (New York: Benzinger Bros., 1947), 2.1.94.4.
52. Hauerwas, *Peaceable Kingdom.*
53. Hauerwas, *Peaceable Kingdom*, 55–57. In his explanation of these "abstractions," Hauerwas does not interact with mainstream voices in the Christian moral tradition that have explicated the natural law tradition through the ages, rendering it difficult to understand how the emphasis on natural law indeed distorts Christian ethics.
54. Hauerwas, *Peaceable Kingdom*, 58. In response, it is fair to state that because the Christian ethic is not known—or acknowledged—by all people, it becomes impossible, apart from the natural law and its attendant grammar, to build any sort of morally meaningful bridge between the Christian and non-Christian. For this very reason, Aquinas vigorously argued that the presence of the natural law in fact attests to those basic moral realities that are "perfected" through grace. And although it is surely true that the natural law is not the end of ethics, it is necessarily the starting point. While Hauerwas does acknowledge points of contact between Christian ethics and "other forms of the moral life," he believes that these "are not sufficient to provide a basis for a 'universal' ethic grounded in human nature per se" (*Peaceable Kingdom*, 60–61). This position, at bottom, presents inherent theological and ethical problems.
55. Hauerwas, "Why the 'Sectarian Temptation' is a Misrepresentation: A Response to James Gustafson (1988)," in *The Hauerwas Reader*, John Berman and Michael Cartwright, eds. (Durham/London: Duke University Press, 2001), 107–8.
56. Oliver O'Donovan, *Resurrection and Moral Order: An Outline for Evangelical Ethics* (Grand Rapids: Eerdmans, 1986), 15.
57. Hauerwas, *Truthfulness and Tragedy*, 58; and *Peaceable Kingdom*, 51–64.
58. Hauerwas, "Should War Be Eliminated? A Thought Experiment," in *Hauerwas Reader*, 404.
59. Hauerwas, "Should War Be Eliminated?"
60. John Courtney Murray, *We Hold These Truths: Catholic Reflections on the American Proposition* (New York: Sheed and Ward, 1960), 288.

61. Glen H. Stassen, D. M. Yeager, and John Howard Yoder, eds., *Authentic Transformation: A New Vision of Christ and Culture* (Nashville: Abingdon, 1996), 22–24.
62. Stassen, Yeager, and Yoder, *Authentic Transformation.*
63. Stassen, Yeager, and Yoder, *Authentic Transformation*, 22.
64. Stassen, Yeager, and Yoder, *Authentic Transformation*, 24.
65. I write as a sympathetic reader of *Christ and Culture* and as one who has profited immensely from the typology offered by Niebuhr's classic work. And I would disagree with George Marsden, who has argued that Niebuhr's typology "could be near the end of its usefulness" (Marsden, "Christianity and Cultures: Transforming Niebuhr's Categories," *Insights: Faculty Journal of Austin Seminary* [Fall 1999], http://www.religion-online.org/showarticle.asp?title=517). Niebuhr's typology remains extremely useful because of the perennial nature of the tension between Christian faith and culture. That it needs reformulation in the idiom of the day is *not* to say, with Marsden, that it is insufficient and no longer useful. Such is certainly *not* the case, even when that typology needs rethinking and reformulation for our own time.
66. Even Tertullian, for whom "Athens" has little or nothing to do with "Jerusalem," affirms the natural law [*Prescriptions against Heretics*, in *Early Latin Theology*, ed. and trans. S. L. Greenslade, LCC 5 (Philadelphia/London: Westminster Press/SCM Press, 1956), 31–64].
67. What is supreme irony is that many orthodox Protestants who revere Lewis are oblivious to his argument for the natural law as developed in the very first chapter (tellingly titled "Right and Wrong as a Clue to Meaning in the Universe") of his book *Mere Christianity.*
68. C. S. Lewis, "On Ethics," in *Christian Reflections*, ed. W. Hooper (Grand Rapids: Eerdmans, 1967), 46.
69. Lewis, *Christian Reflections*, 53.
70. At best, we convince ourselves that in our "radical" commitment to the "ethics of Jesus," in our "radical" separation and denunciation of the "powers," in our "radical critique of Constantinianism," or in our apocalypticism we most faithfully embody Christian discipleship and Christian social ethics. At worst, we delude ourselves by being severed from the mainstream of historic Christian thought, even when we believe we are acting "prophetically."
71. It is a supreme irony that many opponents of natural law thinking—indeed, of law as a concept—view the "Sermon on the Mount" as the crux New Testament text for Christian social ethics yet fail to grasp its context, established in Matt. 5:17–20, where ethical *continuity*, not discontinuity, is painstakingly clarified by Jesus.
72. To his credit, German Lutheran theologian Wolfhart Pannenberg presses this point in *Ethics*, trans. K. Crim (Philadelphia/London: Search Press, 1981), 24–41.
73. Cosmic reality, in turn, entails *law*. The structure of law is such that it guides the commandments and forms the basis for ethics. It always has had this function in the divine economy and it always will; the New Covenant does not abrogate this moral reality. Therefore, law cannot be severed from authentic *Christian religion* and *Christian social ethics*. While love speaks to the proper motivation to obey, law provides the necessary God-given structure within which obedience is performed. St. Paul and James speak with one voice in this regard: love fulfills the law. And short of the *eschaton*, law will always and everywhere be necessary; for this reason, justice has an abiding character and universal contours.
74. Murray, *We Hold These Truths* (supra), 298.
75. Lutheran theologian Carl E. Braaten is one of the few Protestants in our day who has made this argument. See his essay "Protestants and Natural Law," *First Things* (May 1992): 20–26.
76. Braaten, "Protestants and Natural Law," 320.

WORKS CITED

Aquinas. *Summa theologiae*. Translated by the Fathers of the English Dominican Province. New York: Benzinger Bros., 1947.

Barth, Karl. *Church Dogmatics*. Translated by G.W. Bromiley. Edinburgh: T. and T. Clark, 1961.

———. *Protestant Theology in the Nineteenth Century: Its Background and History*. Rev. ed. London: SCM Press, 2001.
———. *The Church and the War*. New York: Macmillan, 1944.
Braaten, Carl E. "Protestants and Natural Law." *First Things* (May 1992): 20–26.
———. "Russell Hittinger's 'Natural Law and Catholic Moral Theology': A Response." In *A Preserving Grace: Protestants, Catholics and Natural Law*, edited by Michael Cromartie, 31–40. Washington, DC/Grand Rapids: Ethics and Public Policy Center/Eerdmans, 1997.
Budziszewski, J. *What We Can't Not Know: A Guide*. Dallas: Spence, 2003.
Calvin, John. *Institutes of the Christian Religion*. Edited by John T. McNeill. Translated by F. L. Battles. Louisville: Westminster John Knox, 2006.
Cessario, Romanus. *Introduction to Moral Theology*. Washington, DC: The Catholic University of America, 2001.
Ellul, Jacques. *The Theological Foundation of Law*. Translated by M. Wiesner. New York: Seabury, 1969.
———. *To Will and To Do*. Translated by C. E. Hopkin. Philadelphia/Boston: Pilgrim Press, 1969.
Garcia, Jorge. "A Public Prophet?" *First Things* 90 (Feb. 1999): 49–53.
Grabill, Stephen J. "Rediscovering the Natural Law in Reformed Theological Ethics." In *Emory University Studies in Law and Religion*. Grand Rapids/Cambridge, UK: Eerdmans, 2006.
Harding, T., ed. *The Decades of Heinrich Bullinger*. 4 volumes. Cambridge: The Parker Society, 1849.
Hauerwas, Stanley. *The Hauerwas Reader*. Edited by John Berman and Michael Cartwright. Durham/London: Duke University Press, 2001.
———. *The Peaceable Kingdom: A Primer in Christian Ethics*. Notre Dame/London: University of Notre Dame Press, 1983.
———. *Truthfulness and Tragedy: Further Investigations in Christian Ethics*. South Bend: University of Notre Dame, 1983.
Hill, Charles L., ed. and tr. *The "Loci Communes" of Philip Melanchthon*. Boston: Meador, 1944.
Hittinger, Russell. Response to "Natural Law and Catholic Moral Theology."
Lewis, C. S. "On Ethics." In *Christian Reflections*, edited by W. Hooper. Grand Rapids: Eerdmans, 1967.
———. "Right and Wrong as a Clue to Meaning in the Universe." In *Mere Christianity*, 3–32. Rev. ed. New York: HarperCollins, 2001.
Luther, Martin. *Against the Heavenly Prophets*. In *Luther's Works*, vol. 40, edited by C. Bergendorff. Philadelphia: Fortress Press, 1958.
———. *Against the Sabbatarians*. In *Luther's Works*, vol. 47, edited by F. Sherman. Philadelphia: Fortress Press, 1971.
———. *How Christians Should Regard Moses*. In *Luther's Works*, vol. 35, edited by E. T. Bachmann. Philadelphia: Muhlenberg Press, 1960.
Marsden, George. "Christianity and Cultures: Transforming Niebuhr's Categories." *Insights: Faculty Journal of Austin Seminary* (Fall 1999). http://www.religion-online.org/showarticle.asp?title=517.
McGrath, Alister E. *Iustitia Dei: A History of the Christian Doctrine of Justification*. 2 volumes. Cambridge: Cambridge University Press, 1986.
Murray, John Courtney. *We Hold These Truths: Catholic Reflections on the American Proposition*. New York: Sheed and Ward, 1960.
Nation, Mark Thiessen. "John Howard Yoder: Mennonite, Evangelical, Catholic." *The Mennonite Quarterly* (July 2003): 3–14.
O'Donovan, Oliver. *Resurrection and Moral Order: An Outline for Evangelical Ethics*. Grand Rapids: Eerdmans, 1986.
Pannenberg, Wolfhart. *Ethics*. Translated by K. Crim. Philadelphia/London: Search Press, 1981.
Stassen, Glen H., D. M. Yeager, and John Howard Yoder, eds. *Authentic Transformation: A New Vision of Christ and Culture*. Nashville: Abingdon, 1996.

Tertullian. *Prescriptions against Heretics*. In *Early Latin Theology*, 31–64. Edited and translated by S. L. Greenslade. LCC 5. Philadelphia/London: Westminster Press/SCM Press, 1956.

Wannenwetsch, Bernd. "Luther's Moral Theology." In *The Cambridge Companion to Martin Luther*, edited by Donald K. McKim, 124–25. Cambridge: Cambridge University Press, 2003.

Yoder, John Howard. "Discerning the Kingdom of God in the World." In *For the Nations: Essays Public and Evangelical*. Grand Rapids/Cambridge, UK: Eerdmans, 1997.

———. *Discipleship as Political Responsibility*. Scottdale/Waterloo: Herald Press, 2003.

———. *Karl Barth and the Problem of War*. Nashville/New York: Abingdon, 1970.

———. *The Politics of Jesus*. Rev. ed. Grand Rapids: Eerdmans, 1994.

Zwingli, Huldrych. *Zwinglis sämtliche Werke*. Edited by Melchior Schuler and Johann Schulthess. Zürich: Schulthess, 1828–42.

Chapter Seven

The Natural Law—Again, Ever

Hadley Arkes

A dear friend, who has done premier work in the neural sciences and several books on philosophical psychology, remarked that he wanted, as the epitaph on his gravestone, "He died without a theory."[1] A former president of my college remarked that I had a "theory" of natural law. But I can join my friend in saying that I, too, have no theory. To say that someone has a theory of natural law is to suggest that an observer, looking on, can see played out before him people seized with theories—that he may stand there, in a wholesome detachment, seeing theories of various sorts whizzing past. From that vantage point we are encouraged to make judgments about the theories, or fragments of theories, that are plausible or implausible, right or wrong, true or false. I said then: Just tell me the ground on which you are making *those* judgments about the theories that are plausible or implausible, true or false, and you would have been led back to the ground of what I understand as the natural law. For one would have been led back to the ground on which we have confidence in the things we can truly know about the properties of propositions, about the statements that are true and false, and finally then, about the things that are morally right or wrong. We would have been led back to what Blackstone called "the laws of reason and nature."

Many high-flown things have been said about natural law, including many high-flown mistakes by people rather accomplished in the law. And so Richard Posner, a legend in his own time as professor and federal judge, has suggested that the survival of the fittest may be taken as an example of natural law, because it purports to describe a law of behavior that finds its source in the "nature" of human beings.[2] By this reasoning, infanticide and genocide seem to be a persisting, intractable part of the human record, and so it seems plausible that they spring from something deeply planted in human nature. And yet, natural law has ever set itself against the killing of the innocent.

Spinoza identified natural law with laws of nature that governed the ways of each individual thing. And so, as he said, "fishes are determined by nature to swim, the large ones to live off the smaller; therefore fishes are using this greatest natural right when they possess the water."[3] This may be called the Kern and Hammerstein theory of natural law: fish gotta swim, and birds gotta fly. But as one commentator, the redoubtable Samuel von Pufendorf, rightly put it, it was a mistake to confound these meanings of natural law, to confuse the laws of determinism with "laws" and "rights" in their moral significance.[4] It was especially inapt to attribute a moral intention, or a moral understanding, to "animals that are not endowed with reason." The fish may swim, but it would be hard to attribute to them the understanding that they were engaging their *rights* as they glided about.[5]

Over one hundred years earlier (in 1539), Francisco de Vitoria rejected a comparable argument, to the effect that the stars had a natural right to shine, and the sun to emit light. By that reasoning, as Vitoria had pointed out, we would be doing "an injustice against the sun" by closing the blinds and blocking the light.[6] And of course, in these arguments, Pufendorf and Vitoria had been preceded by Aquinas.[7]

These are all venerable confusions, but it is time we stopped falling into them, for they have been persistently countered, with compelling reasons. The expounders of natural law did not confuse natural law with regularities in nature, or with *generalizations* about the behavior of humans over time, drawn from the checkered history of our species. Immanuel Kant had warned about that temptation to draw principles of moral judgment from "the particular natural characteristics of humanity" or the "particular constitution of human nature."[8] The teachers of natural law began, rather, with an understanding of the things that were higher and lower in human nature. Which is to say, they had to begin with an understanding of what was in principle higher or lower. On that point, they could take their bearings in part from Aristotle, on the things that made human beings decisively different from animals. Animals could emit sounds to indicate pleasure or pain, but human beings could "declare what is just and is unjust"; they could give reasons over matters of right and wrong.[9] In the culminating lines of his First Inaugural Address, Lincoln appealed to "the better angels of our nature." He could invoke the understanding of what was higher and lower in the nature of human beings.

With Aristotle and Lincoln, we had an appeal to what could be called a "commonsense" understanding: we would begin with the kinds of things that were accessible to ordinary folk, without the need for any specialized, scientific vocabulary. That kind of perspective found its understanding of the "human" by separating human things from the things that were *subhuman* or *superhuman*. And there it would begin with the things nearest at hand, in the difference between men and animals.

What seems to come as a surprise to many accomplished lawyers, who affect dubiety over "natural law," is that the natural law may take its bearing from this very notion of the things that mark a distinctly human nature. Which is to say, what seem to have fled from the memories of the lawyers are the plainest things that Aristotle taught in that first book on politics and law. And lost in the same way is the recognition of how widely the reasoning of natural law has been absorbed in the common sense of ordinary people. That point was less obscure in a time when the language of moral reasoning was used by political men with the art of speaking to the multitude, or making themselves understood among a large, public audience. When Lincoln spoke of natural rights he spoke rather plainly, but tellingly, of the rights that arise distinctly from human nature. To read him again is to recall how he could weave the strands of the arguments in a manner that was instantly intelligible. And so Lincoln would say,

> Equal justice to the south, it is said, requires us to consent to the extending of slavery to new countries. That is to say, inasmuch as you do not object to my taking my hog to Nebraska, therefore I must not object to you taking your slave. Now, I admit this is perfectly logical, if there is no difference between hogs and negroes.[10]

Or, in the same speech, the famous Peoria Speech (October 1854), Lincoln notes that even people from the South had not understood black people to be really nothing more than horses or cattle. He noted that, in 1820, congressmen from the South had joined congressmen from the North almost unanimously in outlawing the African slave trade as a form of "piracy" and "annexing to [that crime] the punishment of death":

> Why did you do this? If you did not feel that it was wrong, why did you join in providing that men should be hung for it? The practice was no more than bringing wild negroes from Africa, to sell to such as would buy them. But you never thought of hanging men for catching and selling wild horses, wild buffaloes or wild bears.[11]

And then in a passage as moving as it was analytically pointed, Lincoln observed that

> there are in the United States and territories, including the District of Columbia, 433,643 free blacks. At $500 per head they are worth over two hundred millions of dollars. How comes this vast amount of property to be running about without owners? We do not see free horses or free cattle running at large. How is this? All these free blacks are the descendants of slaves, or have been slaves themselves, and they would be slaves now, but for SOMETHING

> which has operated on their white owners, inducing them, at vast pecuniary sacrifices, to liberate them. What is that SOMETHING? Is there any mistaking it? In all these cases it is your sense of justice, and human sympathy, continually telling you, that the poor negro has some natural right to himself—that those who deny it, and make mere merchandise of him, deserve kickings, contempt and death.
>
> And now, why will you ask us to deny the humanity of the slave? and estimate him only as the equal of the hog? Why ask us to do what you will not do yourselves? Why ask us to do for nothing, what two hundred million of dollars could not induce you to do?[12]

Lincoln would deftly bring his listeners back to that original ground, the difference between men and animals. That was the ground that marked, for Aristotle, the difference in nature that defined what was distinctly human—and explained why only humans were suited by nature for political life. In the hands of Lincoln, and in the crisis engulfing the America of his time, his casting of the argument was critical to the point that the rights articulated in the Declaration of Independence had a *natural* foundation. They were not "rights" that were merely established or posited in any place by the people with the power to lay down rules, like the right to use the library in town or the squash courts at the club. They were rights that would arise for all human beings by nature, and they would remain the same in all places where that nature remained the same. Drawing on the same ancient understanding, John Locke would put the matter in this way:

> For men being all the workmanship of one . . . wise Maker . . . and being furnished with like faculties, sharing all in one community of nature, there cannot be supposed any such subordination among us that may authorize us to destroy one another, as if we were made for one another's uses, as the inferior ranks of creatures are for ours.[13]

And in his own work on the Social Contract, Jean-Jacques Rousseau could add, "Since no man has natural authority over his fellows, and since Might can produce no Right, the only foundation left for legitimate authority in human societies is agreement."[14] As the understanding ran then, no man was by nature the ruler of other men in the way that God was by nature the ruler of men and men were by nature the ruler of horses and cows. Therefore, in the second step, if we find a state of affairs in which some men are ruling over others, that situation could not have arisen from *nature*. It must have arisen from convention, agreement, or consent. To deny that understanding, said Jefferson, was to suggest that the "mass of mankind" had been "born with saddles on their backs," and that a favored few had been born "booted and spurred, ready to ride them legitimately, with the grace of God."[15]

Even in this age of animal liberation we do not find people signing labor contracts with their horses and cows, or seeking the informed consent of their household pets before they authorize surgery upon them. But we continue to think that beings who can give and understand reasons deserve to be ruled with a rendering of reasons, in a regime that elicits their consent. And yet, in our own day, these classic arguments, grounded in the plainest things we can know, have actually been derided and rejected by the orthodoxies now dominant on the American campuses. The fashionable doctrines of postmodernism and radical feminism have denied that we can know moral truths, let alone truths that hold across different countries and cultures. And at the foundation of everything, the exponents of these doctrines often deny that there is really a human nature. What we take to be human nature they regard as social constructs that vary from one place to another according to the vagaries of the local cultures. I have had the chance to address this problem in another place,[16] but it is worth noting yet again that the people who take this line nevertheless keep casting moral judgments across cultures: they condemn genocide in Darfur, as they had condemned a regime of apartheid in the old South Africa, and they seem able to discern "wrongs" done to women. In fact, they seem to be able to recognize *women* when they see them, even in exotic and primitive places. And so, in the world of the postmodernists now on the campuses, there are human rights to be vindicated all over the globe, but strictly speaking there are no *humans*. For there is no human nature. And since there are no moral truths, there are no human "rights" that are truly *rightful*.

If we follow again Aristotle's understanding, the nature that is enduring becomes the source in turn of laws that spring enduringly from that nature. Aristotle would speak then about the law that is peculiar to any place or people and the kind of law that would be true in all places. And Cicero could write then in his *Republic* that "there will not be different laws at Rome and at Athens, or different laws now and in the future, but one eternal and unchangeable law will be valid for all nations and all times."[17] The late Heinrich Rommen drew upon recognitions of this kind when he remarked of the natural law that it was "an imperishable possession of the human mind."[18] It was an imperishable part of the things we could know, either because there was something permanent and enduring in the truths that it grasped, or something enduring in the nature of a creature that had a distinct access, through his reason, to those truths. It should occasion no surprise then that, in countless ways, those truths break through in the most ordinary cases. A visitor from London gets off a plane in New York, and we do not think we have to look at his passport, or take note of his citizenship, before we protect him from an unjustified assault in the street. But we seem to understand that the same man may not take himself over to the City College of New York and claim admission, or claim the same, subsidized rate of tuition that the people of New York are willing to make available to citizens of New York. The latter is a claim or right that arises in a particular place, out of a particular association (like the right to use the squash courts at Amherst College). But the right to be protected against an unjustified assault is a right we would expect to be respected in all places by governments that purport to be decent and lawful governments.

During the recent, tumultuous demonstrations on immigration, we found many illegal aliens and their sympathizers carrying banners urging the conferral of citizenship even on those who came to this country illegally (in violation of the positive laws). What the demonstrators were arguing, I take it, was the rightfulness of conferring citizenship upon them quite apart from what the positive law had stipulated. They themselves were not citizens, but they wished to be, and they believed they had a *rightful claim* to be recognized as citizens. But again we may be surprised by the obvious: since these people are not citizens, the "rights" they are invoking cannot spring from any rights they possess now *as citizens*. They must be invoking an understanding of right and wrong that stands quite apart from the positive law, the law that is posited, set down, enacted in any place. The demonstrators were evidently invoking a standard of right and wrong that could be posed against the positive laws in judging the rightness or wrongness of those laws. In other words, they were appealing, in effect, to an understanding of natural right or natural law. And once again, they were doing it without any particular awareness that they were doing anything distinctly philosophic or juridical.

In the same way, we find that ordinary people show a commonsense understanding of the properties of a moral argument, even if they have not had a college education. And so, without making too much of it, people seem well aware of the difference between the things that are of the day, evanescent, and the things that are permanent, the things that are always. Or they grasp the difference between the things whose goodness is merely *contingent* upon their results, as opposed to things good or bad in themselves. Even people who have never been instructed in philosophy, and do not have the terms or the jargon, are aware of things whose goodness and badness is contingent on matters of degree and circumstance. They may readily grasp that the taking of an alcoholic drink is not always harmful; that it matters notably if it is taken in moderation, or taken in excess, without restraint. But we do not find the same people saying that "genocide, if taken in moderation, may be harmless or inoffensive." Ordinary people may have a keen sense of those things whose wrongness will not be effaced by matters of degree and circumstance. In that vein, we may find ourselves raising the question of whether racial discrimination—the willingness to assign benefits and disabilities to people solely on the basis of their race—is in principle wrong or merely contingently wrong, depending on its result from case to case. If it is in principle wrong, we would be led to conclude that it is wrong even if we do it just a bit of the time or, as they saying goes, that "we take race into account" at the margins of certain cases. Imagine saying that "it is wrong to kill on the basis of race, but perhaps legitimate to 'take race into account,' to let any decision on killing hinge on the matter of race." And so, if it is wrong in principle to make decisions on admission to universities hinge on race, then it would be quite as wrong to "take race into account" in making decisions in marginal cases. Just how we show that something is indeed in principle or categorically wrong in this sense is a matter that may run well beyond the facility of the man on the street. And yet there is, without doubt, an awareness among ordinary people that there are certain things so wrong that their wrongness will not be diminished even if they are done only occasionally, in small doses.

It is one of the oddities of our recent experience that we can count on ordinary people to have the sense of these things, even as academics contrive theories to talk themselves out of these moral recognitions. But that may confirm the ancient truth that these are the kinds of things that we are simply constituted, in our nature, to understand. Still, even a generation of Founders who were quite clear about natural right and natural justice could find certain advantages in a written constitution. Many of them thought, with Scalia, that a written constitution, published and confirmed over the years, would make it far easier for the public and for lawyers to become clear on the meaning of the "fundamental law."

But as I have tried to show, with a certain persistence in my own writing, none of this dispenses with the need and the utility of natural law reasoning. At almost every practical turn, as we try to apply the Constitution to the cases that come before us, we find the need to move beyond the text of the Constitution to those premises, or principles, that were antecedent to the text.[19] They were the first principles of "lawfulness," so fundamental that few people thought it necessary even to state them. (One of them, for example, was the principle that barred ex post facto laws.) But in their axiomatic quality, they touched the first principles in logic or the "laws of reason." James Wilson, one of the truly premier figures among the Founders and the members of the first Supreme Court, put it most aptly when he observed that, as we sought the ground of the law, we were brought to nothing less than the "principles of mind" or to the grounds on which we can claim truly to *know* anything.[20] The first generation of jurists made these moves with little strain. And yet, it seems to come as a surprise to many jurists and lawyers today that they are relying on these axioms of reason when they are "doing" law, or that these axioms of reason are indeed at the foundation of what the Founders understood as the "laws of reason and nature."

In that vein, one of the first things we understand about the domain of moral judgment is that we cast judgments only on those acts that take place in the domain of freedom, where people are free to choose one course of action over another. We do not say that it was right or wrong for the earth to revolve about the sun. As Thomas Reid observed then, one of the first principles of moral reasoning is a proposition I have recast in this way: that we don't hold people blameworthy and responsible for acts they were powerless to affect.[21] If Smith is thrown out the window and on the way down lands on Jones, we don't hold him responsible for an assault. If Smith was born after the crime was committed we take that as powerful evidence of his innocence. If Smith was acting under hypnosis, so that his acts were directed by someone else, and sprung from no reasons or motives of his own, we take those facts as diminishing or dissolving his fault. If Smith met some clinical test of insanity, if it could be shown that he had not really been in control of himself, that too would argue against his guilt. All of these are but instances informed by the same principle. As it turns out, there are no contingencies or circumstances in which that underlying principle will fail to be true. And yet from that proposition may spring, as I say, things like the insanity defense or the wrong of people suffering discrimination over something like their race, which is beyond their control.[22]

But of course race is not entirely beyond one's control: there are many black people of light skin who passed for white, and in this age of many mixed racial marriages, we find offspring who have choices in the racial definition they offer of themselves. The wrong of racial discrimination reaches a slightly different variant with the same ground of principle. For the issue is bound up with the enduring question of "determinism" as the radical denial of "freedom." I have argued this matter at length in other places,[23] and it may be enough to offer this more compressed account. Behind the will or passion to discriminate on the basis of race is a species of determinism: the notion that race exerts a kind of deterministic control over the character and moral conduct of persons. Under this persuasion, people may slide into the assumption that if they know someone's race, they can draw some plausible moral inferences about him: whether he is, on balance, a good or bad man; whether his presence in the firm or the neighborhood would improve the business or the community, or whether that presence would have a degrading effect. To know someone's race, then, on these premises, is to know something about that person that would mark him, with a high probability, of being fit or unfit for any place, more or less deserving of hiring and promotion. In short we would have the clearest ground for assigning benefits and disabilities to people on the basis, decisively, of their race.

But if this sense of things were true, then none of us could plausibly bear responsibility for his own acts. It might be said, in this respect, that the willingness to discriminate on the basis of race denies that moral autonomy, or freedom, that is the very premise of our standing as moral agents. If we were not in control of our own acts, we would never deserve punishment at the hands of the law—and neither would we ever deserve praise. And so in all strictness it could be said that if discrimination on the basis of race were not wrong, then nothing literally could ever be wrong, for there would be no plausible standards of right and wrong to which persons may be held accountable. The whole language and logic of moral judgment, and of legal judgment, would be stripped of its meaning. These words of *right* and *wrong* would be reduced to the oddity of words without meaning or function. They may imply a vague approval or disapproval, but not strictly a ground for casting judgments of right and wrong on other people.

When understood in this way, the wrongness of racial discrimination is anchored in the very logic of law and moral judgment. The wrong then is not merely contingent on circumstances, or on its effects in any case, but it is *categorical*: there are no circumstances under which it fails to be wrong. That sense of the matter would stand in sharp contrast to the way in which the case against racial segregation was made in the federal courts, in that celebrated pattern of litigation carried through from the 1930s to the 1950s, with *Brown v. Board of Education*. And so the argument was heard that discrimination in colleges and law schools would be wrong because black students would be deprived of the acquaintances and "contacts" that would enlarge their horizons and the prospect for their careers.[24] Or with the *Brown* case, the argument was made that the separation of children on the basis of race would impair the motivation of black children to learn and, with that, their performance in school.[25] Never mind that there were cases of all-black high schools, with motivated pupils, families, and teachers, that went on to produce many black people for professional life.[26] And never mind, too, that these conjectures were inherently probabilistic: in the nature of things, one could not know for sure that, by bringing together people of the same race, the mixture would beget affection, conversation, and friendships carried over into business. These were all predictions quite hostage to the results. And the radical defects in this mode of argument would make themselves manifest as soon as one posed the question in this way: If we separate students on the basis of race and their reading scores *go up*, would that mean that the racial segregation would cease to be wrong? Or are we inclined to say, rather, that the segregation is wrong *in principle*? I once offered the example of the redoubtable Cecil Partee, the legendary black ward committeeman in Chicago. In Partee's account, he had graduated from the University of Arkansas in 1938 near the top of his class, and he applied to the law school. But Arkansas would not permit blacks to attend the law school of the public university. The state offered instead a voucher that would permit Partee to pursue his studies even in law schools outside the state. And so, barred by law from the law school of the University of Arkansas, Partee was compelled to choose instead between the law schools of the University of Chicago and Northwestern. As Partee later put it, "I laughed all the way to Chicago."[27] Cecil Partee did not suffer a material harm as a result of the policy of segregation in Arkansas;

but he was wronged. He was treated according to the maxims of an unjust principle.

To take the matter from yet another angle, a sober reckoning of violent crime in New York or other cities would point to a clear demographic cohort, quite likely to produce assaults well beyond the levels shown by other groups. Young black and Hispanic males, between fourteen and twenty-five, are far more likely to commit violent, armed assaults than white male accountants or female lawyers in their forties and fifties. If it were a matter of strictly of playing the odds, or being governed by the probabilities, it would be entirely conceivable at least to cast an argument on utilitarian grounds for a certain preventative detention, or perhaps "closer official governance," of young males in this category. Balancing risks against gains, it is certainly arguable that the community would be a net gainer in the lives saved and the families preserved against the loss of productive members. And yet no one would come even close to offering such a proposal for discussion, let alone a serious plan to act upon. When we recoil from a scheme of that kind, the aversion can be explained only by the recognition that a policy of that sort would catch, in its sweep, many innocent people. They may be poor, but they may have no disposition to make their way in life by hurting others. But that is to say, when we hold back from that scheme, we seem to recognize that ethnicity and race, mingled with poverty, do not control or determine character. We back into the recognition that we are imputing, even to ordinary folk, a certain capacity to hold themselves back from the ethic that may be dominant in their neighborhood or among their racial group, and reach their own judgments about the things that are right or wrong. To put it another way—without royalties to Immanuel Kant—we are recognizing a certain *moral autonomy* that must be characteristic of human beings. And it must be indeed the predicate of that freedom we impute to moral agents.

It is another of those curiosities of our own day that the notion of "moral autonomy" has been taken by liberals as the anchoring ground for new rights of sexual liberation. And at the same time, those extravagant claims have stirred a recoil among conservatives. In both instances, the notion of autonomy is gravely misunderstood. We may coherently impute a certain moral autonomy only to moral agents—those creatures who are capable of deliberating about the grounds of their well-being, and giving reasons. But it is in the nature of moral agents also that they have an understanding of right and wrong. They could grasp then, as Aquinas and Lincoln recognized, that there cannot be a "right to do a wrong." They could grasp, in other words, the things they can have no right to do or to claim in the name of their "autonomy." To invoke "autonomy" is not to invoke a license for a freedom emancipated from moral restraint, in private or in public. But when we fill in the portrait of that creature bearing this moral autonomy, we are describing again that creature described by Aristotle, standing somewhere between the beasts and the gods. It is the only animal fitted for political life and law because it is the only creature who can frame propositions, grasp the nature of an obligation, and respect a law beyond himself; a law that runs counter to his own inclinations or his interests. When viewed through the lens of the American Founders, they are the creatures encompassed by that "proposition," as Lincoln called it, "All men are created equal." The political Left in our own day reproaches the American Founders for their putative failure to respect that principle. In that vein, the Founders have been indicted for the accommodations they made with the evil of slavery. But as we have seen, the embarrassment for writers on the Left is that they deny that there is a nature that provides the ground for the claims of equality and rights. They take a moral high ground in relation to the Founders, and yet they deny that there are moral truths that reason can know. And so, while they elevate equality as a principle, they deny that principle, or any other moral principle, the standing of a truth.

The confusion suffered here by the Left may be bound up with certain confusions suffered by many other people on what it means to regard "All men are created equal" as a self-evident or necessary truth. A "self-evident" truth is not one of those things "evident" to every "self" happening along the street. It was closer to what Aquinas described as a truth that had to be grasped *per se nota*, as something true in itself. Aquinas remarked that it was one of those "evident" principles of what he called "speculative reason," a truth that is "the same for all, but . . . not equally known to all. Thus it is true for all that the three angles of a triangle are together equal to two right angles, although it is not known to all."[28] If a person could not grasp the law of contradiction—that two contradictory propositions both could not be true—there would be no way of explaining it to him. For virtually anything we said could be contradicted, and if he thought that everything said was equally plausible—if he could entertain at the same time propositions that were at war with one another—there would be nothing he could ever literally come to "know." If we sought to stage a controlled experiment—say, with a ball rolling down an inclined plane—we might test a plane with a slight angle set against a plane with a steeper angle. We could measure then what effect the steepness of the angle had on the acceleration of the ball. But we would need to understand at once that we were dealing with two different angles—that we have angle A, we might say, set against non-A. And yet, if we did not know the law of contradiction, we could hardly understand the significance of comparing two or more distinct angles. We would have to know that A does not equal non-A if the experiment is to make sense. In other words, someone would have to understand the law of contradiction before he could understand an experiment. And if he professed not to understand the law of contradiction, then *there would be no way to convey the point to him in the form of an experiment.*

That the American Founders understood this matter of truths that had to be grasped *per se nota* was nowhere confirmed with more eloquence or clarity than by Alexander Hamilton in his opening paragraph for the *Federalist*, No. 31. I have had the occasion to quote this passage before, but it is never out of season to quote it, for it still offers the most compelling example of what that generation of lawyers and Founders understood about the nature of axioms. This is the way Hamilton set up the problem in the *Federalist*, No. 31:

> In disquisitions of every kind there are certain primary truths, or first principles, upon which all subsequent reasonings must depend. These contain an internal evidence which, antecedent to all reflection or combination, command the assent of the mind. . . . Of this nature are the maxims in geometry that the whole is greater than its parts; that things equal to the same are equal to one another; that two straight lines cannot enclose a space; and that all right angles are equal to each other. Of the same nature are these other maxims in ethics and politics, that there cannot be an effect without a cause; that the means ought to be proportioned to the end; that every power ought to be commensurate with its object; that there ought to be no limitation of a power destined to effect a purpose which is itself incapable of limitation.[29]

Hamilton, in this passage, clearly grasped the properties of a first principle. The question persistently arises as to what kind of a proposition, exactly, was "All men are created equal" if that proposition really had the standing of a first principle. Some people have regarded it as an *inductive* proposition—that it is drawn as a generalization from experience, in taking account of the differences between men and animals, differences accessible to people of common sense. But as Thomas Reid pointed out, an inductive proposition claims to offer nothing more than a generalization drawn from experience, and therefore it cannot rise above a statement of probability.[30] If "All men are created equal" were really an inductive proposition, it would have to be recast as "Most men are created equal, most of the time."

In my childhood, in the early days of television, there was a program called *Candid Camera*, and in one of the early episodes the producers set up a microphone in a mailbox. The mailbox then would engage the people dropping in letters. The mailbox would say something like, "Is it still raining?" And what was astonishing was just how many people, without skipping a beat, would answer and fall into a conversation with the mailbox. It occurred to me recently that we could put the question: If most of us don't talk to mailboxes, do we make that judgment *inductively* or *deductively*? That is, if we are asked why we don't speak to the mailboxes, are we inclined say, "They usually don't talk to me"? That is, do we induce what strikes us as a general rule, likely to be true, as we draw the lessons from experience in the past? Or is it that we grasp something about the nature of mailboxes, and we have no expectation of carrying on conversations with mailboxes, household appliances, or other inanimate objects?

As Reid taught, a first principle had to state a necessary proposition, and "propositions of this kind, from their nature, are incapable of proof by induction." They could not be demonstrated by experiments because experiments depended on experience, and "experience," he said, "informs us only of what is or has been, not of what must be":

> Though it should be found by experience in a thousand cases, that the area of a plane triangle is equal to the rectangle under the altitude and half the base, this would not prove that it must be so in all cases, and cannot be otherwise.[31]

The hard fact was that one could not "experience" a necessary proposition. Experience could tell us only of the things experienced, and we have no experience of the future. At the most, we might say that, in certain cases, the future is likely to be similar to the past and yield similar outcomes. That the advent of major league baseball in any city will foster many new jobs and lift the level of prosperity may be a high probability indeed. Still, that relation of cause and effect would not be true of necessity. But that it is "wrong to hold people blameworthy or responsible for acts they are powerless to affect" would in fact be true under all conditions and circumstances, now and in the future. A necessary proposition would hold true at all times, in all cases. When Lincoln said that the American republic began, not with the Constitution, but with that "proposition" that "all men are created equal," he seemed to regard that proposition as conveying the principle that defined the character of the regime. From that proposition, everything else radiated. That proposition, he said, marked "an abstract truth applicable to all men and all times." And with that, he left us the clearest sense that this principle, the founding principle of the regime, was nothing less than a first principle, with nothing merely contingent or probabilistic about it.

The natural law finds its ground then in these "axioms" or "first principles," as Hamilton understood; and one clear sign of their standing as necessary truths is that any effort to deny them will find the deniers twisting in self-contradiction. And one of the most notable howlers here is also one of the most well-travelled fallacies in our public discourse, committed by writers on the Right as well as the Left. It usually runs in this way: "If there were moral truths that held universally, they would be acknowledged in all places. The fact that they are not—that we find instead a widespread disagreement over the things that are right and wrong—stands as prima facie evidence that those 'universal moral truths' do not exist." As I have pointed out in another place, that argument really reduces to this proposition: that the absence of consensus or agreement indicates the absence of truth. Now of course I would have to register my own disagreement with *that* proposition, and on its own terms that should be enough to establish its falsity.

There are no tricks, and this is not a game with words. It is a matter of people simply falling into what the philosophers call a self-refuting proposition. What is odd is to see how many people experienced in law still regard that proposition with evident seriousness, and that some judges are willing to take it as a foundational point in their jurisprudence. There is surely no more telling example on that head than that proposition offered earnestly by Justice Harry Blackmun:

> When those trained in the respective disciplines of medicine, philosophy, and theology are unable to arrive at any consensus [on the question of when human life begins], the judiciary, in this point in the development of man's knowledge, is not in a position to speculate as to the answer.[32]

Actually, there was no want of consensus in the textbooks on embryology and obstetric gynecology on this matter of when human life began. That point was amply established by the Senate Committee on the Judiciary in 1981, when it surveyed all of the leading textbooks in the field.[33] Obviously, Blackmun had undertaken no survey to gauge the absence of a consensus; he was simply stating what he took to be a truism. But if he had been alert to the property of propositions he might have recognized that he too had simply backed into a self-refuting proposition.

What seems to come as a surprise for lawyers and judges, whether conservative or liberal, is that natural law is bound up with the laws of reasons, or the canons of logic—the canons by which we gauge the things we can claim to know. One of the most gifted lawyers this country has produced, a man who made his way into the profession by "reading at law," gave us the simplest example of natural law reasoning. And in the spirit of natural law, it could be grasped readily even by people without training in law. In a fragment he had written for himself, Abraham Lincoln imagined himself in a conversation with the owner of black slaves, raising the question of how he could justify making a slave of black people:

> You say A. is white, and B. is black. It is color, then: the lighter having the right to enslave the darker? Take care. By this rule, you are to be slave to the first man you meet, with a fairer skin than your own.
>
> You do not mean *color* exactly?—You mean the whites are *intellectually* the superiors of the blacks, and therefore have the right to enslave them? Take care again. By this rule, you are to be slave to the first man you meet, with an intellect superior to your own.

> But, say you, it is a question of interest; and, if you can make it your *interest*, you have the right to enslave another. Very well. And if he can make it his interest, he has the right to enslave you.[34]

Lincoln offered, in the most concentrated form, a model of principled reasoning: there was nothing one could cite to disqualify the black man as a human being, and the bearer of rights, that would not apply to many whites as well. There was an apt lesson to be drawn in pointing out that nowhere, in this chain of reasoning, was there an appeal to faith or revelation. Lincoln's argument could be understood across the divisions of religion or race or class—it could be understood by Catholics or Baptists, by geologists or carpenters, and even by people unburdened with a college education. It could be understood then by ordinary people, using the wit of rational creatures, and in my own experience no one, hearing the argument, has failed to grasp it. For the natural law to function as law, it has to be accessible, fairly commonly, to those creatures of reason who walk among us.

As Aquinas observed, the divine law we know through revelation, but the natural law we know through that reason that is natural to human beings, accessible to ordinary folk as creatures of reason. That understanding was carried down over the years to the American Founders through other sources confirming that teaching. James Wilson often cited the formidable Jean-Jacques Burlamaqui, in his classic work on *The Principles of Natural and Politic Law* (1748); and Burlamaqui thought it critical to get clear on why natural law could not be dependent on revelation. No doubt, he wrote, "God was at liberty . . . to create or not create man," and to impart to him quite a different nature. But "having determined to form a rational and social being, he could not prescribe any thing unsuitable to such a creature." In fact, Burlamaqui suggested that the notion of law and its principles would be subverted if they were thought to depend on "the arbitrary will of God": "For, if these laws were not a necessary consequence of the nature, constitution, and state of man, it would be impossible for us to have a certain knowledge of them, except by a very clear revelation, or by some other formal promulgation on the part of God. But . . . the law of nature is, and ought to be, known by the mere light of reason."[35] Long before Burlamaqui and the teachers of international law, the same point was made by "the judicious Hooker," as Locke called him. Richard Hooker, in his *Laws on Ecclesiastical Polity*, explained the elementary point that the natural law would be known through that reason that is distinctive to human beings, the "law rational," as Hooker condensed the matter, "which men commonly use to call the law of nature, meaning thereby the law which human nature knoweth itself in reason universally bound unto, which also for that cause may be termed most fitly the law of reason."[36]

But long before Hooker were the Church fathers—*vide* St. John Chrysostom (d. 407): "We use not only Scripture but also reason in arguing against the pagans." And of course, running back to the beginning of the Church, St. Paul in Romans: "When the gentiles, which have not the law, do by nature the things contained in the law, [they] are a law unto themselves" (Romans 2:14). On the central place of reason, then, in natural law, there is a convergence of teaching emanating from both Jerusalem and Athens, with the moderns as well as the ancients. In fact, as John Paul II and his successor have argued in our own day, the tradition of philosophy coming down from the Greeks has been, as John Paul II said, "the hedge and protective wall around the vineyard" of the Church. For the discipline of philosophy has been critical in helping to discriminate between readings of revelation that were plausible or spurious. John Paul II thought that it was the considerable service of the "fathers of philosophy to bring to light the link between reason and religion. As they broadened their view to include universal principles, they no longer rested content with the ancient myths, but wanted to provide a rational foundation for their belief in the divinity. . . . Superstitions were recognized for what they were and religion was, at least in part, purified by rational analysis."[37] The tie to philosophy, even for religion, marked the unity of knowledge, and it provided the anchoring point of conviction that there could be no real division between religion and science. As John Paul II observed,

> the two modes of knowledge lead to truth in all its fullness. The unity of truth is a fundamental premise of human reasoning, *as the principle of non-contradiction makes clear*. Revelation renders this unity certain, showing that the God of creation is also the God of salvation history. It is the one and the same God who establishes and guarantees the intelligibility and reasonableness of the natural order of things upon which scientists confidently depend.[38]

I would not want to claim that John Paul II was coinciding with Immanuel Kant in all critical respects; but I would point out that the Holy Father saw no strain in finding the ground of moral reasoning, as Kant did, in the laws of reason, anchored in the law of contradiction. It should not have come as news to writers in our own day, and yet it seems to come as a kind of revelation to discover that natural law does not depend on religious beliefs, ever evading the test of reason. Quite to the contrary, natural law has ever been bound up with the laws of reason, and the laws of reason find their own touchstone, or their anchoring ground, in the law of contradiction.

But the further revelation is that, by the time we have taken these simple steps, tracing back the tradition, we will have backed into Immanuel Kant's recognition: that what we mean by the "moral laws" is nothing more than those laws of reason themselves. They are the *laws of reason*, the canons of logic, that command our judgment in the *domain of freedom*. For it is only in the domain of freedom that a practical judgment becomes possible. It is only when we have the freedom to choose that we are drawn outward to the standards that govern our choice between the things that are good or bad, right or wrong, just or unjust. Kant used that curious expression "the laws of freedom" to mean the "moral laws." At first glance that might sound like an oxymoron, for if there are laws governing us we would not be free exactly to do as we wished. But the point rather was that the "moral world," with the casting of moral judgments, makes sense only in that domain in which people are *free* to choose one course of action over another. The laws of freedom are those laws of reason that command our judgment in the domain of freedom. We do not impute wrongs to the movement of rocks in a landslide; we do not say it would be morally *wrong* if Smith, falling out of a window, fell down upon someone else. The moral world begins with the domain of freedom, and finds its limit where freedom is overborne by the laws of nature. The laws of freedom would refer then to those laws of reason that command and guide our acts in the domain of freedom. But they are laws only if they have about them the quality of necessity. And they can have that quality only if they find their ground indeed in the laws of reason, or the first principles of our reasoning—in propositions we cannot deny without falling into contradiction.

Still, one might ask, how are they laws like the "laws of physics"? After all, we cannot repeal the law of gravity. And those strike us more forcibly as laws: laws that cannot depend on our will or intentions, laws that we are obliged to respect because they are forces of nature. In contrast, people are every day violating the law of contradiction; they often find ways of being inconsistent, especially on things that matter to them. The laws of reason, anchored by the law of contradiction, would be a different species of law. And what makes them a species of law is that they have the force of being inescapably true. The ceiling does not fall in when we do things that are contradictory. The law of contradiction claims the standing of law because it has the sovereign attribute of being not only true, but true of necessity. It commands our respect then as creatures of reason in the domain of freedom. These are creatures who have reasons for their acts, and beyond that, creatures who may be concerned to describe, in their own acts, a principled course of conduct.

As Aristotle reminded us, we would not assume that all human beings, at all ages or stages of maturity, would have that concern as a concern of high rank in their lives. For those people, as he said, life may consist of a series of disconnected emotional episodes, so that the decision taken yesterday bears no relation to the decision taken today.[39] Yet, even ordinary people, not especially reflective, will show that concern in one degree or another; and even if they do not, the main point is not dislodged. To the extent that we would govern our acts by principles of judgment that are true, the standards that are grounded in this way, in propositions that must be true of necessity, have an unsurpassed claim on us. To the extent that we are governed and guided by them, they offer the grounds on which we can give a compelling account of our own acts. And if our acts find their ground in the laws of reason, in propositions that are true of necessity, *those reasons will hold in all places*. They will hold, that is, in all places where human creatures can be found and the laws of reason are intact. Hence the understanding summarized in such a compressed way in the categorical imperative: Act only on that maxim fit to be installed as a universal rule. The subject of this sentence is the unexpressed "you," a person in the domain of freedom who faces a choice over different courses of conduct. To the extent that he allows himself to be governed by the laws of reason, by propositions that must be true of necessity, his acts are guided by a proposition "fit to be installed as a universal law." If a proposition is true of necessity, then as we say, perforce it must be true in all places. It must be universal in its reach or application.

Let me recap quickly and offer an example. We know that we are dealing with a proposition true of necessity when we confront a proposition that cannot be denied without falling into contradiction. The skeptic who denies that we are in the domain of freedom manifests his own freedom to stand apart and refuse his assent to our claim that freedom, as a practical matter, does exist. To the extent that he insists that we are "wrong" or mistaken to assert the existence of freedom—or assert the truth of anything—he does not merely register his feelings or his personal aversion. He is telling us that we are *wrong*, that we are mistaken. But that move must imply that he has access to standards of reason, accessible to us as they are to him—standards of judgment that would tell us that we are wrong. He has merely found another way of confirming his own access to the laws of reason. With these moves he not only backs into self-contradiction; he also confirms the Kantian proof of what we mean by moral truths: (a) that in some parts of our lives at least we are in the domain of freedom, with the freedom to choose our own course of conduct, and (b) that we have access to the laws of reason in gauging whether the maxims, or reasons, underlying our acts are true or false, right or wrong.

But if all of that is the case, then we would confirm in the same way that proposition I mentioned earlier, as the first implication springing from the logic of morals: namely, that moral judgments cast upon others make sense only if we can assume that people had been free to form their own acts. With but a short step, we may add the implication that springs up for racial discrimination: we cannot assume that race essentially controls or "determines" the moral character of any person. For under those conditions, no one would be responsible for his own acts, and no one could possibly merit either praise or blame, rewards or punishments. With those elementary points in place, consider one application of the Kantian understanding:

Let us suppose that we have two owners of restaurants in that liberal town called Amherst, Massachusetts, a college town, peopled richly with persons of the most advanced liberal reflexes. The two owners decide to arrange their establishments on the rule that there shall be no discrimination on the basis of race in admitting customers to their places of business. But we know that people may act in the same way even when their conduct springs from reasons or maxims that are strikingly different. Restaurant Owner A is working on the maxim that "it is good to accord the rules of one's business with the local ethos or the 'culture' of that community in which the business is located. It would be thoroughly bad for business in liberal Massachusetts if the word got out that the proprietors of this restaurant were racist, that they were willing to find certain customers undesirable solely on the basis of their race."

In contrast, Restaurant Owner B works on this maxim: "It would be incoherent to assume that race determines moral character, and that I could draw any interesting inferences about my potential customers based upon their race. It might be reasonable to discriminate, say, on the basis of a dress code, but it would utterly indefensible to mark my customers worthy or unworthy solely on the basis of their race."

But then, in the usual license of a thought-experiment, let us imagine that both Owners are somehow transported to South Africa during the regime of apartheid. Restaurant Owner A holds to his maxim as one that is eminently portable, but he is now in a different place, with a different ethos, and so the result is that he now flips in his operating rule. All around him people make the most important discriminations based on race, and he will not offend the local culture; he will adopt its racial principles as his own. With Restaurant Owner B there is the same willingness to stick with the same maxim, because it has not been affected by the shift in locale. He still understands that it would be not only wrong, but incoherent, to indulge the assumption that people are controlled or determined in their conduct by their race. The difference, however, is that Owner B's maxim is grounded in a law of reason, a proposition that is true of necessity. We need not be overly romantic and suppose that Owner B is utterly indifferent to "results." It may matter profoundly to him that he might not be able to stay in business, and make a living, if he adheres to the maxim that claimed his respect, and governed his acts, when he was in Amherst, Massachusetts. He is bound to understand all of that. It is just that, in all honesty, he still finds that the principle he recognized earlier has not been diminished at all in its validity merely because he has moved from Massachusetts to South Africa. If he would be governed by a moral principle that is true and commands his allegiance, he simply reports that he can do no other. Lincoln once remarked on the young man aspiring to be a lawyer that, "if in your own judgment you cannot be an honest lawyer, resolve to be honest without being a lawyer. Choose some other occupation, rather than one in the choosing of which you do, in advance, consent to be a knave."[40] Advice aptly and soberly offered to lawyers would not become wildly utopian when addressed to the owners of restaurants.

But what we have then, with Owner B, is the case of an actor in the domain of freedom who had accorded his conduct with a maxim fit to be installed as a universal rule. The maxim was as valid in South Africa as in Amherst, and the validity of that maxim was utterly unaffected by the prospect that the results could be dire, that he could fall out of that business. And that is what we may tenably mean by that language, often appearing grandiloquent, that something categorically wrong retains its standing as a wrong even if the results are unhappy and even ruinous.

If that construction is intelligible, then we could see more readily what Kant meant when he said that everything that has standing as a moral principle has that standing as it is drawn as a logical implication from this core: an actor in the domain of freedom, seeking to accord his acts with a maxim grounded in the laws of reason. And so as Kant said, "we ought . . . to derive our principles from the general concept of a rational being as such, and on this basis to expound the whole of ethics."[41] The body of principles we draw in that way may be quite economical or parsimonious. We are not asking, "What do most people around here regard as good or bad, right or wrong?" We would be lifting the bar—which is to say, we would be far more demanding and cautious before we invoke the language of "morality" and impose those judgments as law. But what comes as surprising in another degree is just how much, in our public discourse, or in our moral judgments, may be drawn as implications from this limited, precise sense of the "logic of morals" itself.

In fact, I think we would find that most of our judgments would fall into a class of propositions that are understood readily, even instantly, by ordinary people, even if they have no awareness that they are seeing merely instances of the same, simple principle at work. And what I have in mind are those recognitions, grasped by virtually everyone, of the attributes or conditions that have "no moral significance" and cannot supply the ground of any adverse moral judgments. To put it another way, the point is so obvious that we may be startled even to hear it raised as a question. If we were told, for example, that a person were tall or short, thin or heavy, that he had dark hair or light hair, would we think that any of these points had given us the ground for any inferences on whether we were dealing with a person who was brilliant or dim, admirable or corrupt, someone who deserved praise or blame? We grasp these points readily, but if there were a need to explain the ground of the understanding, it would lie once again in the problem of determinism: we know that none of these features—height, weight, color of hair—"determines" in any way the moral character of any person, and therefore none of them would supply a ground for any inferences as to whether this person deserved to be celebrated or shunned, rewarded or punished.

Traced to its core, this is how we would explain what we mean when we say that these features are utterly wanting in moral significance. But they are but part of a larger scheme that actually does find expression in our law, for the same underlying principle would finally explain why it would be unwarranted to draw adverse inferences about people who are suffering from various disabilities. People quite brilliant may be afflicted with stuttering, or with diabetes, with poor eyesight and tremors. Their maladies may act as barriers to many activities—the stutterer may not work well as an actor or as an announcer on the BBC; the nurse afflicted with poor eyesight may be disqualified to participate in serious surgery. But their disabilities would not bar them from many other occupations, and that sense of things would stand behind the laws that now bar certain discriminations based on disabilities. In the infamous case of Baby Doe on Long Island in the 1980s, the child was afflicted at birth with spina bifida and Down's syndrome.[42] The parents, in league with the doctors, refused to provide medical care to this newborn, with the sense that she had, with these afflictions, a life not worth living. The case became difficult to disentangle as the Reagan administration was perpetually stymied in the effort to gain access to the records of the hospital and to determine the ground on which the medical care had been withheld from this newborn. If the situation had been inoperable, the administration had not been seeking to press people into futile surgery. But if the withholding of care turned on a moral judgment—for example, that people afflicted with Down's syndrome or spina bifida had lives "not worth living," lives that could be terminated without the need to render a justification—then that was a case that came within the moral understanding that barred discriminations based on disability. The discriminations in these cases involved nothing less than a willingness to end the life of a person on the premise that a person with these afflictions did not really deserve to live.

In the cases that keep arising over a "right to die," the courts are persistently being asked to confirm the rightness, the moral justification, for ending the life of a patient because he may be afflicted with AIDS, or with cancer, and perhaps even with deafness. Deafness could be the most disabling of conditions for a conductor in an orchestra, and there are surely people who will claim that, for them, a life without music is a life not worth living. But to leap then to a moral conclusion—that a person afflicted with deafness has no means of living a life of moral consequence—is to make an extravagant and deeply incoherent move. A man may have the means of taking his own life, but something else needs to be said in order to establish that it is "rightful" to end any life, even one's own, on the basis of "reasons" that are irretrievably false and indefensible. And of course it is only when those premises are put in place—that it is somehow rightful to end the life of a patient with AIDS—

that the ground is laid for relatives or even strangers to assist in the ending of that life. For if Jones has a "right" to end his life, why should he be deprived of that right when he is incapable of acting himself to end it? Why should he not be free to authorize someone else to act as an agent in vindicating his right? If he happens to be an orphan, or one without relatives or friends, why should an administrator in a hospital not be able to take up that mandate and act as an agent in helping this man act out his "right"?

My purpose here, though, is not to probe the deeper argument that is engaged in the matter of suicide, assisted or unassisted. I am only pointing out here that what is engaged in these cases is a problem that runs to the same root in principle, on the matter of determinism. That point, quite primary and simple, shows itself in instances spread widely in our law and public life. But to put this point into place is to provide the ground for some lessons that may be received as fairly astounding among lawyers and judges who have been the most dismissive of natural law as an enterprise too ethereal, too hazy to provide any practical import for the law.

We may take again as an example the judgment on deafness and disabilities—the wrong, say, of drawing adverse inferences about any person, or even ending a life, on the basis of deafness. It makes the most profound difference to know that this judgment is anchored in the laws of reason themselves. It is bound up with the rejection of determinism in all of its varieties. But if we come to understand the matter in that way—if we understand just why it would be deeply indefensible to punish people on account of their height, their weight, their deafness, their afflictions—we would understand that this moral reflex of ours does not represent merely some local custom, or *some peculiarity of this tribe of Americans*. We may ask then, where in the world would it be wrong to withhold medical treatment from a newborn—or for that matter, from any other person—because he is afflicted with Down's syndrome or deafness? Would it not be as wrong in Lichtenstein, the Ivory Coast, or New Jersey? The decisive point will ever hinge on the question of whether it is plausible to draw adverse moral inferences about a person based on his deafness or Down's syndrome. And the answer I would earnestly offer is that this act of withdrawing care, on those grounds, would be wrong anywhere, everywhere, where the laws of reason are intact, and where creatures of reason bother to consider whether they truly have reasons to justify their acts.

I would submit then to a candid world—and to some of our friends among the judges—that there is nothing here the least opaque, foggy, imprecise; nothing that depends on the manipulation of words or a rarified vocabulary. What is offered here is grounded in the first premises of moral judgment, and in things that are readily grasped by ordinary people even without an education in philosophy. And the judgment that is offered here would be concrete, precise, not the least hazy—and universal in its reach.

When we have put these things in place, I think we would have sketched an understanding of the grounds of moral judgment that are rooted in the nature of "a rational creature as such," as Kant put it. Kant is not associated with natural law, at least as natural law was identified with the general tendencies that were thought to be characteristic of human beings, or necessary for the "flourishing" of human beings. Indeed, Kant had gone out of his way to stress that the ground of obligation "must be looked for, not in the nature of man nor in the circumstances of the world in which he is placed, but solely a priori in the concepts of pure reason."[43] But at the same time, the principles of pure reason were accessible only to a certain kind of creature. The moral law, drawn from this source, "gives him laws a priori as a rational being."[44] And so, from that idea of a creature of reason, in the domain of freedom, facing the task of practical judgment, Kant could draw out the principles of right and wrong that could have the standing of real principles. They would not be true most of the time, or true under certain contingencies; they could be true of necessity and have the standing then of genuine first principles. As Kant observed, "nothing but the idea of the law in itself . . . can constitute that preeminent good which we call moral," and that idea of law is "present only in a rational being."[45] Once again, only a being with reason can conceive the notion of a "good," or a principle of justice that may override his own self-interest. And, as Kant went on to say, "since moral laws have to hold for every rational being as such, we ought . . . to derive our principles from the general concept of a rational being as such."[46]

There is a danger of being ensnared by the tyranny of labels and missing the substance of the teaching. Kant is not linked to the teachers of natural law, but in the substance of the matter, he found the ground of moral judgment in the same nature that provided the ground for Aristotle. The enduring, irresistible fact of the matter, taught at the beginning by Aristotle, was that law itself sprung from the nature of a certain kind of creature. If we are dealing with a world of framing reasons and propositions, and respecting the force of principles or propositions beyond our own appetites and wills, we are speaking of creatures with the capacity for reason. It has taken generations of lawyers to make obscure and to forget the most obvious things around us—or within us. And perhaps those primary things are so easily overlooked precisely because they are so evidently with us.

It frequently happens that some of our friends who are most skeptical of natural law discover that they have been practicing it handsomely for many years without quite realizing it—much like that character in Moliere who discovers that he has been speaking prose all his life. It is rather like the man who asks, "Can I order coffee without using syntax?" He may not realize that of course he is using syntax and speaking prose without quite recognizing the conceptual world he inhabits or the understandings that are woven into his own nature. It is no wonder that we find some of our best natural lawyers among the distinguished jurists who have been the most skeptical of natural law. They may go on to discover, as a late colleague once said, that we have principles we have not even used yet. But for many of us, the task of bringing out those principles and explaining them has become, happily, steady work.

In that work we may find our model again in Plato's *Meno*: Socrates feeds the right questions to a slave boy, and—wonder of wonders—the boy is soon working out, step by step, the principles of geometry. As the understanding ran, those principles were already within his comprehension; they merely had to be unlocked. In this charming scheme, knowledge was a matter of remembering. It was a matter of unlocking what is always within us, always there to be discovered anew. And the sense of the matter, experienced by our students today as ever, is that when they discover those things they know, about the grounds of their moral judgment, what is buoying in the experience is the recognition that they have known them all along.

NOTES

1. This chapter has drawn upon material from within "The Natural Law—Again, Ever," in Hadley Arkes, *Constitutional Illusions and Anchoring Truths*, 43–79 (Cambridge University Press, 2010), copyright Hadley Arkes, 2010, reproduced with permission.
2. See Richard Posner, *The Problems of Jurisprudence* (Cambridge: Harvard University Press, 1990), 235–36, 238–39, 376, 396–405.
3. Baruch Spinoza, *Theological-Political Treatise*, chap. 16.
4. Samuel von Pufendorf, *Two Books of the Elements of Universal Jurisprudence* (1660; trans. 1672; Oxford: Clarendon Press, 1931), xxxi.
5. Pufendorf, *Elements*, 159.
6. Francisco Vitoria, *Reflections in Moral Theology* (1696; Washington: Carnegie Institution, 1917), 248; from a lecture delivered at the University of Salamanca in 1539.
7. See Aquinas, *Summa theologiae* 2.1.92.2.
8. Immanuel Kant, *Fundamental Principles of the Metaphysics of Morals*, trans. Thomas K. Abbott (1785; repr., Indianapolis: Bobbs-Merrill, 1949), 42, 58.
9. See Aristotle, *Politics* 1252a–53a.
10. Lincoln, "Speech at Peoria" (Oct. 16, 1854), in *The Collected Works of Abraham Lincoln*, ed. Roy P. Basler (Brunswick, NJ: Rutgers University Press, 1953), 2:264.
11. Lincoln, "Speech at Peoria."
12. Lincoln, "Speech at Peoria," 264–65.
13. John Locke, "Second Treatise on Civil Government" (1690), bk. 2, chap. 2, in *Social Contract*, ed. Sir Ernest Barker (London: Oxford University Press, 1960), 5–6.
14. Locke, "The Social Contract" (1762), bk. 1, chap. 4, in *Social Contract*, 173.
15. Thomas Jefferson to Roger Weightman, June 24, 1826, in *The Political Thought of American Statesmen*, eds. Morton G. Frisch and Richard G. Stevens (Itasca, IL: EE. Peacock, 1973), 13.
16. See my own *Natural Rights and the Right to Choose* (Cambridge and New York: Cambridge University Press, 2002), 18–19.
17. See Cicero, *Republic* 3.22.
18. Heinrich Rommen, *The Natural Law*, trans. Thomas R. Hanley (1936; trans. 1947; Indianapolis: Liberty Fund, 1998), 190. It is notable that the original title in German was *Die Ewige Wiederkehr des Naturrechts* (The perpetual return of natural law).
19. See my own *Beyond the Constitution* (Princeton: Princeton University Press, 1990).

20. See Wilson in Chisholm v. Georgia, 2 U.S. 419 (1793), at 453–54: Before Wilson would invoke the authority of any case at law or any writer on matters legal, he would invoke the authority of "Dr. [Thomas] Reid, in his excellent enquiry into the human mind, on the principles of *common sense,* speaking of the sceptical and illiberal philosophy, which under bold, but false pretentions to liberality, prevailed in many parts of Europe before he wrote." But even more fully on this point, see Wilson's lectures on what could be called the "epistemology" of constitutional government—his lectures on "The Philosophy of Evidence," and "Of Man, As a Member of Society," in *The Works of James Wilson*, ed. Robert Green McCloskey (Cambridge: Harvard University Press, 1967), 1:370–98, 197–226, respectively. But see also the new edition of Wilson's writings, including the lectures on jurisprudence, published in 2007 by the Liberty Fund: Kermit L. Hall and Mark David Hall, *Collected Works of James Wilson*, 2:792–826 (on the philosophy of evidence) and 1:621–44 (on man as "a member of society").

21. Reid cast the matter in this way, that "what is done from unavoidable necessity . . . cannot be the object either of blame or moral approbation" (Reid, *Essays on the Active Powers of the Human Mind* [1788; Cambridge: MIT Press, 1969], 361).

22. For the fuller exposition of this account of the domain of freedom as a necessary condition of moral judgment, see my own *First Things* (Princeton: Princeton University Press, 1986), 88, 92–93, 97.

23. See my own *First Things* and *The Philosopher in the City* (Princeton: Princeton University Press, 1981), chaps. 2–3 on "Civility and the Restriction of Speech" and on the matter of "determinism," 46–48 and passim.

24. See, for example, McLaurin v. Oklahoma State Regents, 339 U.S. 637 (1950), and Missouri ex rel. Gaines v. Canada, 305 U.S. 337 (1938).

25. See Brown v. Board of Education, 347 U.S. 483 (1954), at 494–95.

26. See Thomas Sowell, "Black Excellence: The Case of Dunbar High School," *The Public Interest* (Spring 1974): 3–21.

27. Quoted in the interview with Partee conducted by my late, beloved professor, Milton Rakove; see Cecil Partee, interview by Rakove, in *We Don't Want Nobody Nobody Sent* (Bloomington: University of Indiana Press, 1979), 156.

28. Aquinas, *Sth* 2.1.94.4.

29. Hamilton, "The Federalist, No. 31," in *The Federalist* (New York: Random House, n.d.), 188.

30. See Reid, *Essays on the Intellectual Powers of Man* (1814–15; Cambridge: MIT Press, 1969), 654.

31. Reid, *Intellectual Powers of Man*, 654.

32. Roe v. Wade, 410 U.S. 113 (1973), at 159.

33. Report from the Senate Committee on the Judiciary, drawn from Hearings before the Subcommittee on the Separation of Power, Committee on the Judiciary, U.S. Senate; 97th cong., 1st sess., on sec. 158 ("a bill to provide that Human Life shall be deemed to exist from conception"), Apr.–June, 1981. The findings of the Committee on the Judiciary were amply confirmed recently in a comparable survey of the most recent books and revised editions of the books cited by the Committee. See Ryan Anderson, "The Beginning of Life: An Update of the Medical Texts," Witherspoon Center (Princeton) May 2006.

34. Lincoln, "Fragment on Slavery" (Apr. 1, 1854?), in *Collected Works* (supra), 2:222–23.

35. Jean-Jacques Burlamaqui, *The Principles of Natural and Politic Law* (1748), pt. 2, chap. 5.

36. Richard Hooker, *Of the Laws of Ecclesiastical Polity* (1593–97, 1648–61; Cambridge: Cambridge University Press, 1989), 82; originally published in parts in 1593 and 1597, with the latter sections not being published until 1648 and 1661.

37. Pope John Paul II, *Fides et Ratio*, sec. 36.

38. John Paul II, *Fides et Ratio*, sec. 34 (my italics).

39. See Aristotle, *Nicomachean Ethics*, 1.3: Every man is a good judge of what he understands: in special subjects the specialist, over the whole field of knowledge the man of general culture. This is the reason why political science is not a proper study for the young. The young man is not versed in the practical business of life from which politics draws its premises and its data. He is, besides, swayed by his feelings, with the result that he will make no headway and

derive no benefit from a study the end of which is not *knowing* but *doing*. It makes no difference whether the immaturity is in age or in character. The defect is not due to lack of years but to living the kind of life which is a succession of unrelated emotional experiences. To one who is like that, knowledge is as unprofitable as it is to the morally unstable. On the other hand, for those whose desires and actions have a rational basis, a knowledge of these principles of morals must be of great advantage.

40. Lincoln, "Fragment: Notes for a Law Lecture" (July 1, 1850?), in *Collected Works* (supra), 2:82n22.

41. Kant, *Groundwork of the Metaphysics of Morals*, trans. H. J. Paton (1785; New York: Harper and Row, 1964), 79; 412 of the standard edition of the Royal Prussian Academy (hereafter, RPA ed.).

42. See the discussion of this case in my book, *Beyond the Constitution* (supra), 232–45n13. The case was *Bowen v. American Hospital Association*, 476 U.S. 610 (1986).

43. Kant, *Groundwork*, 57n44; 389 of the RPA ed.

44. Kant, *Groundwork*.

45. Kant, *Groundwork*, 69; 401 of the RPA ed.

46. Kant, *Groundwork*, 79; 412 of the RPA ed.

WORKS CITED

Aquinas. *Summa theologiae*.

Aristotle. *Nicomachean Ethics*.

Arkes, Hadley. *Natural Rights and the Right to Choose*. Cambridge and New York: Cambridge University Press, 2002.

———. *Beyond the Constitution*. Princeton: Princeton University Press, 1990.

———. *First Things*. Princeton: Princeton University Press, 1986.

———. *The Philosopher in the City*. Princeton: Princeton University Press, 1981.

Burlamaqui, Jean-Jacques. *The Principles of Natural and Politic Law* (1748).

Cicero. *Republic*.

Hamilton, Alexander. "The Federalist, No. 31." In *The Federalist*. New York: Random House, n.d.

Hooker, Richard. *Of the Laws of Ecclesiastical Polity*. 1593–97, 1648–61; Cambridge: Cambridge University Press, 1989.

Jefferson, Thomas. Thomas Jefferson to Roger Weightman, June 24, 1826. In *The Political Thought of American Statesmen*, edited by Morton G. Frisch and Richard G. Stevens. Itasca, IL: F. E. Peacock, 1973.

John Paul II, Pope. *Fides et Ratio*.

Kant, Immanuel. *Fundamental Principles of the Metaphysics of Morals*. Translated by Thomas K. Abbott. 1785; reprinted in Indianapolis: Bobbs-Merrill, 1949.

———. *Groundwork of the Metaphysics of Morals*. Translated by H. J. Paton. 1785; New York: Harper and Row, 1964; Royal Prussian Academy standard ed.

Lincoln, Abraham. *The Collected Works of Abraham Lincoln*. 9 volumes. Edited by Roy P. Basler. Brunswick, NJ: Rutgers University Press, 1953.

Locke, John. *Social Contract*. Edited by Sir Ernest Barker. London: Oxford University Press, 1960.

Partee, Cecil. Interview by Milton Rakove. In *We Don't Want Nobody Nobody Sent*. Bloomington: University of Indiana Press, 1979.

Posner, Richard. *The Problems of Jurisprudence*. Cambridge: Harvard University Press, 1990.

Pufendorf, Samuel von. *Two Books of the Elements of Universal Jurisprudence*. 1660; translated 1672; Oxford: Clarendon Press, 1931.

Reid, Thomas. *Essays on the Active Powers of the Human Mind*. 1788; Cambridge: MIT Press, 1969.

———. *Essays on the Intellectual Powers of Man*. 1814–15; Cambridge: MIT Press, 1969.

Rommen, Heinrich. *The Natural Law*. Translated by Thomas R. Hanley. 1936; translated 1947; Indianapolis: Liberty Fund, 1998.

Sowell, Thomas. "Black Excellence: The Case of Dunbar High School." *The Public Interest* (Spring 1974): 3–21.
Spinoza, Baruch. *Theological-Political Treatise*.
Vitoria, Francisco. *Reflections in Moral Theology*. 1696; Washington: Carnegie Institution, 1917.
Wilson, James. *The Works of James Wilson*. Edited by Robert Green McCloskey. Cambridge: Harvard University Press, 1967.
———. *Collected Works of James Wilson*. Edited by Kermit L. Hall and Mark David Hall. The Liberty Fund, 2007.

Chapter Eight

Thomas Aquinas's Concept of Natural Law

A Guide to Healthy Liberalism

Christopher Wolfe

The Western world has perennially grappled with the question of an adequate public philosophy. This is a difficult task, because "Western culture" is so complex. It is clearly rooted in Greek and Roman civilization and in Christian medieval civilization. Yet it is also deeply shaped by the Enlightenment, which was hostile to those earlier sources in some profound ways. The tensions between the classical-Christian and Enlightenment worldviews—elaborated so well in the works of Alasdair MacIntyre—are reflected in the tensions between Thomistic natural law political philosophy and many versions of the political philosophy of modern liberalism (e.g., John Locke, John Stuart Mill, and John Rawls).

My general thesis on the relationship between natural law and liberalism is this: people of sound judgment and good will, including natural law theorists, should be willing to be considered liberals. Equality and freedom, the central guiding principles of liberalism, are integral and foundational principles (though not the only ones) for any adequate public philosophy. At the same time, people of sound judgment and good will should be uncomfortable about being *simply* liberals. If the liberal tradition has grasped much of the truth about political life, it has also found it difficult to embrace some elements of that truth—elements found especially in Thomas Aquinas's concept of natural law. And current or contemporary forms of liberalism tend greatly to exacerbate the weaknesses of liberal political theory.

To save liberalism, with all its valuable contributions to human well-being, from its typical weaknesses—the dangerous inclinations it must resist—should be a major goal of contemporary political theory and practice. In this paper, I will focus briefly on four issues. The first concerns the tendency to understand the scope of the common good too narrowly, by failing to see the depth of the inevitable character-shaping influence of political regimes. The other three issues concern essential components of the common good—namely, truth, faith, and family—that have a somewhat tenuous status in liberal regimes, and are always in danger of being undermined or reduced to empty formalities.[1] Each of these weaknesses can be mitigated by recurring to St. Thomas's concept of natural law.

THE INFLUENCE OF THE REGIME

The first problem with liberalism is that it fails to recognize sufficiently the influence of "the regime," a notion that is so central to classical political philosophy.[2] (This blind spot is tied up with liberalism's view that political life is conventional—man-made—rather than natural.) The vision of political life in the liberal tradition is that it exists to establish a framework for the protection of individual rights. Government should remove the barriers to individual "pursuit of happiness." Even when it acts positively (e.g., in modern liberal economic redistribution), this is viewed simply as providing means to self-development, not actually determining or shaping the direction that development—it is providing means rather than dictating ends. But classical natural law theorists (as well as postmodernist theorists) correctly doubt that liberalism can avoid shaping ends as well as means.

Jeremy Waldron defends liberalism against a more modern form of this criticism:

> Sometimes liberals are accused of taking the beliefs and preferences of individuals as given and hence of ignoring the fact that forms of society may determine forms of consciousness and the structure and content of preferences. But liberals need not be blind to the possibility of preferences changing, either autonomously or along with changes in social structure and social expectations. Provided this possibility of change is in principle something that people as they are can recognize in themselves and take into account in their reflective deliberations, then it can be accommodated perfectly well in a liberal account of freedom.[3]

The confident "can be accommodated perfectly well" may distract us from the tenuousness of the assumption on which it rests. Liberals can recognize, Waldron says, that people's ends may be chosen due to "changes in social structure or social expectations," that is, due to the shape and tone and influences of the communities of which they are a part. This should not bother liberals, however, as long as "in principle" people "as they are" can recognize this fact and take it into account in their reflective deliberations. Waldron appears to assume that this condition is not problematic. It seems to me deeply so.

The force of the "in principle" is not clear. Is this to be opposed to "in practice"? If it refers merely to the theoretical *possibility* that some people, some of the time, may recognize social and political influences on their lives, that is certainly true, but it's not clear how that constitutes a defense of liberalism against the charge that liberal citizens often do not—perhaps even typically do not—recognize the way that living in a liberal society subtly forms their preferences. How likely, in fact, are people to recognize such influences? Waldron appears to go beyond just theoretical possibility when he specifies that it must be people "as they are." So that is the question: *do* (not just "can") people, as they are, recognize the extent to which their preferences—their ends, their goals, their assumptions about what is good in life—are shaped by the social ecology of liberalism?

This is the kind of empirical question that is very difficult to answer on the basis of anything other than our own experience with human beings. On the basis of my experience, I am simply puzzled that Waldron seems so confident that this condition is met. The people I have dealt with in the course of my life, the students I have taught—even, I confess, some of the scholars with whom I have interacted—have not *consistently* demonstrated this awareness and control over such influences in their "reflective deliberations." It *is* common to see reflection and critical awareness with respect to a certain range of issues—especially the ones that are more subject to controversy in our society at a given time—but this is compatible with little or no reflection of other broad attitudes toward life (especially where there is a broad social consensus). In fact, I am impressed over and over again with how many people seem simply to absorb many of their most important attitudes toward life from their surroundings, the culture or subcultures of which they are a part, with relatively little or no critical distance from those influences. (Some simple examples: assumptions about what is the "minimum" standard of living for a "decent" human life, broad dating and courtship patterns, ideas about the "right" size for a family, the notion that a church is a "voluntary association," which areas of thought can attain genuine certitude.) The idea that people "as they are" engage in a high level of self-critical analysis, then, strikes me as an extraordinarily optimistic assessment. It seems to be a very good example of a kind of romanticism that is at the heart of much modern liberalism.

But someone might say, "So what if liberalism shapes people, as long as its shapes them well?" Should we be bothered about the way liberalism shapes people?

I should point out immediately that much of that influence is quite beneficent. For example, liberalism, on the whole, encourages people to be tolerant and peaceful, to be active in pursuit of opportunities, and to have an awareness of their own dignity and rights. We can, and should, recognize the many ways in which liberalism shapes people for the good. It is easier, of course, to do so when we look at nonliberal societies—whether in history, or in today's post–9/11 world—and see the suffering and insecurity occasioned by intolerance and inhumanity. Tocqueville observes this trenchantly in his chapter on "how customs are softened as social conditions become more equal," in which he describes letters from an aristocratic woman to her daughter indulging in "cruel jocularity" regarding certain "horrors" in the punishment of commoners.[4] For this, and many other reasons, Tocqueville rightly decides in the end that, despite the defects of modern democracy, of which he is clearly aware, a "state of equality is perhaps less elevated, but it is more just; and its justice constitutes its greatness and its beauty."[5]

But this decision in favor of liberal democracy—a good and right decision—is not the last word. Having made that decision, it is still necessary to recognize the limits and defects of liberal democracy, in order to mitigate them. Or, as Tocqueville says at the end of *Democracy in America*,

> For myself, who now look back from this extreme limit of my task and discover from afar, but at once, the various objects which have attracted my more attentive investigation upon my way, I am full of apprehensions and of hopes. I perceive mighty dangers which it is possible to ward off, mighty evils which may be avoided or alleviated; and I cling with a firmer hold to the belief that for democratic nations to be virtuous and prosperous, they require but to will it.[6]

I want to turn, then, to ask now about some of the more problematic aspects of liberalism, and about three tendencies in particular, relative to truth in general, to religion, and to family.

LIBERALISM AND TRUTH

The first problematic tendency of liberalism is to emphasize freedom at the expense of an emphasis on truth about ultimate realities. The claim to know the truth about human purposes has so often been associated with abridgment of freedom that liberals are understandably cautious, not to say suspicious, of truth claims about human ends. The post-Reformation religious wars (international and domestic) are the most commonly invoked example, from Hobbes and Locke to Rawls, and in the contemporary world their place has been admirably filled by figures such as the Ayatollah Khomeni and Osama bin Laden (with whom contemporary liberals lump the dreaded "Religious Right" in America). This suspicion of dogma is compatible with an acceptance of certain truth claims, above all, the claims of modern science and liberalism's "procedural" principles.[7] (Indeed, the prestige of modern science and its methods—its status as the most credible form of knowledge—helps to account for the widespread doubt that moral philosophy can attain any certitudes.)

The notion that truth is downplayed in a liberal society is not so much a philosophical claim about any supposed inevitable logical consequence of liberalism's principles leading to relativism, but rather a sort of "sociology of knowledge" in liberal societies. It is similar to Tocqueville's claim that, in modern liberal democracies based on equality, the "philosophical method" tends to be "that in most of the operations of the mind each American appeals only to the individual effort of his own understanding."[8]

Over time, it seems that the citizens of liberal democracies tend to move from "tolerance of other people" (that is, their right to have an opinion) to "relativism about ideas of the good" (that there is no single, right opinion, at least about "values"). The virtue of nonjudgmentalism, taken even to the point of a kind of principled agnosticism, eclipses the virtue of wisdom.[9] Some people consider this skepticism (more or less qualified) as one of liberalism's attractive features, but those who believe, like natural law theorists, that human beings are very much worse off when they do not understand the most fundamental truths about human life are concerned about the tendency of freedom to overshadow truth so dramatically.

LIBERALISM AND REVEALED RELIGION

The second tendency, somewhat related to the first, is the tendency of liberal democracy to undermine revealed religion. One of the broad "tendencies" of liberalism, as a tradition of "enlightenment," has been toward secularism or rational religion. Part of this, as Tocqueville argued, was due to the "accidental" (that is, historical, and not necessary) social and political connections between representatives of established churches based on revealed religion and nonliberal regimes, especially continental European monarchies. But there are other, deeper factors as well, which are also noted by Tocqueville.

Tocqueville is well known for his statements about the importance of religion in America. Indeed, he called it "the first of their political institutions," even though he also emphasized the separation of church and state (one of the primary reasons, he said, for the "peaceful dominion of religion").[10] But there is another side to Tocqueville that is less noted.[11] In particular, it is interesting to note that at the end of *Democracy in America*, in his recommendations for how to prevent democratic despotism, he says nothing about religion. I think the explanation for this is that Tocqueville was aware of the tenuous status of revealed religion in modern liberal democracy.

Tocqueville thought that liberal democracies would be suspicious of tradition, and that the "philosophical method" of Americans would be to rely on themselves. But this strikes at the heart of a certain kind of religion: namely, revealed religion, which rests precisely on the "handing down" (*traditio*) of the message that has been revealed to mankind by a God who has intervened in a particular moment of human history. Tocqueville recognized that the natural tendency of modern liberal democracy was the more diffuse and indefinite religion of pantheism.

Tocqueville likewise recognized that liberal democracies would incite and cater to the human desire for physical well-being. So powerful was this tendency that "the heart, the imagination, and life itself" might be given to the pursuit of physical gratifications, "till, in snatching at these lesser gifts, men lose sight of those more precious possessions which constitute the glory and greatness of mankind."[12] He specifically pointed out that one of the advantages of religion was its tendency to curb or moderate this desire. But a moment's reflection shows that this can be turned around: if religion can benefit democracy by acting *against* one of its strongest tendencies, democracy can undermine religion by propagating that tendency.

For these and other reasons, Tocqueville, I think, had some doubts about how efficacious a restraint on liberal democracy religion might be in the long run. I think that American history bears out those concerns. Those who take a more benign view of that history point out the surprising strength of religion in America, especially when compared to Europe.[13] While this strength should not be ignored, a closer attention to the character of that religious belief raises serious questions. In many respects, traditional Christian beliefs, for example, seem to have been modified to accommodate liberal democratic tendencies. Nowhere is this seen more clearly than in the progressive decline of marriage as an institution in American society, a process in which many churches as well as religious believers have simply accommodated dramatically changing sexual mores.

Why is liberal democracy's tendency to undermine revealed religion a "problem"? If liberalism is characterized by an elevation of reason, might not a decline of belief in revelation be one of its beneficial effects, as many liberals, historically, have thought?

There are two answers to this question. First, liberal democracy itself depends for its well-being on religion. This familiar argument was made by Washington, in his Farewell Address, where he argues that liberal democracy depends for its well-being on morality, and that religion is at least an essential component in the foundations of social morality. It is also made by Tocqueville throughout *Democracy in America*, which argues that the freedom of the political world is made possible by the fixed moral framework that religion provides.

A second reason why the undermining of revealed religion is a problem is that refusal to consider carefully the claims of revelation is itself illiberal. There is much to be said for reason, but contemporary liberals themselves are often among the first to emphasize its limits. (What Rawls says about "the burdens of reason" suggests such limits.) One position that an honest exponent of reason would consider is that reason's own capacity may be limited, and that claims of a divine revelation might just be correct. Reason might point beyond itself to faith.

John Paul II raised this possibility powerfully in his encyclical *Fides et Ratio*:

> Step by step, then, we are assembling the terms of the question. It is the nature of the human being to seek the truth. This search looks not only to the attainment of truths which are partial, empirical or scientific; nor is it only in individual acts of decision-making that people seek the true good. Their search looks towards an ulterior truth which would explain the meaning of life. And it is therefore a search which can reach its end only in reaching the absolute. Thanks to the inherent capacities of thought, man is able to encounter and recognize a truth of this kind. Such a truth—vital and necessary as it is for life—is attained not only by way of reason but also through trusting acquiescence to other persons who can guarantee the authenticity and certainty of the truth itself. There is no doubt that the capacity to entrust oneself and one's life to another person and the decision to do so are among the most significant and expressive human acts. . . .
>
> From all that I have said to this point it emerges that men and women are on a journey of discovery which is humanly unstoppable—a search for the truth and a search for a person to whom they might entrust themselves. Christian faith comes to meet them, offering the concrete possibility of reaching the goal which they seek.[14]

My purpose in quoting this passage is not to prove anything about revealed religion and whether it provides the answers to life's questions, but simply to argue that it is incumbent on all rational people to take the question of revealed religion seriously. Insofar as liberal societies indirectly but powerfully undermine revealed religion by the attitudes and habits of mind that it encourages—a distrust of certain kinds of knowledge, individualism, materialism—they divert their citizens from confronting some of the most important answers to the profoundest questions of human existence.

LIBERALISM AND THE FAMILY

A third problematic tendency of liberalism is the undermining of the stability of the family. Some scholars argue that the family is just as strong as it has been in the past, but has simply assumed new forms.[15] It is certainly true that we should resist the tendency to view the history of the family with an unjustified nostalgia. There were plenty of problems with families in the past, including an excessive rigidity in social gender roles, toleration of spousal abuse, sexual "double standards," and many informal as well as formal ways of "breaking up" a family (desertion being one frequent form).

Nonetheless, I think that it is wrong to think that there have *not* been recent dramatic changes that have greatly weakened the family in performing its essential functions, most importantly, the raising of children.[16] In the past there were many violations of the ideal of marriage and family, but today the notion that there is an ideal or norm is itself under assault. As the late Elizabeth Fox-Genovese argued,

> Today, if we credit our senses, we are witnessing a concerted attempt by a portion of the elite to deny the value of the norm. In its place we are offered marriage as the personal fulfillment of the individual, who must be free to switch partners at will. And we are offered family as "families"—whatever combination of people choose to live together on whatever terms for whatever period of time. It is possible that adults may survive this madness, although one may be permitted to doubt. It is doubtful that any significant number of children will survive it, as the mounting evidence of their distress amply warns.[17]

And, while it is also true that many of the forces undermining the family are part of modernity in general, there seem to be reasonable grounds for finding in liberal democracy itself tendencies contrary to stable family life, such as excessive individualism, affluent materialism, and doubt about absolute substantive moral principles.

LIBERALISM AND NATURAL LAW

It does not at all follow from my analysis that, because the influence of the regime is so great, and in some cases the influence of liberal regimes is not benign, we ought to abandon liberalism. The alternatives, after all, might be worse. I, for one, certainly have no desire to return to the Greek polis or the Roman republic. Medieval Christendom might seem to some people (especially some Catholics) to be more attractive, but I would warn such people not to romanticize the actual once-existent forms of that ideal either. As Tocqueville suggested about the aristocracy of the ancien régime, one can be distracted by the high points so much that one fails to see the enormous amount of human misery and injustice. Rather than some return to a preliberal political philosophy, I would argue for the articulation and development of a "natural law liberalism."

Natural law philosophy in its traditional form (especially in St. Thomas) has traditionally been seen as an opponent of liberalism—indeed, the very target of liberalism in its origins. I think that there is some truth in this argument, but also much that is wrong. First, it must be conceded that representatives of classical natural law political theory did sometimes adopt positions incompatible with liberalism, and, more importantly, with sound political principles. The most notable example of such a mistake was the issue of religious liberty. Contemporary natural law theorists, such as John Finnis and Robert George, argue—compellingly, I think—that natural law theory, properly understood, concurs with liberalism in defending fundamental rights to religious liberty.[18]

Having said that, however, I think the more important fact is that many of the social and political institutions and practices in pre-liberal regimes that liberalism condemned and sought to change—especially the great inequality, class divisions, hereditary privilege, political despotism, and arbitrary power—were in no way essential parts of or reflections of the fundamental principles of natural law political philosophy. The very real social ties between church and state in the ancien régime caused people to assume that there was an essential tie between autocracy and Catholicism (the main "carrier" of classical natural law philosophy in the modern world). But, as Tocqueville rightly pointed out, these ties between both Catholicism and classical natural law, on one hand, and pre-liberal regimes, on the other, were generally accidental, not essential. In fact, natural law theory (and its understanding of the requirements of the common good) can and should be understood to ratify many of the essential features of liberalism: fundamental political equality, broad political participation, institutional features such as separation of powers, limited government, a broad range of liberty rooted in a healthy distinction between the public and private, and so on.

At the same time, the closing of the gap between liberal political theory and natural law theory is not a simple, uncritical embrace of liberalism by proponents of natural law. Contemporary forms of liberalism, such as the work of John Rawls, have moved in a direction antithetical to many of the principles of natural law and earlier forms of liberalism, especially in its hostility to preservation of a "moral ecology" that is as essential to the common good as society as it is to individual well-being. The importance of natural law liberalism today lies in the role it can play in preserving liberalism from its own worst tendencies.

Natural law liberalism can help people in a modern liberal democracy to be more self-critical about aspects of liberalism that are less attractive, and in particular about (1) its tendency toward a certain narrowness in its notion of the common good, and (2) its tendencies to gravitate toward or promote certain defective understandings of essential components of the common good (especially truth, faith, and family).

A "natural law liberal public philosophy" would resist these tendencies—which are, after all, tendencies, and not essential constituents of liberalism. Natural law liberals should remind their fellow citizens, for example, of the sobering passage with which Tocqueville concludes his discussion of the "advantages" of democracy in America, in which he notes the deep tendency of liberal democracy to gravitate toward the "middling state of things," the downside of which is mediocrity.[19] And they should also try to "high-tone" liberalism to the extent that they can—for there is a wide range of forms of liberalism, and some of them shape people in much better ways than others.

There is distinguished precedent, I think, for this approach to the question of liberalism. It parallels closely Aristotle's handling of the topic of democracy in his *Politics*.[20] An examination of his account of the various forms of democracy would find that he describes a range of democracies that are on a spectrum from less to more democratic. The democracy he considers best is one that would be at the somewhat less democratic end of that spectrum. (The same would be true of oligarchy.) Underlying his judgment is the principle behind the "mixed regime": the recognition that any form of government has its own defects, and benefits from an infusion of the principles of other forms of government. Just as democracy is best when it is a moderate democracy, liberalism is best when it is a moderate liberalism—a "natural law liberalism."

NOTES

1. This paper draws heavily on parts of my book *Natural Law Liberalism* (New York: Cambridge University Press, 2006).
2. The notion of the "regime"—which combines politics and sociology and economics and culture—is particularly central to and well set out in the work of Leo Strauss.
3. Jeremy Waldron, *Liberal Rights* (New York: Cambridge University Press, 1993), 41. Waldron, in an omitted footnote, cites Rawls's use of this argument against utilitarianism.
4. Alexis de Tocqueville, *Democracy in America*, ed. Phillips Bradley (New York: Alfred A. Knopf, 1972), 2:165.
5. Tocqueville, *Democracy in America*, 2:333.
6. Tocqueville, *Democracy in America*, 2:334.
7. For an example of the procedural principles, see Oliver Wendell Holmes Jr.'s ode to freedom of speech—replacing the "fighting faiths" of the past with a faith that the marketplace is the best test of truth:

> Persecution for the expression of opinions seems to me perfectly logical. If you have no doubt of your premises or your power, and want a certain result with all your heart, you naturally express your wishes in law, and sweep away all opposition. To allow opposition by speech seems to indicate that you think the speech impotent, as when a man says that he has squared the circle, or that you do not care wholeheartedly for the result, or that you doubt either your power or your premises. But when men have realized that time has upset many fighting faiths, they may come to believe even more than they believe the very foundations of their own conduct that the ultimate good desired is better reached by free trade in ideas—that the best test of truth is the power of the thought to get itself accepted in the competition of the market, and that truth is the only ground upon which their wishes safely can be carried out. (Abrams v. U.S., 250 U.S. 616 [1919], at 630)

Holmes never explains why faith in free speech is not simply one of those "faiths" that will be upset like all the others.

8. Tocqueville, *Democracy in America*, 2:3.

9. The widespread hold of nonjudgmentalism on the contemporary American mind is emphasized (and regarded too benignly) in Alan Wolfe's *One Nation After All* (New York: Viking, 1998).

10. Tocqueville, *Democracy in America*, 1:305, 308.

11. For a fuller discussion of this point (and more extensive citations), see my "Tocqueville and the Religious Revival" *This World* no. 1 (Winter/Spring 1982): 85–96.

12. Tocqueville, *Democracy in America*, 2:132.

13. *Unsecular America: Essays by Paul Johnson*, ed. Richard John Neuhaus (Grand Rapids, MI: William B. Eerdmans, 1986).

14. John Paul II, *Fides et Ratio*, Vatican Website, sec. 33, http://w2.vatican.va/content/john-paul-ii/en/encyclicals/documents/hf_jp-ii_enc_14091998_fides-et-ratio.html.

15. One example is Stephanie Coontz, *The Way We Never: American Families and the Nostalgia Trap* (New York: Basic Books, 1992) and *The Way We Really Are: Coming to Terms with America's Changing Families* (New York: Basic Books, 1997).

16. Elizabeth Fox-Genovese, "Thoughts on the History of the Family," in *The Family, Civil Society, and the State*, ed. C. Wolfe (Lanham, MD: Rowman and Littlefield, 1998).

17. Fox-Genovese, "History of the Family," 10–11.

18. See my chapter on religious liberty in *Natural Law Liberalism* (New York: Cambridge University Press, 2006), 217–47.

19. Tocqueville, *Democracy in America*, 1:252–53.

20. Aristotle, *Politics*, in *The Basic Works of Aristotle*, ed. Richard McKeon (New York: Random House, 1941), 4.4.

WORKS CITED

Alexis de Tocqueville. *Democracy in America*. Edited by Phillips Bradley. New York: Alfred A. Knopf, 1972.

Aristotle. *Politics*. In *The Basic Works of Aristotle*, edited by Richard McKeon. New York: Random House, 1941.

Coontz, Stephanie. *The Way We Never Were: American Families and the Nostalgia Trap*. New York: Basic Books, 1992.

———. *The Way We Really Are: Coming to Terms with America's Changing Families*. New York: Basic Books, 1997.

Fox-Genovese, Elizabeth. "Thoughts on the History of the Family." In *The Family, Civil Society, and the State*, edited by C. Wolfe. Lanham, MD: Rowman and Littlefield, 1998.

John Paul II, Pope. *Fides et Ratio*. Vatican Website. http://w2.vatican.va/content/john-paul-ii/en/encyclicals/documents/hf_jp-ii_enc_14091998_fides-et-ratio.html .

Johnson, Paul. *Unsecular America: Essays by Paul Johnson*. Edited by Richard John Neuhaus. Grand Rapids, MI: William B. Eerdmans, 1986.

Waldron, Jeremy. *Liberal Rights*. New York: Cambridge University Press, 1993.

Wolfe, Alan. *One Nation After All*. New York: Viking, 1998.

Wolfe, C. *Natural Law Liberalism*. New York: Cambridge University Press, 2006.

———. "Tocqueville and the Religious Revival." *This World* no. 1 (Winter/Spring 1982): 85–96.

Afterword

A Natural Lawman at the O.K. Corral

Ralph McInerny

I have been asked to speak of natural law in my lifetime. The title makes it unclear as to whose biography is involved, mine or the law's. I suppose you could dramatize the way this account of the wellsprings of human action was marginalized or forgotten in the fifties, ridiculed in the sixties, replaced, as one thought, by virtue ethics and then, slowly rising again like a flag above Fort Sumter, fluttering over the past decade or two, during which proponents of natural law have actually enjoyed the luxury of civil war, disputing among themselves the niceties of the theory. But that story line confuses the external observer with the intramural.

Consider first then what is confidently regarded as the mainstream of twentieth century philosophy even though its course has been as variable as the Mississippi's, meandering toward its delta of destruction.

When I began graduate studies at the University of Minnesota in 1951, "ethics," like a discouraging word, was seldom heard. There was an essay on it by a member of the Vienna Circle—I thought of this as a kaffeeklatch whose members sat in a circle with their embroidery on their laps, the Madame Lafarges of the revolution—which anticipated the sassy little book by A. J. Ayer, *Language, Truth and Logic*.

My major mentors at Minnesota were two, Wilfrid Sellars and Paul Holmer. With Herbert Feigl, Sellars had produced the most influential anthology of what could be called the philosophy of logical empiricism. With him, I studied Descartes, Leibniz, Kant. Minnesota was on the quarter system so one took lots of courses. I also had Sellars for his own theory of knowledge. As I recall, Russell's *Philosophy of Logical Atomism* was held in higher esteem than Wittgenstein, hardly surprising since only the *Tractatus* was then in print. In his "Some Aristotelian Philosophies of Mind," Sellars adopted the Averroist reading of the *De anima*. (He was the only one there who seemed to know much pre-Cartesian history of philosophy; but then Reichenbach's *The Rise of Scientific Philosophy* told us that philosophy began with Kant, much as Quine told us that logic had not really begun until the nineteenth century.)

If I heard of ethics at all, it was in courses given by Paul Holmer. It is to Holmer that I owe my introduction to Kierkegaard. David Swenson, Holmer's predecessor as token wild card on the faculty, had discovered and translated Kierkegaard, setting in motion what has since become an industry. With Kierkegaard, ethics fell under the rubric of his definition of subjective truth: an objective uncertainty held fast in an appropriation process of the most passionate inwardness. In my presumptuous and premature master's dissertation (*A Thomistic Evaluation of Kierkegaard*) I compared Kierkegaard's subjective truth with the practical syllogism of Aristotle and Thomas. Does that fifty-five-year-old dissertation still waste its sweetness on the conditioned air of the University of Minnesota library?

Armed with an MA (philosophy and classics), I transferred to Laval to study with Charles De Koninck. He had lectured in the Twin Cities during that year, he had been the mentor of my first philosophy teacher at the St. Paul Seminary, Father William Baumgaertner, and De Koninck was what I wanted to be. I earned a doctorate at Laval, taught a year at Creighton in Omaha, and in 1955 came to Notre Dame.

Like most philosophy departments in Catholic colleges and universities of the time, the department at Notre Dame could be described as consciously countercultural. The Program of General Studies had been founded by Otto Bird in 1950 and it represented the mutual admiration between Catholic higher education and such places as Chicago, St. John's, and the program at Columbia. Their aim was to revive liberal education and the assumption was that Catholic colleges had kept that tradition more or less alive. In the parlous condition of American higher education, it was imperative that students be rescued from a stultifying specialization and be made literate in the great tradition in which we stand. All but one member of the philosophy department was a Thomist, but "Thomist" was not a univocal term—there were Louvain Thomists, Toronto Thomists, Catholic University Thomists, and, of course, Laval Thomists. Like those we joined in the attempt to revive the liberal arts tradition, we held a pretty dim view of what had been going on in modernity.

Nowadays when just about everyone has his little list of howlers from the days of the Enlightenment Experiment, there is perhaps less tendency to dismiss with a smile the little lists we all had then: where Descartes went wrong, the errors of Kant, etc. Of course Descartes had gone wrong, we all know it now; and Kant was a bottomless source of error. It had dawned on more than one observer that modern philosophy was in many ways the Protestant Reformation carried on under different auspices. It was pretty clear that if one were guided by this or that modern philosopher—of course they seldom agreed with one another—a first casualty would be the Catholic faith. Who could fail to feel a frisson at Hume's insolent treatment of the Eucharist in his discussion of miracles? No student of modern philosophy is likely to think of it as neutral with respect to religion.

At Notre Dame we had the Natural Law Institute, whose journal eventually became the *American Journal of Jurisprudence*. (What waffling lay behind that change of name?) My first years in South Bend were preconciliar of course and in 1959–60 I went off on a Fulbright to Louvain, where I wrote *The Logic of Analogy*. As a Thomist one felt part of a vast global band of brothers—some sisters too—with our superstars—Maritain and Gilson—and a passel of three star and two star generals. Publications in every language, journals, series of historical and other works, minute exegesis of the text of Thomas, meetings, medals, camaraderie. When I was given tea in the sitting room of the director of the *Institut Supérieure de Philosophie*, Canon De Raymaeker, the elegant little ceremony seemed to include the ghosts of Cardinal Mercier and of other early heroes of the Thomistic Revival. Latin then made Catholics feel at home throughout the world; analogously, a Thomist felt comfortably *chez lui* in otherwise foreign settings.

It could be said—it began to be said at the time—that we were living in utter indifference to what was going on in philosophy elsewhere. The term *ghetto* was used. One who had been on both sides of the line knew of course that the ignorance of and indifference in secular universities to what we were doing was total. But of course a Catholic philosopher could not rest content with such indifference to the philosophies of the day. We did not hold a *kind* of philosophy, one species among others, chosen randomly; we were doing philosophy tout court and the assumption was that nothing philosophical could be alien to us. Wrong, maybe, but not alien. In short, we felt an obligation to what would come to be called dialogue.

The great heroes of Thomism were our guides in this. Try to imagine a Maritain or a Gilson failing to relate what he thought to what was going on around him. I emphasize this analogue of the missionary spirit because it would prove to be a virtue that transformed itself into a vice before the 1960s were out. We did not think of ourselves as on the banks of the mainstream. We were the mainstream, tracing our lineage back through the debris of modern philosophy to the Middle Ages, principally to Thomas Aquinas, and then back through Boethius, Augustine, the other fathers, to Plato and Aristotle. Our friends seeking to revive liberal education in secular colleges and universities shared this view of a tradition in which we stood. It was from all this that one modern philosopher after another had turned away, dismissing it as a house of cards, then tried to replace it with one implausible construct after another.

Something happened. It began around 1960, it gathered momentum during the years of the council—Vatican II, 1962–1965—and by the end of the decade the great assumption of our common effort had been questioned, then lampooned, finally set aside. Erstwhile Thomists turned into a variety of butterflies and fluttered off to beat their gossamer wings against the indifferent pane of modernity. What was happening was the academic version of the chaos in the Church that followed Vatican II. Where once we had lived consciously and proudly in a tradition, now we were assured that the tradition had been jettisoned. Why, the fathers of the council had deposed Thomas Aquinas. I wrote a book about this at the time, *Thomism in an Age of Renewal* (1966). It may not explain much, but it does evoke those times.

Into this melee came a little book by Monsignor John Tracy Ellis, chiding Catholic colleges and universities for not being excellent. By excellence he meant meeting the criteria by which success was gauged in the Ivy League. With the collapse of the old consensus among us, Ellis indicated a path for personal and institutional renewal. We knew where to look for the criteria of success, we knew who we were to emulate. Within a decade, you could shoot a cannon through a Catholic campus and not hit a Thomist.

No need to underscore the irony of all this. Iconoclasts are always easy marks. But recall that where once we had shared with others interested in the revival of liberal education the judgment that something was radically wrong with the secular universities of the country, now we were asked to take those same universities as our guide into the promised land of excellence. If that earlier criticism were valid, the results of this pursuit of "excellence" were predictable. What has been called the secularization of our institutions had begun. Thomism was in diaspora at best. Consider what this meant in the area of ethics.

It has been said that twentieth-century Anglo-American moral philosophy emerged out of G. E. Moore's *Principia Ethica*. Consider what was perhaps its most influential claim, the so-called "naturalistic fallacy." This alleged fallacy, not to put too fine a point upon it, consisted in assuming that the natural properties of what you called "good" were the basis for calling it good. Moore showed to his own satisfaction and that of generations to come that any such effort landed you in a tautology. So what did it mean to call something good? Well, what does it mean to call something yellow? You just know.

The criticism, the acceptance of the naturalistic fallacy and the determination to avoid it at all costs, characterized British and American moral philosophy almost to the end of the twentieth century. The positive accounts of what *good* and *bad* meant varied, but not the assumption that there was a gap between the natural world and the world of "values." Shades of Kant, of course, though perhaps Moore never read him.

One account of the behavior of ethical terms (we all began to talk this way) had been given by that little book of Ayer's I mentioned earlier. If calling a thing good or bad cannot be explained by features of the thing being evaluated, value terms express our subjective attitude of approval or disapproval. The religious and aesthetic were similarly subjectivized by Ayer.

By the time Ernan McMullin and David Solomon put on a famous summer ethics program at Notre Dame, such figures as R. M. Hare, who was there, along with Philippa Foot, Marcus George Singer, and others, were satisfied to do metaethics. A philosopher didn't presume to tell anyone what to do, what was right or wrong, good or bad. How could he? What he could do was analyze the different accounts of evaluation that had been proposed. Hare applied something like the structure of Aristotelian logic to moral discourse, and this led him back to basic premises, starting points, principles, the claims on which all subsequent argued-for claims depended. One who had been well brought up might think of natural law precepts. Did Hare hold that there are principles which are simply true?

No. He spoke of a decision of principles. The starting points weren't inescapably imposed on us. We had to choose our principles. Of course, like Moore, Hare imagined there would be agreement among decent folk like ourselves, but it turned out that there was no rational protection at all from, say, a Nazi who wanted to rid the world of a race or two.

It was at that summer conference that my own interests turned again to moral philosophy. The lectures I gave there were meant to be a little précis of Thomistic moral philosophy; perhaps I was expected to grunt like a dinosaur as I gave them. They became *Ethica Thomistica*. David Solomon, when he joined the department, had sat in on a graduate course I was giving on the *Prima secundae*. He was astounded that this sort of thing was still embraced and argued for. Once he asked me, wearing a very serious expression, if I didn't realize that something absolutely radical had ushered in modernity. Like Wilfrid Sellars some years before, Dave seemed to think I hadn't yet heard the news. It was when Dave himself turned a critical eye on the critical turn that the transformation began that has made him the hero of ethics and culture at Notre Dame.

This impressionistic and barefoot trip over the terrain of recent philosophy can suggest either that there are lots of freebooting gunslingers or, more accurately perhaps, two large groups, with many internal disagreements that do not obscure the general agreement that all those on their side are wearing the white hats and those on the other black hats. What to do?

It is precisely the question of how people in radical disagreement with one another can communicate that has drawn much attention of late. As a matter of human psychology, we all occupy the stance we do, a stance which, however odd it may look to others, has become so familiar to us as to seem self-evident. Alasdair MacIntyre spoke of philosophical traditions—he isolated three—which seem to have nothing in common on the basis of which they could communicate with one another. An occupant of one tradition can listen in to another, learning its language, and would of course pass a critical judgment on it. And vice versa. But that seems to come down only to this, that from the standpoint of tradition A, tradition B is false, and vice versa. And this in turn would sound like saying they don't speak French in Tokyo. In his Gifford lectures, MacIntyre developed an ingenious method by which this difficulty in noncommunication can be overcome.

There is another method—at least initially it will seem different from MacIntyre's—and that is the method suggested by John Paul II's *Fides et Ratio.* In the introductory section of that encyclical, the Holy Father makes the apparently astonishing claim that not only are there common questions that all men ask, there are common answers to them that all men hold. These answers he labels "implicit philosophy." The Pope is suggesting that all men implicitly hold the same answers to such questions as: Who am I? Where have I come from and where am I going? Why is there evil? What is there after this life?

Now surely in the light of the philosophical Babel all around us this must seem a daring claim. The major role that implicit philosophy plays in the encyclical is to provide a set of criteria to appraise the bewildering variety of philosophical systems. A knowledgeable reader like yourself will see in the Pope's remarks about the contents of implicit philosophy echoes of Aristotle and St. Thomas, and the fear could arise that what he is really doing is using one philosophical system to appraise the others and then we are quite clearly back to MacIntyre's problematic. In reading the encyclical, you will find in the reference to the principles of contradiction, finality, and causality, the echoes I have mentioned; when the Pope adds the concept of person as a free and intelligent subject, with the capacity to know God, truth and goodness, you will perhaps throw up your hands and whisper "Thomism." When the Pope goes on to say, "Consider as well certain fundamental norms which are shared by all," what else can you say except, "Natural law."

You need not worry. The Holy Father is not here invoking the "philosophical system" of Thomism; he will speak of that much later in Chapter IV. Rather he is pointing to something that commends Thomism, as well as at least some other philosophical systems. And that is their incorporating and moving off from the principles of implicit philosophy. These common principles, implicitly held by all, are the starting points of any philosophy that can commend itself to the human mind. These principles function in Thomism but they are not Thomistic in any narrow sense. The discussion and elaboration of them by an Aristotle or a Thomas amounts to pointing to what everybody already knows, implicitly. Wouldn't it be odd to call the principle of contradiction Thomistic, or label it from any other system? Of course it would.

So what is the meaning of *implicit*? When one first hears the principle of contradiction formulated—it is impossible for a thing to be and not to be at the same time and in the same respect—he is doubtless hearing a sentence he never himself formulated. Yet when he grasps what is being said he thinks: I already knew that. He is coming explicitly to see what he always implicitly knew. He knew it in the way that he knew that "Yes" and "No" as possible answers to a question are such that he has to choose the one and reject the other. He knows it in the way that he knows it is nonsense to say that the cat is on the mat when the cat is not on the mat. And so, the Pope is suggesting, it goes with the other items he mentions. But we are interested in those "fundamental norms which are shared by all."

When St. Thomas makes these explicit in his discussion of natural law, he fittingly compares them to the first principles in the theoretical order, for example, the principle of contradiction. That principle, stated abstractly, stands for all the quite particular instances in which it is embedded. We do not deduce the latter from the former; we arrive at the principle by generalizing from the myriad situations in which we realized you can't have it both ways, both yes and no. In much the same way, the corresponding principle in the practical order—good must be done and pursued and evil avoided—has a daunting generality, but it immediately commends itself to us because we have known it as embedded in countless choices and decisions. It is sometimes complained that this first practical principle is vacuous and unhelpful; and so it would be if we ignored that this generality is merely making explicit what everyone knows whenever he acts.

Perhaps we have not always made it as clear as we should that the account of natural law that Thomas Aquinas gives is not the proposal of some novel theory of starting points for action, but rather making explicit what every human agent implicitly knows.

But surely it is disingenuous to suggest that it is only the account of natural law and not the implicit knowledge it articulates that has come under fire from opponents. It is no secret that the theory of natural law, and its presuppositions too, are rejected by many philosophers. What to do?

Have we taken sufficiently into account the analogy St. Thomas draws between the principle of practical reasoning—natural law—and the principles of theoretical reasoning, reasoning in general? The latter are characterized as self-evident, per se nota, what everybody knows. Nonetheless such principles have been rejected. The response to this, as both Plato and Aristotle have shown, is to show that the rejection involves one in incoherence, self-contradiction. Think of Plato's handling of the Sophistic principle "What's true for me is true for me, what's true for you is true for you." Can denials of fundamental moral principles be handled in this way? They can.

For many of us, the so-called "mystery clause" in Justice Anthony Kennedy's *Planned Parenthood v. Casey* opinion has become a favorite. It still surprises one to read what the Justice had to say, set out in black and white, in a presumably serious text. Why is it that even the most minimal restrictions on access to abortion must be struck down? Because each of us has a fundamental right to define life, the world, existence as we please. That is not a direct quote, but it accurately captures the decision's basis for striking down a law. You can define life, existence, the world any way you like, and so can I and everybody else. Presumably such freedom does not extend to English, or *can* we define words too any way we like. Could my "No" be your "Yes"? In any case, the Supreme Court is clearly part of the world as Kennedy defines it. Can I exclude it from mine, along with its decisions? Could I define *life* in such a way that Supreme Court justices are undeserving of it?

Obviously what the Justice has written is nonsense. His effort to bypass fundamental and common moral principles lands him in a wonderland of nonsense. This may seem an altogether too easy target. But it is one to practice on before drawing on less simplistic denials of natural law.

MacIntyre's algorithm for adjudicating between conflicting systems is to seek to show that a tradition, on its own principles, falls into contradiction. But doesn't the application of this invoke principles common to any tradition? Obviously it does. So there is a nice complementarity between MacIntyre's important contribution and John Paul II's *Fides et Ratio*.

I could go on. And on. Garrulousness is the vice of age. I needn't tell this audience how the treasure that was all but lost is being found again. We may be tempted merely to be amused by all those who hankered for the flesh pots of Egypt. They sold their birthright for a mess of pottage and got a potted message. Let me end with a little avuncular advice.

If I had to single out the one most devastating mark of the dark decades to which I allude, it would be the loss of the sense of Christian philosophy. By that I mean the context and ambience within which we pursue our tasks. Philosophy is formally distinct from theology of course. But philosophizing is the activity of a person whose habits and convictions and beliefs inevitably affect the questions he raises and where he is likely to look for answers. Have we been persuaded that this is peculiar to believers? That secular philosophers are engaged in an uncircumstanced pure reasoning and that it is our obligation to adopt a kind of practical apostasy if we would be real, professional philosophers? A moment's thought will reveal that anyone's philosophizing is a concrete act influenced by many factors.

The difference is that the believer here has a tremendous advantage. The faith can guide his philosophizing. For example, when he encounters attacks on religion and the mysteries of the faith (Hume on the Eucharist), he knows in advance these attacks are wrongheaded. That conviction does not provide him with any arguments, of course—all that lies ahead. The secular philosopher has no such guide in the existential circumstances that govern his philosophizing. He is bereft of that simple logic of the believer: if a claim is in conflict with the faith, it is false.

Well, this is a vast subject, and it may have been unwise to introduce it without being able to pursue it. Then again it may have been wise. I offer you the slogan that Jacques Maritain took from John of St. Thomas: *philosophandum in fide — philosophize within the ambience of the faith.*

Index

About the Contributors

Hadley Arkes is William Nelson Cromwell Professor of Jurisprudence and Edward Ney Professor of American Institutions Emeritus at Amherst College. He is the author of *Natural Rights and the Right to Choose* (2002), and *Constitutional Illusions and Anchoring Truths: The Touchstone of the Natural Law* (2010). He is Founder and Director of the James Wilson Institute.

Steven Brust is assistant professor of Political Science at Eastern New Mexico State University. He received his PhD in Political Theory from the Catholic University of America, and he is the author of "Ancient and Modern: Natural Moral Law and Universal Moral Principles." in *The Catholic Social Science Review*, and "Retrieving a Catholic Tradition of Subjective Natural Rights from the Late-Scholastic Francisco Suárez," in the *Ave Maria Law Review*.

J. Budziszewski is professor of government and philosophy at the University of Texas at Austin, where he also teaches courses in the law school and the religious studies department. He specializes in natural law, with a special interest in moral self-deception, and more generally the ethical foundations of political and social life. Among his books are *The Line Through the Heart: Natural Law as Fact, Theory, and Sign of Contradiction* (2009) and *Commentary on Thomas Aquinas's Treatise on Law* (2014).

J. Daryl Charles is the 2018–2019 Acton Institute Affiliated Scholar in Theology and Ethics. He has previously taught at Taylor University, Union University, and Berry College, and he has served as director and senior fellow of the Bryan Institute for Critical Thought and Practice as well as visiting fellow at the Institute for Faith and Learning, Baylor University, and as William E. Simon Visiting Fellow in religion and public life at the James Madison Program for American Ideals and Institutions, Princeton University. He is the author of *Natural Law and Religious Freedom* (2017), *Retrieving the Natural Law: A Return to Moral First Things* (2008), and *The Unformed Conscience of Evangelicalism: Recovering the Church's Moral Vision* (2002).

Fulvio Di Blasi is an Italian attorney and international scholar in moral philosophy and natural law theory. He is the president of the Thomas International Online University. He has a PhD in philosophy of law from the University of Palermo and has taught in several universities both in Europe and in America. His books include *God and the Natural Law* (2003), *John Finnis* (2008), *Ritorno al diritto* (2009), *Questioni di Legge Naturale* (2009), *Ancient Wisdom and Thomistic Wit* (2017), and *From Aristotle to Thomas Aquinas: Natural Law, Practical Knowledge, and the Person* (2018).

Steven A. Long is professor of theology at Ave Maria University and a member of the Pontifical Academy of St. Thomas Aquinas. He is the author of *The Teleological Grammar of the Moral Act* (2007) and coauthor of *Thomism and Predestination: Principles and Disputations* (2017).

Ralph McInerny was professor of philosophy at the University of Notre Dame for fifty years, as well as director of the Jacques Maritain Center. He is the author, among many other books, of *Aquinas on Human Action* (1992) and *Praeambula Fidei* (2006).

Michael Pakaluk is professor of ethics in the Busch School of Business at the Catholic University of America. A member of the Pontifical Academy of St. Thomas Aquinas, he is the author the Clarendon Aristotle on *Nicomachean Ethics VIII and IX* (1998), and *Aristotle's Ethics: An Introduction* (2005), and co-author of *Moral Psychology and Human Action in Aristotle* (2011). His most recent book, *The Memoirs of St. Peter*, a new translation and commentary on the Gospel of Mark, is forthcoming with Regnery Gateway.

Christopher Wolfe is designated affiliate professor of politics at the University of Dallas and president of the American Public Philosophy Institute. He is also the former codirector of the Thomas International Center in Raleigh, North Carolina, and Emeritus Professor of Political Science at Marquette University. He is the author of *The Rise of Modern Judicial Review* (1986) and *Natural Law Liberalism* (2006).

www.ingramcontent.com/pod-product-compliance
Lightning Source LLC
Chambersburg PA
CBHW051252200926
51612CB00001B/12
9781498576420